Booker T. Washington and Black Progress

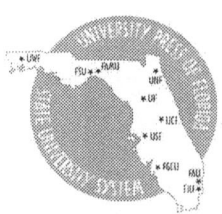

Florida A&M University, Tallahassee
Florida Atlantic University, Boca Raton
Florida Gulf Coast University, Ft. Myers
Florida International University, Miami
Florida State University, Tallahassee
University of Central Florida, Orlando
University of Florida, Gainesville
University of North Florida, Jacksonville
University of South Florida, Tampa
University of West Florida, Pensacola

Booker T. Washington and Black Progress

Up From Slavery 100 Years Later

Edited by W. Fitzhugh Brundage

University Press of Florida
Gainesville · Tallahassee · Tampa · Boca Raton
Pensacola · Orlando · Miami · Jacksonville · Ft. Myers

Copyright 2003 by W. Fitzhugh Brundage
Printed in the United States of America
All rights reserved

First cloth printing, 2003
First paperback printing, 2004

Library of Congress Cataloging-in-Publication Data
Booker T. Washington and black progress: Up from slavery 100 years later /
edited by W. Fitzhugh Brundage.
p. cm.
Includes bibliographical references (p.) and index.
ISBN 0-8130-2674-1(cloth); ISBN 0-8130-2814-0 (pbk.)
1. Washington, Booker T., 1856–1915. Up from slavery.
2. Washington, Booker T., 1856–1915—Criticism and interpretation.
3. Washington, Booker T., 1856–1915—Political and social views.
I. Brundage, W. Fitzhugh (William Fitzhugh), 1959–.
E185.97.W4B666 2003
370'.92—dc21 2003050400

The University Press of Florida is the scholarly publishing agency for the State University System of Florida, comprising Florida A&M University, Florida Atlantic University, Florida Gulf Coast University, Florida International University, Florida State University, University of Central Florida, University of Florida, University of North Florida, University of South Florida, and University of West Florida.

University Press of Florida
15 Northwest 15th Street
Gainesville, FL 32611-2079
http://www.upf.com

Contents

Preface   vii

1. Reconsidering Booker T. Washington and *Up From Slavery*   1
   W. FITZHUGH BRUNDAGE

2. *Up From Slavery* as History and Biography   19
   LOUIS R. HARLAN

3. In Search of Booker T. Washington:
   Up From Slavery, History, and Legend   38
   WALDO MARTIN

4. Understanding the Wizard:
   Another Look at the Age of Booker T. Washington   58
   ROBERT J. NORRELL

5. What Made Booker Wash(ington)?
   The Wizard of Tuskegee in Economic Context   81
   PETER A. COCLANIS

6. More Than an Artichoke:
   The Pragmatic Religion of Booker T. Washington   107
   WILSON J. MOSES

7. "Curious Silence"?
   African American Women in *Up From Slavery*   131
   PATRICIA A. SCHECHTER

8. Booker T. Washington's Strategies of Manliness,
   for Black and White Audiences   149
   DAVID LEVERENZ

9. Moving Beyond the Accommodation/Resistance Divide:
Race and Gender in the Discourse of Booker T. Washington   177
LOUISE NEWMAN

10. *Up From Slavery* for South Africans:
Booker T. Washington's Classic Autobiography Abridged   193
HUNT DAVIS

Contributors   221

Index   223

Preface

In the fall of 2000, Robert "Jeff" Norrell suggested that the centenary of the publication of Booker T. Washington's *Up From Slavery* deserved recognition. We talked about organizing a panel at the Southern Historical Association meeting in the fall of 2001. In the process of coordinating that panel, I became increasingly intrigued by the idea of engineering a conference devoted to Washington and his famous autobiography. Although historians have, and have had, much to say about Washington, he remains far less studied than some of his other contemporaries. Moreover, whereas other noted African American activists of his era, especially Ida Wells and W.E.B. Du Bois, remain objects of continuing interest, Washington, in the eyes of many, seems to have been adequately "explained" and "revealed." Scholars seemingly have concluded that they understand Washington and that their research and interpretative efforts should be directed elsewhere. But as the conference ("Rethinking Booker T. Washington's *Up From Slavery*: A Centenary Conference," held at the University of Florida October 4–6, 2001) and this collection of essays show, Washington continues to warrant careful and sustained analysis.

This collection, appropriately, has been a collective effort. It would not exist without the generous support and active encouragement of many people at the University of Florida. There, Winfred M. Phillips, vice president for research and dean of the Graduate School, Neil S. Sullivan, dean of the College of Liberal Arts and Sciences, and David R. Colburn, provost, provided the funds that made possible the conference out of which this collection grew. Likewise, the Humanities Council, led by Sheldon R. Isenberg and John Leavey, provided crucial support and inspiration for the conference. Barbara Corwine and Jose Maria Corona, in the Department of History, did a magnificent job of handling the logistics of the conference. At the University Press of Florida, Meredith Morris-Babb has been an early and warm supporter of this project. Finally, the participants in the conference and contributors to this collection deserve my warmest thanks for sharing their collective interest in and fascination with Booker T. Washington with audiences in Gainesville and readers everywhere.

1

Reconsidering Booker T. Washington and *Up From Slavery*

W. FITZHUGH BRUNDAGE

The hundredth anniversary of the publication of Booker T. Washington's *Up From Slavery* in 2001 provided an opportunity to revisit the book's enduring place in the canon of American autobiographies as well as its author's controversial but far-reaching impact on American life. Until the publication of Malcolm X's life story in 1965, *Up From Slavery* was the most widely read and reprinted African American autobiography. It was translated into countless languages and inspired readers as diverse as the future Pan-Africanist Marcus Garvey in Jamaica, an obscure teacher in India (who subsequently translated the book into Urdu), and Japanese students who traveled to Alabama to study at the Tuskegee Institute, over which Washington presided as principal. Bespeaking the book's enduring appeal, it has remained continuously in print since it was first serialized in *Outlook* magazine more than a century ago.

Up From Slavery is interesting not only for what it divulges about Washington, but also for what it reveals about the era from which it sprang. Washington's early chapters recount the transition from slavery to freedom in the South, and highlight the eagerness with which freed people seized the opportunities now available to them. His catch-as-catch-can efforts to acquire an education typify the exertions made by many freedpeople. *Up From Slavery* also provides a primer about vocational education, which Washington encountered at Hampton Institute in Virginia and which he later replicated at Tuskegee. As such, the book was one of the most influential compendiums of the arguments for industrial education. Beyond offering Washington's distinctive perspective on the economic opportunities for blacks after slavery, the book reveals much about notions of personal worth and success in late-nineteenth-century America. Finally, *Up From Slavery* exposes the shifting, always treacherous complexities of racial etiquette in the United States that Washington and other African Americans had to contend with in the age of Jim Crow.

Washington's autobiography provides a valuable lens through which to view his age because few, if any, of Washington's black contemporaries were as prominently involved in so many facets of national public life. Indeed, Washington loomed over the last decade of the nineteenth and the first decade of the twentieth century to such a degree that the era has appropriately been labeled "the age of Washington." In 1882 he took over as the principal of the newly established Tuskegee Institute, Alabama, a state-funded school modeled after Washington's alma mater, Hampton. After a decade of tireless labor laying a solid foundation (figuratively and literally) for the school, Washington launched the Tuskegee Negro Conference, which annually brought hundreds of blacks to the campus to discuss programs for social welfare, economic development, and educational reform. He cemented his national reputation when he delivered his celebrated address at the Atlanta Cotton States Exposition in 1895. This brief speech summarized the program of education, self-help, and racial cooperation that he had been practicing at Tuskegee. To the delight of his white listeners, Washington seemingly renounced social equality and advocated that blacks and whites work separately for their shared common good. Whites concerned about the nation's "Negro problem" heard a palatable solution in his ostensibly simple message. After the speech northern philanthropists, ranging from industrialists Andrew Carnegie and John D. Rockefeller to Sears and Roebuck magnate Julius Rosenwald, sought Washington's advice about the best means to promote black advancement. Washington became the conduit through which white charitable donations reached black institutions and causes. In 1900 he founded the National Negro Business League with the goal of fostering black entrepreneurship. His influence soon extended to the corridors of national politics, where Presidents Theodore Roosevelt and William Howard Taft discussed race relations with him and solicited his advice regarding patronage appointments. Indirectly he exerted pervasive influence on the black community by backing newspapers and organizations.[1]

By the turn of the century, no meeting or discussion that touched on racial topics was complete without an appearance or a comment by Washington. In 1903, W.E.B. Du Bois observed that "easily the most striking thing in the history of the American Negro since 1876 is the ascendancy of Mr. Booker T. Washington."[2] So powerful was Washington and so extensive was his influence that Du Bois and other critics complained that he operated the "Tuskegee Machine," which determined the fortunes of individual blacks as well as the black community at large. Although criticism of Washington began to mount after the turn of the century, his stature as arbiter of white-black relations, at least in the eyes of white racial moderates, remained secure until his death in 1915.[3]

Since the turn of the twentieth century, Washington and his program of racial uplift have provoked sharply differing opinions. As Waldo Martin observes in this collection, the critiques of Washington by Du Bois, William Monroe Trotter, Ida Wells-Barnett, and others have had an enduring impact on perceptions of Washington. For some contemporaries and later critics, Washington epitomized a tragic tradition of purportedly pragmatic but actually naive accommodationism that rendered African Americans dependent on white paternalism. With the publication of August Meier's *Negro Thought in America, 1880–1915* (1963) and subsequently Louis Harlan's magisterial biography of the "Wizard of Tuskegee," Washington emerged as a more complicated figure than either his earlier critics or defenders understood. Whereas Washington previously had been perceived as an apologist for segregation and disfranchisement, he now emerged as a cagey opponent of Jim Crow. His apparently tepid opposition to the disfranchisement of southern blacks was contradicted by his furtive financial support for legal challenges to several state constitutions that deprived blacks of the vote. In 1900, for example, Washington secretly raised money to challenge the constitutionality of the "grandfather clause" in the new Louisiana state constitution, which extended the franchise to illiterate voters whose grandfathers had been qualified to vote, but which effectively excluded blacks. Several years later, he covertly funded two legal challenges, *Giles v. Harris* (1903) and *Giles v. Teasley* (1904), against discriminatory voter registration practices in Alabama.[4]

Although the work of Meier and Harlan reveals that Washington had labored to impede the advance of Jim Crow, it also confirms the existence of the "Tuskegee Machine" that Du Bois and others had denounced.

Washington's published letters in particular unmask Washington's heavy-handed machinations to silence his critics and to establish his power within virtually all black institutions. Washington's carefully nurtured reputation for integrity and his self-professed simplicity now appear to be a veil behind which Washington scrupulously hid his boundless ambitions and petty vindictiveness. Thus, as Robert J. Norrell suggests in this collection, the recent revisionism has not removed the taint of misguided accommodationism or invidious ambition from Washington's life.[5]

This collection is not intended to rehabilitate Washington's reputation. That most of the contributors to this volume reach relatively positive conclusions about Washington and his program is the result of coincidence rather than design. The aim of this volume, and the conference out of which it grew, was to bring together gifted scholars to look closely at Washington's autobiography and his life's work. Neither a critique of nor an apologia for Washington, these essays instead use Washington, his autobiography, and his program as a pretext to consider the meanings of *Up From Slavery*, the plight of African Americans, and possible responses by blacks in the United States and elsewhere to the "highest stage of white supremacy."[6]

For all of its apparent simplicity, *Up From Slavery* is a complex text marked by tactical silences, carefully contrived narrative devices, and artful representations. Literary scholars long have appreciated the subtlety and complexity of the work. One scholar describes the book as "resistant" to analysis while another warns that "no other text in the canon of African American literature offers prose which is so tricky and deceptive."[7] In this collection, historian Louis Harlan, from his vantage as the doyen of Washington historians, assesses the merits and limits of *Up From Slavery* as an accurate and full accounting of Washington's life up to 1900. Harlan, like other commentators on *Up From Slavery*, highlights Washington's carefully crafted self-representation. Washington's concern about self-representation helps to explain why he wrote two autobiographies, *The Story of My Life and Work* (1900) and *Up From Slavery* (1901), within a two-year span.[8] Intended for a black audience, the first volume focused on Washington's program for racial self-help. His second and more famous autobiography was intended to elicit support from sympathetic whites. Consequently, Washington adopted distinct voices that he believed were appropriate for the different audiences of the two volumes. In an era when blacks, and especially black men, were depicted in popular culture as either buffoons or menacing criminals, Washington intended his autobiography to be a counter-representation of African American character and identity. By no means was Washington's autobiography the only challenge to racist depictions of blacks, but few autobiographies exerted more influence on blacks' perceptions of themselves or on the image of blacks in the white mind. After surveying some of the editorial decisions Washington made and representational strategies he adopted when he wrote for a white audience, Harlan concludes that *Up From Slavery* is a masterful autobiography but hardly good history. Harlan suggests that Washington's lack of candor was prompted by his intent to keep the inspirational message of his autobiography simple and to avoid revealing behavior that contradicted his carefully constructed public persona.

Washington's artifice, in *Up From Slavery* and throughout his career, is a major focus of Waldo Martin's essay. Martin acknowledges the harrowing context in which Washington worked—when lynching was an everyday occurrence and when black civil rights were under attack across the nation. But Martin is more concerned with Washington's chosen modes of self-representation and leadership, or, in other words, those things over which Washington had a substantial degree of control. At the most fundamental level, Washington's style of leadership, as revealed in *Up From Slavery* and in his life, rested upon exceptional self-mastery. To conduct a public life so riddled by hidden agendas and contradictions must have required extraordinary self-possession, circumspection, and duplicity. Martin concludes that this strategy required even more deftness than the "Wizard of Tuskegee" possessed and that the contradictions between Washington's image and his actions have contributed to his controversial and divisive legacy.

Robert J. Norrell also is interested in Washington's tactics, but he insists that any assessment of Washington must take into account the circumstances that he and other former slaves encountered in the South after the Civil War. When emancipated, most southern blacks were impoverished, landless, and illiterate. A few succeeded in acquiring land and a measure of economic autonomy, but most became laborers or sharecroppers. However much sharecropping was an economic necessity in a region where whites owned the land and blacks were the laborers, it offered only limited opportunities for black economic mobility. Hoping that education might provide an alternative path of advancement, freedpeople flocked to the newly established public schools in the South and rates of illiteracy among southern blacks dropped steadily across the late nineteenth century. But southern whites, who believed that formal education inspired blacks to entertain inappropriate economic and social ambitions, remained hostile to black education. Consequently, black schools in the South, including Tuskegee, remained under constant threat from both white vigilantes and parsimonious legislators.[9]

Evidence of the systematic erosion of African Americans' rights mounted across the late nineteenth century. The rising toll of anti-black violence was especially conspicuous. Intensifying white fears about black independence and criminality fueled rampant extralegal violence. In 1882, the year that Washington arrived at Tuskegee, southern mobs executed more than forty-five people. Within ten years that number had more than doubled, and with each succeeding decade the connection between lynching and race became starker. During the years that are the focus of *Up From Slavery* (ca. 1880–1900), southern mobs executed perhaps as many as 2,000 victims. Simultaneously, a growing chorus of white southerners condemned blacks for their purported criminality, laziness, and depravity. When, in 1897, Georgia reformer and newspaper columnist Rebecca Latimer Felton exhorted white southerners to "lynch a thousand a week" in order to defend the "virtue" of white women threatened by black rapists, she gave voice to sentiments shared by many whites.[10] The lawlessness of lynching and race riots sanctioned by these attitudes testified to the resolve of whites to assert their supremacy by any means.[11]

As the prevalence of racial violence demonstrated, the nation's commitment to equality, which began waning during the 1870s, seemed to disappear entirely during the 1890s. Then, laws segregating the races expanded from railroads to many other facets of southern public life. In 1896, in the *Plessy v. Ferguson* decision, the U.S. Supreme Court sanctioned "separate but equal" public accommodations for blacks, thereby endorsing legalized segregation. Campaigns to deprive southern blacks of voting rights, through both constitutional and illegal means, also gathered speed during the 1890s. By the first decade of the twentieth century, voting rolls across the South had been purged of the overwhelming majority of blacks, leaving most without a role in electoral politics.[12]

Both Washington's critics and subsequent historians, as noted above, have chided Washington for doing too little to protest and prevent these worsening conditions. They chastise him for failing to exploit his extraordinary access to influential whites or his international prominence to wage a forthright campaign against Jim Crow. Too often, they claim, he seemed to sanction, if only by his silence, the advance of segregation and disfranchisement. And his furtive campaign to stem this tide was, according to Waldo Martin, both a tactical and strategic failure.[13]

Robert J. Norrell's essay challenges such arguments by reminding us of the precarious position that Washington occupied after 1900. It is tempting to assume that Washington's "acommodationism" made him the toast of the white North and South and rendered him invulnerable to criticism. Indeed, historians tend to pay far more attention to Washington's black critics than to his white opponents after 1900. But Norrell insists that Washington was beset by vigorous and powerful opponents throughout the nation, and especially in Alabama and the Deep South. His program remained controversial, and he could never assume that even southern white "moderates" would defend it. The slightest breach of southern racial etiquette by Washington was likely to prompt a deluge of denunciations by even Washington's purported white southern allies, let alone racist extremists. Norrell contends that if Washington was pragmatic and guarded, it was because the political, social, and economic environment of the era afforded him only the narrowest latitude within which to work. Arguably because of, rather than in spite of, his realistic and accommodationist tactics, Washington was successful. After all, would confrontational strategies have accomplished more in Alabama during the era of Jim Crow?

Whereas Norrell concentrates on the political and cultural contexts in which Washington operated, Peter Coclanis focuses on the economic plight of African Americans and the appropriateness of Washington's "gospel of the toothbrush" to it. Although conceding that Washington's platitudes about cleanliness, rectitude, and hard work may hint at Washington's deepest psychological wellsprings, Coclanis is much more interested in their practical value. Washington's program of education, public health, and capital accumulation, Coclanis argues, was prescient. Given the extremely limited economic resources that blacks had at their disposal, Washington proposed a practical program that offered African Americans a realistic opportunity to improve their circumstances. Rather than dismissing Washington as a purveyor of hackneyed Victorian virtues and a backward-looking champion of nineteenth-century capitalist individualism, Coclanis contends that we instead should recognize that Washington anticipated recent strategies for the economic development of impoverished nations. Coclanis concludes that Washington's program of black economic development was far more reasonable, timely, and apt to the Jim Crow South than previous accounts have recognized.

The ideological context out of which Washington's thought emerged also is at the center of Wilson Moses's subtle essay. Readers of *Up From Slavery* have long recognized the inspiration that Ben Franklin's life and teachings provided for Washington. Moses reminds us that Franklin also figured prominently in the thought of the distinguished sociologist Max Weber. Weber may have codified the idea of a Protestant work ethic (and its seminal contribution to American capitalism), but Washington anticipated Weber's idea and transformed it into an instrument for black progress. Too long caricatured as a shallow, unthinking champion of secular materialism, Washington, as described by Moses, emerges as an imaginative, spontaneously pragmatic thinker who fully recognized and appreciated the power of religion. Washington's approach to religion, like the rest of his ideology, may have been pragmatic and unsentimental, but it was, Moses insists, "clearly conceived, consistently maintained, and imaginatively expressed." In order to promote the behaviors and values that his times required, Washington appropriated the Protestant creed of thrift and diligence and proselytized it with missionary zeal. By doing so, Washington demonstrated, contrary to the claims of his critics, his belief in the primacy of ideas. Perhaps even more revisionist is Moses's claim that Washington never embraced fully the triumphant commercialism of his era and instead remained a steadfast critic of frivolous and unproductive consumption. Implicitly, Moses's essay warns that by continuing to caricature Washington's thought (no less than his politics and his economic ideas), we fail to understand fully Washington's creativity or impact.

At yet another level, *Up From Slavery* provides a revealing insight into the ideology of respectability that gripped Washington and many other members of the black elite. His life, as depicted in his autobiography, personified both black achievement and respectability. Beyond the economic rationale discussed by Peter Coclanis, Washington's stress upon deportment and cleanliness in *Up From Slavery* was an example of his intention to demonstrate blacks' mastery of the etiquette of American public culture. Perhaps the most sophisticated example of the "rags to riches" genre that was so popular in late-nineteenth-century America, Washington's autobiography is a paean to discipline, character, and self-restraint, values then much prized. Washington's obsession with public decorum and preoccupation with propriety and moral uplift take on additional meaning when understood in the context of the racist stereotypes of his age. He intended his autobiography to demonstrate that the present status of blacks was determined by environment—their lack of education, industrial skills, and cultural refinement—not by biological limitations. When Washington vouched for his individual integrity and refinement, he simultaneously attested to his race's collective integrity and, in the language of his day, respectability.[14]

Washington's emphasis on respectability as a strategy for racial advancement appealed to both white and black audiences, but for different reasons. Whites detected in Washington's insistence upon blacks' conformity with Victorian manners and morals evidence of his acceptance of the values of the dominant white society. Black leaders, like Washington, recognized that interracial cooperation was easiest when their work focused on programs that promoted respectability among blacks. But within the black community, "the politics of respectability" was never just an unthinking mimicry of whites. When Washington and other blacks concentrated on individual behavior and attitudes, they asserted their will and agency to define themselves. By adhering to a code of temperance, thrift, polite manners, sexual purity, cleanliness, and rectitude, blacks contradicted racist stereotypes about their alleged inferiority. Blacks also rejected any claim that wealth or status defined their self-worth, thereby extending the claim of respectability to even the most humble members of their community. This inclusiveness across class lines helps to explain why "respectability," whether invoked by Washington or others, had such resonance among blacks.[15]

Extant scholarship on Washington and *Up From Slavery* has duly noted the grip of Victorian notions of respectability on Washington. But Washington's ideas about gender, which were inextricably bound up in contemporary understandings of civilization, culture, and respectability, have been largely unexplored. Louise Newman places Washington's ideas about manliness and womanliness within the larger discourse of civilization and evolution that was so pervasive in turn-of-the-century America. Then, she explains, a crucial measure of one's refinement and respectability was how closely one's life hewed to patriarchal notions of manhood, motherhood, and domesticity. African American domestic life had come under close scrutiny and criticism because of the ways in which Victorian ideologies, especially social Darwinism and evangelical Christianity, linked the private with the public. Hostile whites concluded that because black family life contradicted the rules of civilization, blacks, despite living among the civilized, were doomed to remain a primitive people. Washington and other black activists countered that the race's embrace of the patriarchal family demonstrated the triumph of blacks over the legacy of slavery.[16]

As the patriarch of Tuskegee and of black America (at least in the eyes of many), Washington necessarily grappled with the era's prevailing ideas about masculinity, femininity, and race. Newman, Patricia Schechter, and David Leverenz each explain in their essays that Washington exploited and subtly revised contemporary understandings of gender and race. Schechter rebukes scholars who have exaggerated Washington's apparent reticence to discuss the black women who figured prominently in his life. To the contrary, Schechter contends that Washington is as forthright and effusive about his debt to his mother and his wives as Victorian conventions allowed. Moreover, Washington's patriarchal conduct and vision was consistent with the standard of treatment for black women that Anna J. Cooper and many black women activists advocated: "homage to mothers, credit to wives, protection to girls." Certainly, Washington's commitment to coeducation at Tuskegee and the prominent role of Washington's wives and other women in Tuskegee's operations demonstrate his interest in and respect for educated black women.

David Leverenz draws our attention to the challenges Washington faced as he figured out how to navigate the protocols of Victorian racial and gender etiquette. Leverenz is interested in the telling silences in *Up From Slavery* and what they reveal about how Washington chose to depict himself as a black man before a white audience. To represent himself as a vigorous, competent, and ambitious black man without at the same time arousing white racist stereotypes, Leverenz contends, required all of Washington's prodigious skills. Presenting himself as the embodiment of middle-class black male dignity and self-control, Washington combined assertiveness with civility, avoiding either craven resignation or gauche flashiness. Leverenz further highlights the performative dimensions of Washington's autobiography, or, in other words, how Washington challenged white readers with "the spectacle of his own body as a site of mastery." What Washington achieved, according to Leverenz, was a dignified, nonconfrontational manhood at a time when seemingly any assertion of black manhood was taboo. Together, the essays by Leverenz, Newman, and Schechter bear out Newman's claim that the incorporation of gender in the analysis of Washington and *Up From Slavery* will refresh long-standing and stale debates about Washington as well as open new avenues for discussion.

The multiple meanings and polyvocality of *Up From Slavery* emerge forcefully in Hunt Davis's concluding essay on the reception and dissemination of Washington's autobiography in South Africa. Davis's essay reminds us of Washington's far-flung international influence.[17] Wherever the uplift of "primitive" peoples became a matter of public policy, Washington's program and life story aroused interest among both the colonized and the colonizers. Washington's influence was especially notable in South Africa, where the racial policies imposed by the white minority shared important similarities to those implemented in the United States. Davis explains that Charles T. Loram (and other influential white South Africans) looked to Washington's educational philosophy as an appropriate model for the education of South African blacks. But it is noteworthy that careful editing of Washington's writings by Loram was required in order to render Washington's text consonant with white racial ideology in South Africa. At the same time, D. D. T. Jabavu and other black South Africans discerned in Washington's autobiography a different voice, one that encouraged aspirations far beyond those that even South African white moderates anticipated. It would be inappropriate to exaggerate the influence of *Up From Slavery* on the origins of South African black nationalism, but it also would be a mistake to suggest that Washington's program meshed easily with the unfolding policies of racial segregation in South Africa. Thus, just as Washington found a way to speak to and engage multiple audiences in the United States, so too, Davis explains, was he able to convey multiple meanings to audiences elsewhere.

This volume aims to encourage historians to continue to scrutinize Washington and *Up From Slavery*. Literary scholars remain interested in Washington's autobiography, but historians in recent years have displayed much less interest. Perhaps they have assumed that Louis Harlan's prizewinning biography of Washington is definitive and so have directed their energies elsewhere. Or perhaps many historians have found Washington's "accommodationism" both uninspiring and unworthy of sustained scrutiny at a time when the protest tradition of the modern Civil Rights movement is the particular focus of scholarly attention. In either case, these essays, we hope, demonstrate that there is ample reason to continue to use Washington and his autobiography to think about the era of Jim Crow.

The riddle of Booker T. Washington endures. By no means do the essays in this volume exhaust the subject. Despite ongoing research by literary scholars and classic historical works by Harlan, Meier, and others, important questions remain about Washington's life and programs. The origins of Washington's economic thought, for example, have received too little attention. This lacuna has been partially addressed by Heather Cox Richardson in *The Death of Reconstruction*, which concludes with a reconsideration of *Up From Slavery*. She contends that Washington's autobiography is perhaps the last expression of the abolitionist, free labor ideology that had inspired the antebellum campaign against slavery. By 1900 the faith that white northerners had in the capacity of African Americans to embrace free labor capitalism had eroded to the point that many concluded that blacks were bound to remain in a state of semi-barbarism. In myriad ways throughout *Up From Slavery*, Washington invoked the free labor values trumpeted by northern Republicans before and after the Civil War. He appropriated "the Northern worker myth" and insisted that blacks now embraced it, and that it remained central to the African American experience. Just as there is value in placing *Up From Slavery* within the tradition of slave narratives, so too, Richardson explains, is it appropriate to interpret the book within the tradition of nineteenth-century free-labor tracts. Read this way, Washington's life story, with its often grating (and ingratiating) rags-to-riches moralism was a political act that contested, rather than affirmed, the drift of white mainstream opinion.[18] Richardson's work, as well as Coclanis's essay in this collection, demonstrate that careful scrutiny of Washington's economic thought and its origins may substantially revise conventional wisdom about his program and its efficacy.

Washington's attitudes about religion, as well as the influence of African American Protestantism on Washington, seldom elicit comment. Unusual among scholarly treatments of Washington's thought is David Howard-Pitney's *The Afro-American Jeremiad*, which identifies the African American Protestant millennial tradition that Washington appropriated in much of his public oratory. We may be tempted to view Washington as a profoundly secular figure because of his harsh condemnation of black ministers (who, he joked, preached principally as a means to avoid productive work) and his own brief, unsatisfying, and seldom acknowledged experience as a seminarian in Washington, D.C. But Howard-Pitney contends that Washington's orations were redolent with language, images, and themes derived from mainstream nineteenth-century Protestantism. Moreover, Washington adopted a "priestly" voice when addressing whites, with which he emphasized the ideals that whites and blacks shared, and a "prophetic" voice when addressing blacks, with which he chastised the nation for failing to live up to its God-appointed destiny. Further work along these lines will deepen our understanding of both Washington's rhetorical strategies as well as how audiences heard and interpreted Washington's resonant language and images.[19]

Important questions remain about Washington's educational philosophy. The merits and impact of Washington's program of vocational education, for example, have been extensively debated since the 1890s.[20] Yet, as Peter Coclanis points out, we lack a systematic longitudinal study of the careers of early Tuskegee graduates. Such a survey might revise our assumptions about the efficacy of Washington's pedagogy of uplift by confirming the charges of Washington's critics that Tuskegee, for all of its boasted practical education, was a glorified teachers' college. Or perhaps such a study will confirm that Tuskegee provided its students with the vocational skills, moral training, and support networks that in turn led to greater economic independence, enhanced self-respect, and elevated social standing. Similarly, a careful investigation of women's education at Tuskegee and of the careers of women graduates will clarify the extent to which Washington and his staff disseminated emancipatory notions of gender roles.

Despite recent work, including the essays in this collection, Washington's discursive and performative strategies remain incompletely understood. There is, for instance, no systematic consideration of Washington's modes of addressing different audiences. He routinely relied on improvisation when he delivered public addresses. Considerable evidence suggests that Washington at the very least adopted different styles of speaking depending on his listeners. What specific rhetorical devices and tropes did Washington use with black audiences? With whites? With mixed audiences? And does an analysis of Washington's invocation of gender roles in his public speeches bear out the conclusions of Patricia Schechter, David Leverenz, and Louise Newman about Washington's subversion of prevailing gender conventions? Finally, the performative aspects of Washington's public persona, which David Leverenz highlights, beg to be studied. Because Washington was the most famous and widely viewed black orator of his day, the manner in which he presented himself to audiences is much more than a minor historical detail. We await a sustained analysis of Washington's performances, along the lines undertaken by Leverenz in this collection.

The international influence of *Up From Slavery* and of Washington's program, as Hunt Davis's essay suggests, remains a fruitful field of investigation. A transnational survey of the influence of Tuskegee on colonized societies is long overdue. Was the contradictory impact of Washington's ideas that Davis traces in South Africa replicated in other places? And what does Washington's involvement in agricultural modernization in the African colony of Togo, for example, reveal about his ideas about Africa, Africans, and the universality of his program?[21]

Finally, attention to the iconic representations of Washington and their import for both whites and blacks would be welcome. He was a celebrity, as well as a leader, and was frequently depicted in all manner of material culture. Washington's portrait adorned the walls of countless black homes, just as his name came to grace many black schools (including the one that Waldo Martin attended). Only systematic studies will reveal who invoked Washington, in what contexts, and with what apparent intended purposes. He, for instance, has been the subject of countless children's books since the beginning of the twentieth century. Because Washington and his program were rife with many layers of meaning and contradiction (as the essayists in this collection stress), we may wonder how specific meanings were assigned to Washington and his vision in these children's books as well as other cultural forms. Clearly, iconic representations played a crucial role in crystallizing the historical memory of Washington.

The contributors to this volume will be gratified if their collective work inspires any research on these or other questions related to Washington. These essays, we hope, affirm the importance of moving beyond inherited judgments about Washington in order that we better understand Washington's exceptional life and his age in all of its bewildering complexity. Perhaps in the end, Washington will remain, as Louis Harlan suggests, fundamentally unknowable. But we nevertheless stand to learn much that is valuable about the South, the United States, and the plight of people of color in the Age of Empire by continuing to struggle to get to know Booker T.

Notes

1. The essential starting point for any understanding of Washington's early career is Louis R. Harlan, *Booker T. Washington: The Making of a Black Leader, 1856–1901* (New York: Oxford University Press, 1972).

2. W.E.B. Du Bois, *Writings*, ed. Nathan Huggins (New York: Library of America, 1986), 1: 392.

3. On Washington's later life and career, see Louis R. Harlan, *Booker T. Washington: The Wizard of Tuskegee, 1901–1915* (New York: Oxford University Press, 1983).

4. Louis R. Harlan, "The Secret Life of Booker T. Washington," *Journal of Southern History* 37 (August 1971): 393–416; August Meier, *Negro Thought in America, 1880–1915: Racial Ideologies in the Age of Booker T. Washington* (Ann Arbor: University of Michigan Press, 1963). For a discussion of the evolving historiography surrounding Washington, see Kevern Verney, *The Art of the Possible: Booker T. Washington and Black Leadership in the United States, 1881–1925* (New York: Routledge, 2001), chapter 10.

5. Harlan, "Secret Life of Booker T. Washington"; August Meier, "Booker T. Washington and the Negro Press," *Journal of Negro History* 38 (January 1953): 67–90; Meier, *Negro Thought in America*, chapter 7.

6. John W. Cell, *The Highest Stage of White Supremacy: The Origins of Segregation in South Africa and the American South* (Cambridge: Cambridge University Press, 1982).

7. James M. Cox, "Autobiography and Washington," *Sewanee Review* 85 (spring 1977): 235–61; Frederick L. McElroy, "Booker T. Washington as Literary Trickster," *Southern Folklore* 49 (1992): 100.

8. Booker T. Washington, *The Story of My Life and Work* (Naperville, Ill.: J. L. Nichols & Co., 1900). For comparisons of the two autobiographies, see Roger J. Bresnahan, "The Implied Readers of Booker T. Washington's Autobiographies,"

Black American Literature Forum 14 (spring 1998): 15–20; Charlotte D. Fitzgerald, "*The Story of My Life and Work:* Booker T. Washington's Other Autobiography," *Black Scholar* 21 (1991): 35–40; Donald B. Gibson, "Strategies and Revisions of Self-Representation in Booker T. Washington's Autobiographies," *American Quarterly* 45 (September 1993): 370–93; and Carla Willard, "Timing Impossible Subjects: The Marketing Style of Booker T. Washington," *American Quarterly* 53 (December 2001): 624–69. See also Verney, *Art of the Possible,* chapter 9.

9. For general surveys of the deteriorating race relations in the Jim Crow South, see Leon F. Litwack, *Trouble in Mind: Black Southerners in the Age of Jim Crow* (New York: Knopf, 1998), and Joel Williamson, *The Crucible of Race: Black/White Relations in the American South since Emancipation* (New York: Oxford University Press, 1984).

10. *Atlanta Journal,* August 12, 1897.

11. On lynching and racial violence, see E. M. Beck and Stewart E. Tolnay, *A Festival of Violence: An Analysis of Southern Lynching, 1882–1930* (Urbana: University of Illinois Press, 1995); W. Fitzhugh Brundage, ed., *Under Sentence of Death: Lynching in the South* (Chapel Hill: University of North Carolina Press, 2002); and Philip Dray, *At the Hands of Persons Unknown: The Lynching of Black America* (New York: Random House, 2002).

12. Edward L. Ayers, *The Promise of the New South: Life after Reconstruction* (New York: Oxford University Press, 1992), chapter 6; Alexander Keyssar, *The Right to Vote: The Contested History of Democracy in the United States* (New York: Basic Books, 2000), chapter 4; J. Morgan Kousser, *The Shaping of Southern Politics: Suffrage Restriction and the Establishment of the One-Party South, 1880–1910* (New Haven: Yale University Press, 1974); Michael Perman, *Struggle for Mastery: Disfranchisement in the South, 1888–1908* (Chapel Hill: University of North Carolina Press, 2001).

13. For a critique of Washington's tragically circumscribed vision, see Houston A. Baker Jr., "Men and Institutions: Booker T. Washington's *Up From Slavery,*" in *Long Black Song: Essays in Black Literature and Culture* (Charlottesville: University Press of Virginia, 1972), 84–95. For a critique of his leadership style, see Nathan Huggins, "Afro-Americans," in *Ethnic Leadership in America,* ed. John Higham (Baltimore: Johns Hopkins University Press, 1978), 91–118.

14. On respectability, see James T. Campbell, *Songs of Zion: The African Methodist Episcopal Church in the United States and South Africa* (New York: Oxford University Press, 1995), chapter 2; Kevin K. Gaines, *Uplifting the Race: Black Leadership, Politics, and Culture in the Twentieth Century* (Chapel Hill: University of North Carolina Press, 1996), introduction and chapter 1; John F. Kasson, *Rudeness & Civility: Manner in Nineteenth-Century Urban America* (New York: Hill and Wang, 1990), especially chapters 4 and 7; and Deborah Gray White, "The Cost of Club Work, the Price of Black Feminism," in *Visible Women: New Essays on American Activism,* ed. Nancy A. Hewitt and Suzanne Lebsock (Urbana: University of Illinois Press, 1993), 247–69.

15. Evelyn Brooks Higginbotham, *Righteous Discontent: The Women's Movement in the Black Baptist Church, 1880–1920* (Cambridge: Harvard University Press, 1993), chapter 7.

16. See especially Gail Bederman, *Manliness & Civilization: A Cultural History of Gender and Race in the United States, 1880–1917* (Chicago: University of Chicago Press, 1995), chapters 1 and 2; and Louise Michele Newman, *White Women's Rights: The Racial Origins of Feminism in the United States* (New York: Oxford University Press, 1999), chapter 1. See also Tunde Adeleke, *Unafrican Americans: Nineteenth-Century Black Nationalists and the Civilizing Mission* (Lexington: University Press of Kentucky, 1998), chapter 1; and Wilson Jeremiah Moses, *Afrotopia: The Roots of African American Popular History* (New York: Cambridge University Press, 1998), chapters 4 and 6.

17. For another glimpse, which treats Washington's influence on the Jamaican Marcus Garvey, see Verney, *Art of the Possible*, chapter 8.

18. Heather Cox Richardson, *The Death of Reconstruction: Race, Labor, and Politics in the Post–Civil War North, 1865–1901* (Cambridge: Harvard University Press, 2001).

19. David Howard-Pitney, *The Afro-American Jeremiad: Appeals for Justice in America* (Philadelphia: Temple University Press, 1990), 55–72.

20. Sharply critical accounts of Washington's program of vocational education include those of James D. Anderson, "Education as a Vehicle for the Manipulation of Black Workers," in *Work, Technology, and Education: Dissenting Essays in the Intellectual Foundations of American Education*, ed. Walter Feinberg and Henry Rosemont Jr. (Urbana: University of Illinois Press, 1975), 15–40; James D. Anderson, *The Education of Blacks in the South, 1860–1935* (Chapel Hill: University of North Carolina Press, 1988), 33–109; Houston A. Baker Jr., *Turning South Again: Rethinking Modernism/Re-reading Booker T.* (Durham: Duke University Press, 2001), 79–98; and Donald Spivey, *Schooling for the New Slavery: Black Industrial Education, 1865–1915* (Westport, Conn.: Greenwood Press, 1978), 45–70. More measured accounts include those of Eric Anderson and Alfred A. Moss Jr., *Dangerous Donations: Northern Philanthropy and Southern Black Education, 1902–1930* (Columbia: University of Missouri Press, 1999), especially chapters 1 and 2; Meier, *Negro Thought in America*, chapter 6; and William Toll, *The Resurgence of Race: Black Social Theory from Reconstruction to the Pan-African Conferences* (Philadelphia: Temple University Press, 1979), chapter 2.

21. On Washington's ideas about and Tuskegee's involvement in Africa, see Edward H. Berman, "Tuskegee in Africa," *Journal of Negro Education* 41 (spring 1972): 99–112; Louis Harlan, "Booker T. Washington and the White Man's Burden," *American Historical Review* 71 (January 1966): 441–67; Manning Marable, "Booker T. Washington and African Nationalism," *Phylon* 35 (December 1974): 398–406; Kendahl L. Radcliffe, "The Tuskegee-Togo Cotton Scheme, 1900–1909" (Ph.D. diss., UCLA, 1998); Michael O. West, "The Tuskegee Model of Development in Africa: Another Dimension of the African American Connection," *Diplomatic History* 16

(summer 1992): 371–87; Andrew Zimmerman, "Booker T. Washington in German Togo: Labor and Race in the Atlantic World" (unpublished paper, in author's possession); and Andrew Zimmerman, "From Primitives to Proletarians: The Tuskegee Institute in German Togo and the Emergence of 'Free Labor' in the Atlantic World" (manuscript in progress).

2

Up From Slavery as History and Biography

LOUIS R. HARLAN

Booker T. Washington's autobiography *Up From Slavery* is still in print after a hundred years and is still inspiring readers with its African American version of the American success story. As a work of popular literature, it is a classic.[1] This confronts the scholarly reader with a paradox, because, as a source of information about the man whose ideas and personal leadership dominated African American life in the early twentieth century, the book is less than dependable. In its hundredth year of publication, it is fitting that we reexamine this work and its impact. Let us consider, first, the genesis of *Up From Slavery*, its critical reception in Washington's own time, its publishing history and worldwide influence, and second, its merit as a biographical and historical source.

Washington began to consider writing an autobiography soon after he flashed into American public consciousness in 1895. Up until that year, when he was thirty-nine years old, his principal achievement had been the building of Tuskegee Normal and Industrial Institute in rural Alabama. He had been one of a half-dozen lesser-known African American leaders in the shadow of Frederick Douglass, but when Douglass died after a long career as an abolitionist leader and black spokesman, Washington moved with uncharacteristic boldness to fill the leadership vacuum. In September 1895 he delivered his eloquent Atlanta Compromise Address on the opening day of the Cotton States Exposition in Atlanta.[2] That Washington was the only black person on the platform was cause enough for wonder. He was not intended to give the principal speech of the occasion, but his speech eclipsed that of the designated chief orator and captured national newspaper headlines the next day because he proposed a solution of the southern race problem. The South was the most depressed part of a nation that was in the worst economic depression in its history up to that time. The South was also in the throes of a white supremacy movement that sought to overturn the Reconstruction era's few gains in black status and opportunity. Beginning in Mississippi in 1890, this movement rolled eastward and northward until it engulfed all of the former Confederate states and strongly influenced the racial attitudes of the entire nation. An amalgam of disfranchisement, segregation, violence, and terrorism, white supremacy assumed the God-given and universal right of white men not only to rule but also to subordinate all blacks in a lowly status not far removed from slavery.

Washington asserted in his Atlanta Compromise Address that black people would acquiesce in segregation and cease all agitation for their political and civil rights, at least for the time being, if southern whites would place no impediments in the path of black economic and educational opportunity. "In all things that are purely social we can be as separate as the fingers," he shouted, holding his open hand aloft, "yet one as the hand in all things essential to mutual progress," clenching his fist. Cheers broke out in both parts of the segregated audience, as each racial group heard what it wished to hear. At that moment, or soon thereafter, Washington became America's foremost black leader and spokesman by acclamation rather than by election. Election, of course, was not then available as a means of choosing the race's policy makers.

Southern white leaders never actually accepted Washington's proposed bargain, and white supremacy continued unabated until the middle of the next century. But Washington's speech signaled a shift of black racial strategy from being northern-based to being southern-based, from emphasizing the political to emphasizing the economic, and from being militant to being moderate in tone. Washington's new leadership would disparage black officeholding at a time when few blacks could vote. He would urge blacks to improve their work skills, acquire property, and vote through the teller's window. He would seek, "in every manly way," to mollify whites, seek common goals with whites, and improve black educational and business opportunity. In effect, Washington's accommodating leadership personified the diminished hopes of black people after the end of Reconstruction, in a Progressive Era that was "For Whites Only."[3]

Soon after the Atlanta Compromise Address, Washington might have sensed the desirability of an autobiographical narrative to illustrate not only his success story but also his racial thought. An opportunity presented itself in 1896, when the southern-born editor and publisher Walter Hines Page, then of Houghton, Mifflin and Company, rejected Washington's prospectus for a volume of his speeches, and suggested instead that Washington should write an autobiography.[4] Washington was too busy to respond at that time, however. A year later, Washington quietly and inauspiciously sent the prospectus of an autobiography to the obscure subscription publishing house of J. L. Nichols and Company, of Naperville, Illinois. This company specialized in books by black authors sold from door to door to African Americans too poor or too uncertain of a warm reception to venture into standard bookstores. Book publishing was increasingly segregated, like nearly every other aspect of American life.

Washington hired a young and inexperienced black journalist named Eugene Webber as a ghostwriter and was too busy to supervise him closely. The result of this collaboration was *The Story of My Life and Work*, published in 1900. Discovering too late the book's blemishes and shortcomings, Washington fired Webber and refused to acknowledge in the book the ghostwriter who had in fact written virtually the entire text. In a second printing, Washington even removed the photograph of Webber that the ghost had slyly inserted into a group of portraits of prominent and promising young black men.[5] When *Up From Slavery* appeared less than a year later, the head of the Nichols firm threatened to sue for breach of contract. Washington persuasively argued that, whereas the first autobiography was designed for a black reading public, the new book was written for northeastern white readers who bought magazines and read book reviews.[6]

For the new autobiography Washington chose not only a striking new title, *Up From Slavery*, but also a talented new ghostwriter. He was Max Bennett Thrasher, a white Vermonter who had worked as a Boston newspaperman, as superintendent of a school for indigent boys, and on the Tuskegee payroll as a public relations man.[7] Sometime in 1900 Washington began dictating autobiographical notes to Thrasher as they rode together on trains between Washington's speaking engagements, or between trains in railroad stations and hotels. Washington then wrote a handwritten draft of the book using Thrasher's typed notes and let Thrasher smooth out the rough spots and prepare a typescript of each chapter.

The evidence that Washington was to a large extent the author is a substantial fragment of an early draft of *Up From Slavery*, in Washington's hand, in the Booker T. Washington Papers in the Library of Congress. "Without the painstaking and generous assistance of Mr. Max Bennett Thrasher," Washington wrote in the preface of the first book edition, "I could not have succeeded in any satisfactory degree."[8] Despite this generous acknowledgment, however, the book bears unmistakable marks of Washington's authorship. The wording is similar to that of his speeches, and he had used many of the book's anecdotes in earlier speeches and writings. A letter that Thrasher wrote Washington in October 1900 hints at the creative relationship between author and ghost. Thrasher wrote that the first chapter they had agreed to serialize in *The Outlook* magazine had been "arranged as we decided on the train." He added: "I have not left out anything that you wrote except that one brief paragraph or perhaps a dozen lines in the first copy which you told me yourself you had decided to omit."[9] When *Up From Slavery* began appearing in the weekly issues of *The Outlook,* Thrasher spent most of the time between October and December 1900 in New York checking the galley proofs in the magazine office and making corrections and additions ordered by Washington.

The most cogent advice that Washington received on how to organize and package his past, however, seems to have come from Lyman Abbott, the venerable editor of *The Outlook*. After seeing a portion of an early draft, Abbott wrote to Washington: "The pictorial side of your life, the incidents which you have seen, out of which your own generalizations have grown, will be of the first interest and first value to your readers." He urged Washington to give his readers more information on his boyhood in slavery, his sports (he actually had none), his education, and his work experience. He suggested that Washington write about the Reconstruction period from the black man's perspective. Abbott also had suggestions as to style and order of treatment. He remarked: "I have the impression that this manuscript has been dictated, and that if you were to go over it carefully, you would condense it somewhat by cutting out some repetitions."[10]

Washington promised Abbott that he would see to it that the remainder of the text would be "in better condition as to compactness," and that he would develop more fully the themes Abbott had suggested. He wanted, however, a clear understanding with Abbott about the structure of the book. "When I talked with you and your son I got the impression that you did not care for one of the rather stereotyped styles of autobiographies which as a rule are divided into periods, of childhood, youth, &c., with each period exhausted before another is begun. This I have sought to avoid not only because I thought you desired it but also because it is in keeping with my own method of writing." He then stated his own rules of composition: "My general plan is to give the first place to facts and incidents and to hang the generalizations on to these facts—taking for granted that the average reader is more interested in an interesting fact than in a generalization based on that fact, and for this reason I have sought not to use many generalizations and when they are used to have them well sugar-coated with some interesting incident." As for order of treatment, "while I am at it I say nearly everything that I intend saying about" any subject. Washington privately complained to his friend T. Thomas Fortune of the "captiousness" of *The Outlook*'s staff, but this mood gave way to a sunnier one after Thrasher reported that Abbott was delighted with the new drafts. "Said he could not conceive how anything could be better or more striking," Thrasher wrote.[11]

Up From Slavery appeared in weekly installments in *The Outlook* from November 3, 1900, to February 3, 1901, and Doubleday, Page, and Company published it in book form in March 1901. All during its serialization, Abbott continued his editorial advice. Was Washington giving too much space to Tuskegee and too little to himself? "I should like to know, and our readers I am sure would," Abbott wrote, "what you have done for yourself as well as for others; what recreation you take, if any; what you read; what you have found helpful and suggestive in literature and in your acquaintance with other men; some of your experiences on your speaking tours; how you have been treated by the whites as well as by your own race on these tours; the political aspect of your work, for I do not believe that it will do any injury to the cause which you are fighting for, if you touch on the political side of it." Whereas Walter Hines Page confined his role largely to cheerleading, Abbott actively helped Washington to shape his autobiography to project the most appealing self-image. He invited Washington to dinner to discuss his suggestions more fully.[12] Abbott seemed to have little idea how touchy some of his suggestions were, particularly those on race relations and politics. Washington had reason to sidestep these and other questions (for example, about his reading and his recreation, both of which were practically nil). Nonetheless, Abbott's suggestions were provocative and at least as useful to Washington's writing as the more self-effacing services of Max Thrasher. A close reading of *Up From Slavery* shows that Washington responded to Abbott's advice in his own creative way.

Those who had worked with Washington to publish his new autobiography were among the first to congratulate him on his achievement. Hamilton W. Mabie, associate editor of *The Outlook*, wrote: "I do not think you can over-estimate the influence of your articles ... nothing that I have read in a long time has moved me so much."[13] Not only the senior editors at the magazine but also the clerks, copyboys, and printers thought Washington's story a cut above the magazine's usual offerings, and they held a dinner party in his honor, at which he answered their questions for an hour or more.[14] One of the book's publishers, Walter Hines Page, wrote in his cheerful Christmas letter to Washington in 1901: "how heartily I congratulate you on the results of this year. Tuskegee out of debt and broadening its work all the while, & your book steadily making its way about the world to the broadening of your influence & to the cheering of all earnest men."[15]

As on other occasions when Washington wrote or spoke, readers of diverse viewpoint found what they sought in his ambiguous rhetoric. Black readers particularly identified themselves with Washington and lived vicariously through his hardships, struggles, and successes. The most significant thing about Washington for black readers was that he had been born a slave. They responded to his urging not only to work hard and save money but also to be neat and respectable in their clothing, habits, and households, and to spread "the gospel of the toothbrush." As a struggling black attorney of Nashville wrote to Washington after reading *Up From Slavery:* "[M]y early experience was very similar to your early ones. I only wish the similarity were kept up to this day."[16]

As Washington had anticipated, however, the majority of his readers were whites, as they had the greater affluence, literacy, and access to the book market in an era of gross discrimination and segregation. The elite northern readers of *The Outlook* were particularly welcoming to the chapters as they unfolded. Many copies passed through several hands or were read aloud to the family at the breakfast table or to neighbors in the evening. William T. Harris, the United States Commissioner of Education, wrote to Washington after reading four chapters: "Mrs. Harriet Beecher Stowe wrote 'Uncle Tom's Cabin' and thereby produced a civil war in the Nation. You have written a book which I think will do more than anything else to guide us to the true road on which we may successfully solve the problems left us by that civil war." Mary Mackie, Washington's former teacher at Hampton Institute, declared that the autobiography "sets forth more graphically than any article that I have read the transition from slavery to freedom. It reads like a romance." She said that her sister was reading the chapters aloud every week to the girls in her private school.[17] There were other signs that the movers and shakers of the white community found in *Up From Slavery* a confirmation of their approval of Washington's moderate, nonthreatening leadership of African Americans. Reviews in the white media were almost universally favorable, the only notable exception being one in *Dial* magazine by W.E.B. Du Bois, Washington's leading African American critic. Du Bois complained that *Up From Slavery* was "a partial history" that gave "but glimpses of the real struggle which he has had for leadership" and ignored the compromises that Washington had made to secure white approval.[18] William Dean Howells, the novelist and arbiter of American letters, remarked that Washington seemed to have a greater measure of kindness for whites than many members of his race had cause to feel, and "rather more tolerance for the rich than the New Testament expresses," but he thought that Washington's way was, "at present, the only way for his race."[19]

Up From Slavery cast a broad net throughout the world. There were translations into French, German, Norwegian, Swedish, Danish, Dutch, Finnish, and Russian, and three Spanish-language editions, one of which circulated widely in Latin America. Translations were reported also in Arabic, Zulu, Hindi, Malayalam, Urdu, Chinese, Japanese, and the Indian languages Marathi and Telugu. In most if not all cases, these foreign editions gave Washington no royalties, but they did spread his influence far and wide. White missionaries and aboriginal peoples in the colonialized world both found messages in *Up From Slavery* that suited their purposes and needs. Not only Christians but also Hindus, Buddhists, and Sikhs responded to Washington's story of struggle and success. A Japanese read the book with "zeal" and thought it "one of the best books to encourage the spirit of young folks of the world."[20] A Sikh teacher in a Methodist college in Lucknow, India, wrote of *Up From Slavery*, "It dealt with so many of the problems that face us native Converts that I took the liberty to translate it into Urdu."[21] The Hindu headmaster of a school in the south of India wrote that his Malayalam adaptation of *Up From Slavery* had been adopted as a textbook. "More than 700 boys and girls, between the ages of 12 and 16," he said, "are thereby likely to know something of your labours at Tuskegee, for your race, and I hope they will learn some lessons of self-help therefrom, and learn to recognise the dignity of manual labour and training." He later reported that Madras University had also adopted the book.[22]

Up From Slavery profoundly influenced the Jamaican black nationalist leader Marcus Garvey, who wrote Washington seeking an invitation to visit Tuskegee Institute when he came to the United States. "I read 'Up from Slavery,' by Booker T. Washington," Garvey later wrote, "and then my doom—if I may so call it—of being a race leader dawned upon me in London.... I asked: 'Where is the black man's Government?' 'Where is his King and his kingdom?' 'Where is his President, his country, and his ambassador, his army, his navy, his men of big affairs?' I could not find them, and then I declared, 'I will help to make them.'"[23] Garvey failed to notice that Booker T. Washington had said nothing in *Up From Slavery* about the black man's governments, kings, or presidents, that he abhorred back-to-Africa movements, and that he was a black nationalist only in a cultural sense, if at all. Garvey and many other readers recognized that the autobiography did exude race pride and a desire that black people be accorded all the respect that was due them, and it was this spirit that won Garvey as Washington's enthusiastic disciple. Unfortunately for Garvey, Washington died several months before Garvey reached the United States, but Garvey made Washington a sort of patron saint of his Universal Negro Improvement Association that flourished in America in the 1920s.

Among the important side effects of the publication of *Up From Slavery* was the way it touched the hearts and pocketbooks of the richest white Americans. A few of these, including John D. Rockefeller and Henry H. Rogers of the Standard Oil Company, had begun making substantial gifts to Tuskegee Institute in the 1890s, but George Eastman and Andrew Carnegie were directly inspired to give by their reading of the autobiography. Eastman, the camera manufacturer, wrote Washington in 1902: "I have just been reading your book, 'Up from slavery' and have come to the conclusion that I cannot dispose of five thousand dollars to any better advantage than to send it to you for your institute."[24] He gave that sum every year, later increased it to $10,000 a year, and after Washington's death gave $250,000 to the Washington memorial fund.[25]

Washington had stalked Carnegie, the canny Scottish-American millionaire, for years without success. Soon after *Up From Slavery* appeared, however, the publisher Frank N. Doubleday regaled the retired steel manufacturer with anecdotes from Washington's book between shots of their golf game. These stories piqued Carnegie's interest in the man he had refused to see but whose life seemingly exemplified his own "gospel of wealth." Carnegie was an impulsive giver, and his first impulse was probably to say to his secretary, "Bertram, give that man a library." Learning of Carnegie's interest and surmising that thrift was the surest way to this man's heart, Washington had the school's architect draw up plans for a two-story Carnegie library building on the campus that, with student labor at about three cents an hour, would cost Carnegie only $20,000. Carnegie was so impressed by this example of Washington's ingenuity and economy that he began making a $10,000 annual donation to Tuskegee.

Somehow the annual gifts did not fully express, however, Carnegie's enormous admiration of Washington. So, after passing the donation basket at a huge fund-raising meeting for Tuskegee Institute at Madison Square Garden in 1903, Washington found a little slip of paper from Carnegie pledging $600,000, an astonishing amount for that day among black institutions of learning. Carnegie offered the sum in gilt-edge U.S. Steel bonds, of which $150,000 was for Washington's personal use. The letter of gift warrants full quotation because it expresses how completely *Up From Slavery* had bridged the distance between Washington's "gospel of the toothbrush" and Carnegie's "gospel of wealth." Carnegie wrote of Washington: "To me he seems one of the foremost of living men because his work is unique. The modern Moses, who leads his race and lifts it through Education to even better and higher things than a land overflowing with milk and honey. History is to know two Washingtons, one white, the other black, both Fathers of their People. I am satisfied that the serious race question of the South is to be solved wisely, only by following Booker T. Washington's policy which he seems to have been specially born—a slave among slaves—to establish, and even in his own day, greatly to advance."[26] Almost in one breath Carnegie associated Booker T. Washington not only with Moses and George Washington but with industrial multimillionaires like himself who had become America's new social arbiters. A newspaper cartoon of the day captioned "The 'Modern Moses' Strikes Rocks" caught the essence of Washington's ascending status through the Carnegie connection.[27]

Up From Slavery struck so many responsive chords with readers over so many generations that it may seem ungenerous to raise the question whether it truly represents his life experience. When we closely examine the text, however, and compare it with the other documentary evidence about Washington's life and work, we find discrepancies between its moving account of Washington's rise from rags to riches and the picture of Washington's life that emerges from the million or more letters in his private papers. The question arises whether *Up From Slavery* is essentially fact or fiction.

All autobiography, of course, includes fictional elements to some degree. When we write or speak about ourselves, we fiddle with our past so as to strike just the right note. We almost unconsciously present ourselves to the world as we wish to be seen rather than as we really are or really were. We invent a partly mythical past self and past events to impress the reader. We shift our experiences in or out of shadow, up to center stage, or back into the wings to mold our past or foreshadow our present. Every autobiographer does this to some extent, and more or less successfully, but Washington was even more prone to such fictionalizing than most, and he was more skillful at it because the circumstances of African American life had forced him to wear a mask all his life. He had as much to hide from certain readers as he had to reveal. He also had a message to convey, and he selected certain incidents of his life to illustrate the message. As in Aesop's *Fables*, nearly every anecdote in *Up From Slavery* is preceded or followed by a moral. One wonders which came first to his mind, the story or the moral. Which was tailored to fit the other? Washington's autobiography was important historically because it was the best and most inspirational statement he ever made of his social philosophy and his program for black advancement. As an account of his own life, however, it is in some respects inadequate.

Despite its fictional and moralistic elements, or rather because of them, *Up From Slavery* has worn well with the reading public. Though never a best-seller, it was popular in its own time and has continued to enjoy steady sales even during the decline in Washington's reputation during the Civil Rights era. It has incited countless readers, in America and abroad, among all races, to struggle up from their own lowly condition to successful lives and respectable middle-class status. The work remains in print in several published editions and is also available in cyberspace, not only to buy but to read for free. The entire text of *Up From Slavery* may be read on at least five different web sites. Obviously, the book has struck a responsive chord in many people and continues to have a share in the dialogue among African Americans and between them and white Americans.

One reason for *Up From Slavery*'s wide and lasting readership might be its simple, direct language—the language of speech and oral tradition rather than the more abstract language of the professional men who were Washington's sharpest critics. Washington was a self-made man, a man of the people, not a college graduate. He spoke the people's language, but more skillfully and subtly than most people. On this point we may rely upon the judgment of Barrett Wendell, who wrote to Washington praising *Up From Slavery* after teaching English composition for about twenty years at Harvard. "Certainly I have grown less and less patient of all writing which is not simple and efficient; and more and more of a style which does its work with simple, manly directness," he wrote. "It is hard to remember when a book, casually taken up, has proved, in this respect, so satisfactory as yours. No style could be more unobtrusive; yet few styles which I know seem to me more laden—as distinguished from overburdened—with meaning."[28] A simple, engaging style, however, cannot be the only reason for the success of *Up From Slavery*, for Washington wrote twelve other books in more or less the same style, and none of them were best-sellers or so "laden . . . with meaning."

Up From Slavery had a major impact on readers because it was not simple—it only seemed to be. Washington hired a talented white ghostwriter, but *ghostwriter* is a loose term, and in this case it does not mean the ghost did the writing. Max Thrasher took down Washington's dictated words, typed them up, and helped Washington revise them. Between them, they crafted a masterpiece that not only told Washington's life story but also embedded in it a reassuring message that even the American race system could not keep a good black man down. We today might call it subliminal if that were not an anachronism. Understanding Washington's message requires an understanding of the era in which he sent it. It was the worst time for black people since slavery, a time of lynchings, race riots, personal humiliations, disfranchisement, and the deepening and spreading of segregation. The autobiography intimated that if black people would only follow Washington's leadership in pursuance of an economic rather than a political path to higher status, they too could share in the American dream. Instead of agitating for rights, they would earn them. They would get along with their white neighbors, set attainable goals for themselves, work hard, save their money, and acquire property. They would become respectable, conservative, middle-class citizens—except in income, of course. That would come in time as whites recognized black people's true worth.

As far as we can know from the scanty records, *Up From Slavery* presents the main events of Washington's life up until 1901, but its account of his boyhood and youth is problematical. One of his chief problems in writing the book stemmed from his effort to please both white and black readers with a single text. He dealt with this by employing ambiguity. In discussing his childhood in slavery, for example, he stated that slavery was an evil, but then he added that the white owners were as trapped in the slavery system as were the slaves, and that black people benefited in many ways from what he called "the school of slavery." In discussing voting rights, Washington stated that if there were to be suffrage restrictions, "they should be made to apply with equal and exact justice to both races." He excused southern state disfranchisement laws, however, by conceding that "in the South we are confronted with peculiar conditions that justify the protection of the ballot in many states, for a while at least."[29] He had to choose his words carefully, of course, if he were to satisfy both whites and blacks enough to protect himself and his educational institution, but the final result was often self-contradiction.

At the very outset of his narrative in *Up From Slavery*, Washington felt it necessary to incorporate the plantation legend that had become fashionable in the late nineteenth century, which endowed every southerner with an imaginary antebellum plantation, conveniently burned, of course, by General Sherman. Instead of describing his birthplace accurately as a small farm where his owner and the owner's sons worked alongside about a half-dozen male slaves in the field, Washington calls it a plantation, complete with a Big House, overseer, and slave quarters.[30] Being the slave of a small-scale slaveowner was still slavery, of course, but it was very different from the gang labor and the impersonality of a big plantation. When Washington returned for the first time to his birthplace in 1908, he remarked: "I'm afraid I wouldn't know the place. Every thing is changed. But after all, the most remarkable changes that I notice is in the size of things."[31]

Being only nine years old when he gained his freedom, Washington did not experience many of the harsher aspects of adult slavery. Still, these were the formative years of early childhood, when Washington was socialized into the slave system.[32] One of the most poignant anecdotes in the book is of little Booker losing the sacks of corn off the horse's back on the way to the gristmill, and crying helplessly until an adult passed by and helped him. The problem is that his brother, John, three and a half years older, said that experience had actually happened to him, along with several other incidents that Booker Washington had appropriated to embellish his story.[33]

After slavery, as Washington grew up in Malden, West Virginia, and attended Hampton Institute, his budding career and his thinking seem to have been inordinately influenced by a series of well-to-do white people. The first of these was Viola Ruffner, wife of General Lewis Ruffner, the town's leading citizen, whose houseboy Washington became. She indoctrinated him with the Puritan ethic of hard work and thrift, and with a particular obsession with neatness. He said in *Up From Slavery* that the lessons she taught him were "as valuable to me as any education I have ever gotten anywhere since. Even to this day I never see bits of paper scattered around a house or in the street that I do not want to pick them up at once. I never see a filthy yard that I do not want to clean it, a paling off of a fence that I do not want to put it on, an unpainted or unwhitewashed house that I do not want to paint or whitewash it, or a button off one's clothes, or a grease-spot on them or on a floor, that I do not want to call attention to it."[34] Today we might stifle our admiration by calling him a "neat freak."

It was General Samuel Chapman Armstrong who became the "great white father" of this fatherless youth. Armstrong brought to the founding of Hampton Normal and Agricultural Institute the experience of a son of missionaries in Hawaii and the discipline of a Union officer of black troops in the Civil War. In *Up From Slavery* Washington called General Armstrong "a great man—the noblest, rarest human being that it has ever been my privilege to meet." And not merely great. "I shall always remember," Washington wrote, "that the first time I went into his presence he made the impression upon me of being a perfect man; I was made to feel that there was something about him that was superhuman."[35]

Other Hampton students shared this adulation of Armstrong, but Washington carried it further. He marked down for emulation every gesture, thought, and attitude of the general, even the cut of his clothes. He became Armstrong's favorite pupil, and a few years after graduation he was brought back to Hampton as a teacher and given further indoctrination in Armstrong's ideas. Armstrong considered African Americans to be a "tropical" race, similar to the Polynesians among whom he had grown up. "Of both it is true," he wrote, "that not mere ignorance, but deficiency of character is the chief difficulty, and that to build up character is the true objective point in education."[36] In Armstrong's view, "idleness, like ignorance, breeds vice." On another occasion he expressed the belief that "the differentia of races goes deeper than skin" and that, as "a child of the tropics," the African American was "in the early stages of civilization," not so much inferior as backward. Armstrong's "industrial education," therefore, was not so much a training in the humbler trades as it was the inculcation of industriousness.[37]

General Armstrong's influence may be seen in many of Washington's themes in *Up From Slavery*. For example, Washington interpreted the Reconstruction experiment as "artificial and forced" because it tempted African Americans to seek advancement through political participation and civil rights agitation rather than "perfecting themselves in the industries at their doors and in securing property."[38] This viewpoint Armstrong had expressed thirty years earlier in editorials in the *Southern Workman*, Hampton Institute's magazine. It was not unnatural that a white man of Armstrong's background would have such racial attitudes and such an educational program for young black people recently out of slavery. What was unnatural, and the source of many of Washington's problems as a black leader, was that this young, impressionable black student became the lifelong disciple of a racist white man, benevolently racist if there is such a thing, but still racist. Washington modeled Tuskegee Institute after Hampton Institute, adopted key elements of Armstrong's thinking, and sought to carry out his racial strategy of compromise with southern whites. In the instance of Washington's relationship with Armstrong, at least, we can gain biographical insights from *Up From Slavery*.

A significant omission in *Up From Slavery* is Washington's failure to discuss his search, in the years following his graduation from Hampton, for a career that would elevate him to leadership of the African American community. Hampton had prepared him to be a teacher, but teaching at the black school in his little hometown was not even a living, much less a career. In his earlier autobiography, *The Story of My Life and Work*, Washington speaks of spending about a year at Wayland Seminary, in Washington, D.C., to prepare for a career as a Baptist minister. He is silent on the question of why he left. But in *Up From Slavery* he says nothing about this abandoned career path except to remark parenthetically that "During the time I was a student in Washington" he had observed a superficiality in the lives of black city dwellers.[39] The following year, as he writes in *The Story of My Life and Work* but not in *Up From Slavery*, he assiduously read law books in the office of Romeo Freer, a carpetbagger lawyer in Charleston, West Virginia, and later a Republican congressman, another white hero for Washington. Under Freer's aegis, Washington even began a budding political career by speaking in black communities all through southern West Virginia in behalf of moving the state capital to Charleston.[40]

Why would Washington explicitly treat these alternative career tracks in one autobiography and not the other? The explanation lies in the different audiences the two books addressed. Washington preferred that his white readers not know that he had ever aspired to the somehow threatening professions of the ministry and the law. Whites might associate them with racial agitation or aspirations too high for a member of the subordinated race. Washington merely says in *Up From Slavery* that "The temptations to enter political life were so alluring that I came very near yielding to them at one time, but I was kept from doing so by the feeling that I would be helping in a more substantial way by assisting in the laying of the foundation of the race through a generous education of the hand, head, and heart."[41] Actually, he gave up law and politics because his hero, General Armstrong, offered him a job. Washington's choice of a career as an educator was either shrewdly intuitive or very lucky. Though he could not have known it at the time, he had picked the career most likely to position him for race leadership twenty years later.[42] Black politicians and ministers after Reconstruction both suffered a decline in their leadership status, and educators rose correspondingly to greater prominence, possibly because the white leadership in the South did not perceive them as threatening to white supremacy. One cannot argue with Washington's career choice, but only with his lack of candor about it in his autobiography.

While *Up From Slavery* was a "good read" and persuasive propaganda for Washington's racial philosophy, it is not very useful as a biographical source because it totally omits a large part of Washington's real life, as revealed by his private correspondence in the Library of Congress. While *Up From Slavery* does treat Washington's interracial diplomacy in the famous Atlanta Compromise Address in 1895, it does not so much as mention the Tuskegee Machine, as it was called, a vast nationwide network by which Washington controlled every avenue of black life. After 1895, Washington used his newly acquired fame and power to create an army of black friends and lieutenants in every center of black population. With help from sympathetic whites in positions of political and economic power, he dispensed rewards and punishments, jobs and subsidies, to black newspaper editors, businessmen, lawyers, educators, clergymen, and even officers of fraternal orders such as the Odd Fellows and the Prince Hall Masons, all with the object of creating personal loyalty to himself and suppressing dissent from his racial strategy.

There is also nothing in *Up From Slavery* about what I have elsewhere described as Washington's "secret life."[43] In deepest secrecy Washington hired and directed lawyers in the prosecution of civil rights cases attacking the very racial settlement that Washington publicly endorsed. And in an equally clandestine way he employed spies, paid and unpaid, to infiltrate the organizations of his black and white critics, his "enemies list," in order to counteract their efforts and even sometimes to act as provocateurs. Both Washington's hidden civil rights activity and his covert maneuvers against his rivals were unknown to more than a handful of his contemporaries, and only came to light when his private papers were opened in the early 1960s. The real Washington was then revealed to have been more devious and more morally ambiguous than had been assumed on the basis of his public writings and actions, but also more interesting and more courageous in challenging racial injustice. The image of modesty, rectitude, and compromise that he had presented in *Up From Slavery* needed to be revised.

One must keep in mind that Washington wrote his autobiography when he was only forty-five, and thus *Up From Slavery* does not include treatment of much of the most historically significant period of his public life. He later had an opportunity to rectify this when he wrote *My Larger Education* in 1911, a sort of sequel to *Up From Slavery*, but this later work shows the same lack of candor about his private actions.[44] It is understandable that Washington did not reveal to the reading public that he was a political boss or that he secretly deployed civil rights lawyers and spies to attain some of his ends, but it does limit the usefulness of *Up From Slavery* as a biographical and historical source.

It is safe to say, however, that most people read *Up From Slavery* less for historical information than for personal inspiration. Washington's message was of the "power of positive thinking." His life story was a case in point that anyone in America, even someone beginning life as an abject slave, could achieve the American dream of upward mobility and the pursuit of happiness. Despite its frequent weasel words that Washington felt were necessary to secure the good will or grudging acquiescence of whites, the autobiography holds out the promise—not only to African Americans but also to downtrodden people everywhere—that if they persist and strive, if they improve themselves, and if they seek common ground with their oppressors, good will come of these efforts. As an illustration of his success formula, Washington told the story of his building of Tuskegee Institute from a henhouse on a worn-out farm to a shining example of what black enterprise and hard work could accomplish. The narrative loses force somewhat as Washington sought to describe the period after the success of his Atlanta address in 1895, but the significance of his shaking hands with the president of the United States and having tea with Queen Victoria was not lost on his black readers. Over the century that followed the publication of *Up From Slavery*, few of Washington's followers were able to break through the hard shell of American white supremacy, but that has not stopped men and women from dreaming. Washington could claim only modest gains during his time as a race leader, but, to paraphrase Jesse Jackson, another black self-help promoter, Washington kept hope alive.

Notes

1. Booker T. Washington, *Up From Slavery* (New York: Doubleday, Page, and Co., 1901). Of the several current editions, I have chosen to use the Penguin Classics paperback edition (New York: Penguin, 1986), with an introduction by myself, and page numbers will refer to that edition.

2. Ibid., 218–25. A manuscript version in Washington's hand and the standard

printed version of the speech are presented in Louis R. Harlan and Raymond W. Smock, eds., *The Booker T. Washington Papers*, 14 vols. (Urbana: University of Illinois Press, 1972–89), 3: 578–87 (hereinafter cited as *BTW Papers*).

3. Quoted from C. Vann Woodward, *Origins of the New South 1877–1913* (Baton Rouge: Louisiana State University Press, 1951), 369.

4. Page to Washington, October 14, 1896, *BTW Papers*, 4: 226.

5. Editors' introduction to *The Story of My Life and Work*, in *BTW Papers*, 1: xix.

6. Washington to J. L. Nichols and Company, April 26, 1901, *BTW Papers*, 6: 95–96. For more information on Washington's relationship with this firm and its successor, Hertel, Jenkins and Company, see Louis R. Harlan, *Booker T. Washington: The Making of a Black Leader, 1856–1901* (New York: Oxford University Press, 1972), 244–45 (hereinafter cited as Harlan, *BTW*, vol. 1).

7. On Thrasher's background and relation to Tuskegee Institute, see Harlan, *BTW*, 1: 246.

8. Washington, *Up From Slavery*, preface.

9. Thrasher to Washington, October 11, 1900, Booker T. Washington Papers, Division of Manuscripts, Library of Congress (hereinafter cited as BTW Papers LC).

10. Abbott to Washington, October 1, 1900, *BTW Papers*, 5: 646.

11. Washington to Abbott, handwritten draft, ca. October 8, 1900, *BTW Papers*, 5: 653–54; Washington to Fortune, October 11, 1900, and Thrasher to Washington, October 11, 1900, BTW Papers LC.

12. Abbott to Washington, January 8, 1901, BTW Papers LC.

13. Mabie to Washington, January 14, 1901, BTW Papers LC.

14. Report of the dinner in the *Tuskegee Student* 13 (January 26, 1901): 1, 4.

15. Page to Washington, December 18, 1901, BTW Papers LC.

16. George F. Robinson to Washington, May 5, 1901, BTW Papers LC.

17. Harris to Washington, December 3, 1900, *BTW Papers*, 5:687; Mackie to Washington, November 21, 1900, BTW Papers LC. Harris added that he thought "that in writing this autobiography you have come upon a method by which you can increase your usefulness tenfold and a hundredfold by revealing in a book the spirit of your methods."

18. See account of the reviews, including that of Du Bois, in *BTW Papers*, 1: xxx–xxxiii.

19. Review in *North American Review* 173 (August 1901): 280–88.

20. Laijiro Yamamasu to Washington, March 1, 1915, BTW Papers LC.

21. Lilavati Singh to Washington, June 3, 1901, BTW Papers LC.

22. K. Paramu Pillai to Washington, January 24, 1905, April 25, 1906, and June 12, 1908, BTW Papers LC.

23. Garvey to Washington, April 12, 1915, *BTW Papers*, 13: 261. Garvey's description of the impact of reading *Up From Slavery* is quoted from Amy Jacques-Garvey, ed., *Philosophy and Opinions of Marcus Garvey*, 2 vols. (New York: Universal Publishing House, 1923, 1926), 2: 126. See also E. David Cronon, *Black Moses: The Story of Marcus Garvey and the Universal Negro Improvement Association* (Madison: University of Wisconsin Press, 1969), 16.

24. Eastman to Washington, January 2, 1902, *BTW Papers*, 6: 370.

25. Louis R. Harlan, *Booker T. Washington: The Wizard of Tuskegee, 1901–1915* (New York: Oxford University Press, 1983), 130 (hereinafter cited as Harlan, *BTW*, vol. 2).

26. Carnegie to William H. Baldwin Jr., April 17, 1903, *BTW Papers*, 7: 120. Baldwin was chairman of the Tuskegee Institute board of trustees. I quote from Carnegie's original letter, but another of the same date, written at the request of the trustees, modified somewhat the terms of Washington's personal share of the gift.

27. *Boston Record*, April 25, 1903, clipping, BTW Papers LC.

28. Barrett Wendell to Washington, April 12, 1901, *BTW Papers*, 6: 87.

29. Washington, *Up From Slavery*, 17, 16, 237.

30. Harlan, *BTW*, 1: 6–9.

31. "Tuskegee's Principal at his Old Home," a news item from the *New York Evening Post* reprinted in the *Tuskegee Student*, October 3, 1908, in *BTW Papers*, 8: 637.

32. I am indebted to Orlando Patterson, who, at the University of Florida conference on the reconsideration of *Up From Slavery* in October 2001, made this point about childhood assimilation into the culture of slavery.

33. John H. Washington to Asa L. Duncan, August 20, 1913, *BTW Papers*, 12: 265.

34. Washington, *Up From Slavery*, 44.

35. Ibid., 54–55.

36. Samuel C. Armstrong, "Lessons from the Hawaiian Islands," *Journal of Christian Philosophy*, reprint of January 1884, 213, Hampton University Archives.

37. See the discussion of General Armstrong's educational and social ideas in Harlan, *BTW*, 1: 56–62, 74–75.

38. Washington, *Up From Slavery*, 84–85.

39. My interpretation of the psychological relationship between Washington and Armstrong does not go so far toward the Freudian as that of Houston A. Baker Jr., in *Turning South Again: Re-thinking Modernism/Re-reading Booker T.* (Durham: Duke University Press, 2001), 50–51, 73.

40. Harlan, *BTW*, 1: 92–100.

41. Washington, *Up From Slavery*, 85.

42. See chapter 2, "Changing Attitudes toward Political Activity," in August Meier's pioneer study, *Negro Thought in America, 1880–1915: Racial Ideologies in the Age of Booker T. Washington* (Ann Arbor: University of Michigan Press, 1963), 26–41.

43. See Louis R. Harlan, "The Secret Life of Booker T. Washington," *Journal of Southern History* 37 (August 1971): 393–416, and Harlan, *BTW*, 2: 90–94, 244–47, 364, 376–77.

44. Booker T. Washington, *My Larger Education: Being Chapters from My Experience* (New York: Doubleday, Page, and Co., 1911), especially 3–10, 102–27, 158–82, 239–61.

3

In Search of Booker T. Washington

Up From Slavery, History, and Legend

WALDO MARTIN

> We wear the mask that grins and lies,
> It hides our cheeks and shades our eyes—
>
> Paul Laurence Dunbar, "We Wear the Mask"

Booker T. Washington was the namesake of my elementary school. Like so many black children coming of age in the twilight years of the Jim Crow era, those of us lucky enough to attend the all-black Washington Elementary School in Greensboro, North Carolina, first came to know Washington as the official, All-American Negro hero. In fifties America, he was the quintessential Negro American, the consensus Negro who even received honorable mention in all-white history textbooks. He towered over the historical landscape as the most important twentieth-century leader of black people. Exactly who he was and what he did only emerged for most of us over time, and in fits and starts. Nevertheless, we understood from the beginning that Washington had led our people during some really hard times not too long after emancipation. Through many Negro History Week programs at school and in the community, especially the church, over time Washington's inspiring rise from the obscurity of slavery to greatness as a free and world-famous man became clearer. Like that of his nineteenth-century counterpart, Frederick Douglass, Washington's story personified the enduring African American challenge: to do well in spite of racism so as to redound to the glory of "the race."

Concurrently, mid-fifties America witnessed the blossoming of the modern Civil Rights movement. Not only did that momentous struggle yield another important "Moses" of our people, Martin Luther King Jr., but it also witnessed the epochal *Brown* decision (1954)—the legal death knell of Jim Crow and the overturning of the ruling *Plessy* (1896) precedent. The legal and constitutional basis for the fiction of "separate but equal" black and white worlds was now gone. Yet *Brown II* (1955), the remedy phase of the decision, only exacerbated white resistance with its deliberately evasive decree to integrate segregated schools with "all deliberate speed." We later learned (or recalled) that Washington had been installed as the preeminent Negro leader at the moment of Jim Crow's codification in the *Plessy* decision, deepening our understanding of the difficulties his leadership presented, not just for him, but for black people in the main.

The high tide of the sixties Civil Rights (1945–65) and Black Power (1966–75) insurgency (hereinafter referred to as the Movement) demanded that blacks—indeed the nation—come to grips with the historical Washington and his legacy. While there clearly were other important black leaders during Washington's time, such as W.E.B. Du Bois, and since, such as Du Bois and Marcus Garvey, for the first half of the twentieth century, Washington dominated the leadership pantheon. In fact, it was commonplace until the emergence of King to view black leadership in the period between Washington's death in 1915 and King's spectacular emergence forty years later as an interregnum. The ideological and historical imperatives of the Movement dramatically altered that understanding. In other words, the Movement forced a searching reconsideration of and renewed appreciation for an increasingly diverse array of black leaders before, during, and after the "Age of Washington." It also forced an equally profound rethinking of the very notion of black leadership. For example, we now concern ourselves with issues of class, gender and varieties of leadership, including non-elite and elite, charismatic, facilitative, and local as well as national.[1]

Despite shifting definitions of black leadership in the more than thirty years since the apogee of the Movement, and 100 years after the publication of his classic autobiography *Up From Slavery*, Booker T. Washington remains a canonical figure in the American experience. Washington epitomizes the masterful accommodationist and calculating realist seeking to carve out a viable strategy for black struggle amidst the nadir of race relations in the United States. As methodically and seductively argued in *Up From Slavery*, Washington simultaneously resisted and accommodated the white supremacist offensive sweeping the nation at the time.

This very paradox has rendered Washington a highly controversial, often divisive figure. He has often been derisively characterized by his antagonists then and since as the very embodiment of "Uncle Tomism" precisely because of his thoroughgoing public accommodationism. The cumulative historical weight of this consistent and intensely negative critique has in turn fed an equally negative historical image problem. This has been the case especially since the Movement, when the withering assaults on his accommodationism obscured everything else about him. Countervailing evidence and his continuing legion of supporters notwithstanding, the tar brush of "Uncle Tomism" has stuck to Washington over the course of the twentieth century.

Like his accommodationism, his private radicalism, wherein he vigorously opposed the publicly conciliatory stances he assumed, also failed as a strategy. His private campaigns against lynching, disfranchisement, and Jim Crow remained hidden in his day, and in spite of partisans' and scholars' efforts, remained largely hidden for much of the twentieth century.[2] For obvious reasons, neither in *Up From Slavery* nor in public did Washington comment on this fundamental contradiction of his life: his public accommodationism despite his private opposition to that very same accommodationism. While there are glimpses of resistance in *Up From Slavery* and his public life, his efforts to deny, avoid, and obscure them overshadow all else. In the end, we must see Washington himself as the crucial agent in the construction of his complex historical persona, and *Up From Slavery* as the key text driving the process; he was both creator and hero, on one hand, and victim and antihero, on the other.

When Washington arrived at Hampton Institute in 1872 seeking admission after an arduous trek of 500 miles from Malden, West Virginia, his prospects appeared dim. Miss Mary F. Mackie, the head teacher, saw something in him, though, and asked him to sweep the recitation room. He not only swept the room three times, but he also went the proverbial extra mile. "I got a dusting cloth and I dusted it four times." He left the room squeaky clean. So clean, in fact, that "unable to find one bit of dirt on the floor, or a particle of dust on any of the furniture," Miss Mackie immediately admitted him to Hampton. His excellence at cleaning earned him a job as a janitor, enabling him to cover most of his boarding charge.[3]

In designing his homespun yet artful biographical narrative, this episode, like many of its kind sprinkled throughout the book, proves both revealing and determinative. It affirms the substance and the arc of his self-made ascent from humble, rural origins to national and international renown. Like Benjamin Franklin and Frederick Douglass before him, Washington self-consciously plots his life as both archetypal self-made man and American hero—an exemplar to whites as well as to blacks.[4] No matter how high he rose, or the magnificence of a particular accomplishment, he never forgot his roots: He remained common, an everyman. In fact, he never left his beloved rural South.

Washington's Hampton "entrance exam" showcased certain revealing features about the person. This fixation on cleanliness, hygiene, fastidiousness, and order revealed a deep-seated concern with control, with mastery, and with power. On a quite different yet related level, this same fixation manifested itself in his chronic concern with appearance, with surface representations. This particular episode—in fact, the entire autobiography—illustrated a profound desire for control over the appearance as well as the reality of his private as well as public life. This consuming desire to achieve mastery over his private and public selves went hand-in-hand with an equally deep concern for how others—especially powerful and important people, white as well as black—saw him. The consequences were telling. Most important, his concerns for control over both his self-representation and his reception by others fed off of one another. Mixed with Washington's fundamentally cautious and conservative temperament, they yielded an exceedingly complicated personality with many, at times conflicting, sides.

This fixation with cleanliness and dirtiness likewise exposed a profound ambivalence toward the earth, and ultimately, toward himself. Washington simultaneously embraced the life-giving earth and was bedeviled by the stigma of personal dirtiness, and by extension, personal unworthiness. On one level, he clearly loved the land, the farm world with which his life and beloved Tuskegee were intimately associated. On another level, dirtiness called forth a powerful, perhaps unconscious, identification of himself as a lowly and unclean, thus unworthy, former slave. Hence his fetish of personal hygiene and general cleanliness illustrated deep-seated concerns. For him the interrelated stains of dirtiness and unworthiness had to be wiped away. Louis R. Harlan, Washington's biographer, offered that his elusive subject was in the end a "complex, enigmatic figure."[5]

Washington incessantly traversed the border between accommodation and resistance, seeking a middle ground where resistance conflated with accommodation. Working deftly within this geography, Washington adopted a number of guises. At bottom, as Ralph Ellison has observed of the psychology of masking, for Washington this process signaled "a profound rejection of the image created to usurp his identity," especially negative and racist renderings of blacks. He labored long and hard to realize his own vision of himself. While deeply sensitive to social perceptions of himself, in the end, if push came to shove, he went in the direction of self-definition, especially if a compromise between the two appeared impossible. To a remarkable degree the finesse worked. As W.E.B. Du Bois noted in the early twentieth century, "the most striking thing in the history of the American Negro since 1875 is the ascendancy of Mr. Booker T. Washington." Writing in a similar groove, almost half a century later, August Meier dubbed the period from 1895 to 1915 the "Age of Washington."[6]

Yet as with his autobiographical ancestors Franklin and Douglass, constraints imposed by the historical moment circumscribed the psychological self as well as the narrative self that Washington so ably interwove. The concurrent regime of anti-black terrorism seriously undercut the "Age of Washington." The crafty ambiguity of his studied accommodationism left him open to multiple, often conflicting, assessments. Just who was Mr. Booker T. Washington? Was he the "Sage of Tuskegee," as supporters have seen him? Or, was he the "Wizard of Tuskegee," as detractors have seen him? Was he a realist, a pragmatist, a visionary who did the most and the best he could, given the difficult times in which he found himself? Or was he a "devious behind-the-scenes-wheeler-dealer"? A "shrewd power broker," or a "cynical sell-out"?[7]

Those who have seen Washington in the glowing light cast by *Up From Slavery* typically read that narrative in a relatively straightforward way. When read as a faithful rendition of personal uplift and self-invention, his life story functions as a stirring affirmation of the mythic American Dream (material comfort and respectability) and the mythic American Success Model (hard work, smarts, savvy, and connections leading to the American Dream). Washington's overweening optimism, notably that of *Up From Slavery*, obscured the reality that the dream and the success formula prescribed by American individualism were mythic at best, and far too often a cruel hoax, particularly for blacks struggling within the nadir.

A more cogent way of reading *Up From Slavery* has been to see it as an imaginative and playful text mirroring an adeptly scripted life story. Throughout the text as well as most of his life, Washington skillfully moved from one mask to another, from one element of personal development to another. Throughout it all, he represented the package as reflective of his race's potential and actual advancement. Like Douglass, Washington believed that his uplifting personal saga tellingly signified the movement of his people from slavery to freedom. Consequently, the narrative must be read not simply as an artful series of poses and manipulations. It is that and much, much more. Most important, it is an extraordinarily engaging story. Washington was a supreme ironist and must therefore be read as one. The text must be read figuratively as well as literally; it must be read against itself as well as straight.

For most of the twentieth century, the autobiography has been read straight, emphasizing its truthfulness and transparency. Today, the complex historical Washington has been fully acknowledged. Dissecting *Up From Slavery*'s mixture of self-invention and self-promotion has added significantly to our understanding of this complex historical Washington. "Today it is almost taken for granted," William Andrews has explained, "that Washington wrote behind multiple masks in *Up From Slavery* and seldom lowered them enough to allow his reader to look him full in the face."[8]

Put another way, the autobiography raises the question of who's playing whom? In *Invisible Man* Ellison wrestles with this dilemma in his portrait of Dr. Bledsoe, a character based loosely on Washington. Bledsoe mirrors the complexity of the historical and autobiographical Washington. In Ellison's novel, Washington's accommodationism appears in various guises. Like Washington, operating on the treacherous terrain of Jim Crow America, Bledsoe plays to his different constituencies, white and black, with consummate skill. He is both "sage" and "wizard"; shrewd and candid; selfless and self-centered; race man and race traitor, who rules his Tuskegee-like fiefdom with an iron glove.[9]

The need for an ironic analysis of the paradoxical Washington is nowhere clearer than in the speech and the moment that launched him into fame and notoriety. That five-minute speech at the Atlanta Cotton States and International Exposition on September 18, 1895, was a masterpiece. It spoke brilliantly to the various assembled constituencies and to those throughout the nation, all of whose support he so assiduously courted. His presentation was such that it sealed his elevation to the position of the preeminent national Negro spokesman. This unofficial yet important post had been vacated recently as a result of the death of Frederick Douglass earlier that same year. Washington artfully captured the spirit of the times with his earnest and multilayered accommodationist message.

He argued persuasively for interracial amity and reconciliation, "bootstraps mobility" (Negro uplift through self-help and self-reliance buttressed by the American success ideology and the Protestant work ethic), and acceptance of a status quo in race relations. The tone of the speech—selflessness and Christian forbearance—was quite different from Douglass's uncompromising advocacy of political and civil rights. In Washington's public position, Negroes could now de-emphasize such rights but would earn them in due time by proving themselves worthy. Speaking both metaphorically and straightforwardly, he pointed out that "In all things that are purely social we can be as separate as the fingers, yet one as the hand in all things essential to mutual progress." While embracing the "separate but equal" social logic of Jim Crow, Washington nevertheless asked that influential whites assist Negroes in their self-help efforts. In other words, black "self-help" required white support.[10]

Washington's program in turn gave each segment of his audience something to agree with. Reflective of his multifaceted personality and leadership, to each segment of his audience he pushed aspects of his program. He spoke openly yet also from behind a veil, a series of masks. Southern and northern whites clearly saw appeasement as well as accommodation. Blacks recognized the common black emphasis on self-help, racial and economic nationalism, and community building.

"Seeking to be all things to all men in a multifaceted society," Harlan has argued, "Washington jumped Jim Crow with the skill of long practice, but be seemed to lose sight of the original purposes of his dance." Washington often employed stories and devices drawn from minstrelsy—in other words, he at times rhetorically "jumped Jim Crow"—but he was certainly no minstrel. Eric Sundquist has recently offered a similar appraisal, contending that Washington was an expert at creating "a paradoxical performance at the very boundary of Jim Crow."[11] The dilemma of accommodation—not to mention protest—via "jumping Jim Crow" is acute. On one hand, his approach obfuscates and undermines the politics of resistance. On the other, it likewise obfuscates and undermines the cultural politics of race pride and racial nationalism. Thus, as a potential site of transgression and subversion, it is highly problematic.

Or is it? At points *Up From Slavery* provides a telling critique of existing institutional arrangements. In chapter 15, "The Secret of Success in Public Speaking," he speaks revealingly yet metaphorically to the need for greater national economic parity across races and classes. Harking back to Sunday morning meals as a slave child, where his mother supplemented the "corn bread and pork" with "a little molasses from the big house," Washington now represented those meals as "feasts." Using molasses as a metaphor for the economic playing field, he insisted that there is "more molasses on a plate when it is spread all over the plate than when it occupies a little corner." In this probing critique of economic injustice, notably hoarding and income inequality, he further explained that he "never believed in 'cornering' the syrup." He allowed that he had earlier enjoyed his "share" of the syrup, which was "usually about two tablespoonfuls," far more than the "fourteen-course dinner" he now at times shared with the business-industrial elite. Washington was painfully aware of the personal "costs" of being a witness to such unjust economic privilege and gross excess. He likewise displayed here a noteworthy sensitivity to the plight of those not just denied a seat at the table, but denied anything approximating economic justice.[12]

Speaking from a comparable perspective, Houston Baker has applauded the subversive qualities and modernist aesthetics of Washington's rhetorical appropriation of Jim Crow minstrel material and techniques. More commonly, others, like Adolph Reed, have blasted this appropriation and the very performance itself as the rankest kind of political opportunism and self-demeaning sycophancy. Baker, for instance, at points has interpreted Washington's use of the Negro "chicken thief" stereotype as a kind of transgressive performance. Rather than evidence of innate black immorality, as racists would employ it, Baker argues that Washington used it very differently. In *Up From Slavery*'s initial chapter, Washington speaks approvingly of his mother stealing chickens to feed her family. Instead of buying into the stereotype, Washington appropriates and then reworks it.[13]

For Baker, both the original "theft" and Washington's narrative appropriation of it were subversive, even affirmative moves. "The mother's act," according to Baker, "offers instruction in (and nourishes) a cultural voice won from slavery's victimization and silencing."¹⁴ In other words, slave morality fundamentally opposed the interests of their masters. For slaves to appropriate and redistribute among themselves their master's property for the slave's unpaid labor was thus wholly ethical and justifiable. While regaining cultural voice and all that it entails is essential, equally essential is the moral and political philosophy tied to that voice. These were all crucial considerations in the individual and collective freedom struggle that Washington himself embodied.

In the Atlanta Exposition Address, however, Washington overstepped himself. Here he speaks jocularly of the freedpeople's possessions at the dawn of emancipation as "a few quilts and pumpkins and chickens (gathered from miscellaneous sources)." Here his modernist manipulation of Jim Crow went awry; he overplayed the masking routine. "Scandal," Baker argues, "is the only designation for the appearance of such a sound (a chicken-thieving tonality) in the first address presented in the South by a black man considered a national leader."¹⁵

While the style as well as the substance of Washington's accommodationism have consistently rubbed many blacks the wrong way, many whites have found Washington's unassuming and nonthreatening posture quite palatable. Washington labored diligently to become a trustworthy Negro emissary to the white power structure. "More than Douglass ever had been," Reed notes, "Washington became the singular, trusted informant to communicate to whites what the Negro thought, felt, wanted, needed." Without grassroots support pushing him forward, without a political constituency to answer to, Washington became "the first purely freelance race spokesman: his status depended on designation by white elites rather than by any black electorate or social movement."¹⁶

Washington's personal success and the success of *Up From Slavery* demonstrate vividly his uncanny insight into the possibilities of the historical moment. Washington thus fundamentally revised the African American autobiographical tradition built upon the slave narrative. As a result, he very carefully crafted a persona for himself and his historical cohort as the "New Negro," or freedom's first and subsequent generations.¹⁷ Unencumbered by the moral morass and structural inequalities growing out of slavery and white supremacy, "The New Negro" reflected the New South mythology of regional economic uplift into modernity. A rising economic tide, he contended, would lift all the ships in the South, including Negro ones, and ultimately bring freedom, justice, and equality to the region.

Up From Slavery and Washington himself thus exuded the dominant "Gospel of Wealth," or business/economic ethos of the times. Andrew Carnegie's narrative and his Horatio Alger–like life were a key model here. Even more directly, however, *Up From Slavery* drew upon the nineteenth-century African American autobiographical tradition epitomized by Frederick Douglass's 1845 *Narrative* and his 1855 narrative, *My Bondage and My Freedom*. Washington not only succeeded Douglass as the major African American spokesman of the age, but he also constructed a powerful revisionist slave narrative that basically remade the tradition so as to reflect his own life and ideology. What Andrews refers to as "Washington's skill in masking his personal and social agenda behind an apparently simple, almost folksy brand of unassuming storytelling" has proven to be extremely effective. In terms of sales and influence, *Up From Slavery* soon supplanted Douglass's narrative as the foundational black freedom story. Not until Richard Wright's stunning post-emancipation autobiography *Black Boy* (1945) was there a challenge to *Up From Slavery* as a defining historical and literary framework. In substance and tone, *Black Boy* reprised the realism and spirit of aggressive struggle so central to Douglass's narratives.[18]

The most striking similarities between Douglass's narratives and *Up From Slavery* are philosophical. Both project a profound attachment to the promise of the American Dream. Both believed deeply in the Enlightenment project, especially its emphasis on human perfectibility, human progress, and the power of human reason. Both believed deeply in individual and collective notions of self-help. While both were optimistic, Washington was far more so, especially the public Washington. In the end, through the uncommon force of their spectacular life stories of ascent from slavery to freedom, both men became symbols as well as leaders. Their stories confirmed the potential of the race. In that sense, both were representative race men. Much of their continuing historical significance, then, owes to their willingness and ability to project themselves as emblematic of their people's struggle, not just their own personal struggle.

The divergences between the narratives are equally telling. These critical differences shed light on Washington's complexity and his troubled historical legacy. First, there is the basic conflict between Douglass's commitment to ceaseless agitation and Washington's "calculated accommodationism." Second, there is the related issue of contrasting historicisms, or how best to represent the history of slavery, emancipation, Reconstruction, and the emergence of Jim Crow, disfranchisement, and lynching. Throughout his life, Douglass remained resolute in his belief that slavery and racism were moral monstrosities and national sins that demanded ceaseless struggle to overcome. Whites as well as Negroes themselves, indeed the entire nation, bore responsibility for overcoming them. An uncompromising abolitionist mandate for full equality, Douglass's autobiography personified the tradition of active resistance to wrong. Douglass's stirring victory as a slave over the vicious Covey, "the Negro Breaker," constituted a moral anchor for his narrative. In *Up From Slavery*, there is neither a comparable moment of physical triumph over evil, nor is there a comparable moral anchor.

The logic of accommodation led Washington in other directions, forcing him to make other kinds of choices. Douglass, unlike Washington, who was freed from slavery while a child, had seized his freedom by escaping North with the assistance of his future wife, Anna Murray. Rather than being a brief for abolitionism and full equality, *Up From Slavery* is a primer for black self-improvement, economic uplift, and interracial harmony in the nadir. Andrews has aptly characterized it as a "post-bellum slave narrative." This designation explains much. *Up From Slavery*'s center is economic: the Protestant work ethic and the "Gospel of Wealth" as the bases for Negro uplift. The strategy of appeasement aligned Washington with the plantation, business, and industrial elite in the South and the business-industrial elite in the North. This petit bourgeois program stressed nonunion manual and agricultural labor as well as vocational education for the toiling masses. It also stressed a black business and middle-class elite tied to a captive and supportive black consumer market.

In a related vein, Washington touted the rural South—contrasted against the city and the North—as Negroes' historic home and hence the place where they would best progress. Pro-self-help, pro-business, pro-southern, and pro-rural, Washington's ideology also reflected and reinforced the growing national weariness with the "Negro Problem" as revealed in the swift national retreat from Reconstruction. Washington's narrative thus overloaded the black conscience as it soothed the white conscience. Ultimately, Washington's accommodationism meant avoidance and denial of the ubiquity of white supremacy and racial conflict.

Washington's crucial break with the classic African American autobiographical tradition over the issue of protest was generational and intensely personal as well as ideological and tactical. He saw himself and his generation as needing to define themselves in their own terms on their own turf. Indeed, in his time, Washington was a leading exponent of the "New Negro" philosophy. This historical moment was the place where Washington both revised his people's past and present and envisioned their future. Nowhere was this process more in evidence, often leading to controversy among his people then and since, than in his accommodationism. He often went to extremes to gain what he deemed crucial white support.

Especially striking in this regard was the Christian spirit of generosity, forgiveness, and forbearance he exhibited toward whites generally and white ex-slaveowners especially. Whereas the tone of the classic autobiography was one of moral outrage and righteous indignation, that of Washington's revisionist narrative was moral equanimity and empirical calm. As Washington saw it, moral culpability and victimhood cut both ways, even if whites were more powerful. Racial reconciliation was the paramount goal here. Slavery was a horrible experience, Washington noted, but "not because my owners were especially cruel, for they were not, as compared with many others." Of his unknown white father he maintained: "I do not find especial fault with him. He was simply another unfortunate victim of the institution which the Nation unhappily had engrafted upon it at that time."[19]

Another revealing aspect of Washington's outlook was his exaggerated optimism, his constant ability to see the glass as half-full rather than half-empty. On the contrary, the optimism of the classic narrative had been candid and cautious. Harlan noted that a key part of Washington's wizardry and strength as a leader was, in addition to "his skill of maneuver," his equally impressive "ability to make the most of bad circumstances."[20] This eternal sunniness, this ability to see the silver lining in every cloud, however, too often tested the limits of credulity.

Allied with his belief in progress and providential design, Washington's excessive optimism betrayed roots in a romantic and sentimentalized view of American history. Increasingly memorialized in a pro-southern white reading of that history, in white hands this history embraced a pro-slavery and white supremacist logic. This was evident in the "Moonlight and Magnolia School" of southern history that emerged during the late nineteenth century and that came to dominate American historical consciousness for much of the twentieth century. Powerfully packaged in celluloid classics like "Birth of a Nation" (1915) and "Gone with the Wind" (1939), this history reveled in powerful myths like that of the glorious "Lost Cause" of southern white nationalism during the Civil War. It similarly reveled in the myth of the "dark days" of "Negro misrule" during Reconstruction that demanded the counterrevolution of white Redemption.

Washington's historicism was providential in substance and interpretation. In line with its accommodationist-related policy of appeasement, it was also very sympathetic to southern whites. Slavery, emancipation, Reconstruction, and the "Age of Washington" were God-ordained. For Washington, a usable past also meant accommodating the increasingly dominant white-friendly and pro-white southern view of these pivotal developments. Therefore, while emancipation was a human success, Reconstruction, largely due to black mistakes, was a colossal failure. Ironically, even though the freedpeople were relatively powerless throughout Reconstruction, they—rather than their more powerful white opposition—were seen as more responsible for Reconstruction and its consequences. The upshot of Reconstruction's failure was that black progress suffered a self-inflicted setback. Not surprisingly, therefore, the onus for ameliorating that situation lay primarily with the freedpeople themselves.

Washington worked within and outside the boundaries of this dubious historical framework. He fitfully endeavored to provide a more nuanced and less racially offensive, if not downright anti- or non-racist, rendering of that history. Nevertheless, he neither defined nor challenged the basic parameters of the framework. In large measure his version of this history failed because, regardless of his own, however well-intentioned, representation of this history, the framework itself was grossly erroneous and thus extremely misleading. Once again, as he operated at the border where accommodation shaded into subtle forms of resistance, accommodation all but overwhelmed his efforts, at times with baneful results.

Consistent with this historical understanding, slavery was typically represented as good for the slaves themselves as well as for the masters. Shorn of its blatant racism, a version of this argument had innumerable black and white adherents. In order "to show how Providence so often uses men and institutions to accomplish a purpose," God, operating through the slave trade, had rescued African slaves from savagery and heathenism in West Africa. In return, in the context of New World slavery, these Africans received the inestimable blessings of western civilization and Christianity. Enslavement, in this view, not unlike the view of proslavery apologists, was a school, a powerful acculturative institution. Washington maintained that, "notwithstanding the cruelty and wrong of slavery, the ten million Negroes inhabiting this country, who themselves or whose ancestors went through the school of American slavery, are in a stronger and more hopeful condition, materially, intellectually, morally, and religiously, than is true of an equal number of black people in any other portion of the globe."[21]

Slavery here was clearly the proverbial "blessing in disguise." For "notwithstanding the cruel wrongs inflicted upon us," Washington observed, "the black man got nearly as much out of slavery as the white man did." While slavery sapped "the spirit of self-reliance and self-help out of the white people," it only enhanced self-reliance and self-help among the blacks. On an equally positive note, because blacks had endured and learned so much as slaves, upon emancipation they "were as well fitted to begin life anew as the master."[22]

This particular view of slavery, its consequences, and its meanings cuts at least two ways. Those looking for convergence with aspects of the "Moonlight and Magnolia" school of history could certainly find it. Washington's historicism, notably his treatment of the nineteenth-century history of race relations, could be read as arguing that on balance things were not all that bad for Negroes. His, was, after all, an overly optimistic narrative and history of evolutionary progress. Thus in spite of the alarming growth of "the evil habit of lynching," Washington could conclude *Up From Slavery* on a high note, observing that "There was never a time when I felt more hopeful for the race than I do at the present."[23]

As pupils within the schools of slavery and freedom, blacks, like Washington himself, necessarily deferred to their teachers, white and black. Similarly, as landless agricultural workers, they necessarily deferred to the power of their masters and bosses. As a relatively powerless labor force, they operated within the constraints of slavery, sharecropping, and tenant farming. The pliant and hardworking Negro was a staple in Washington's rhetoric and ideology. Rejecting any intimation of the aggressive Negro, Washington embraced the notion of the faithful and docile black laborer as a counter to that of both the lazy Negro and the militant Negro. His adoption of this image, in part as an element of his appeasement strategy, has consistently infuriated his detractors and at times even confounded his supporters.

Easily the most controversial such image that Washington employed was that of "the faithful slave" as personified by Uncle Tom. The legendary protagonist in Harriet Beecher Stowe's antislavery novel, *Uncle Tom's Cabin*, exemplified black virtue and redemption through suffering. All the while, Uncle Tom elicited waves of sympathy and significant antislavery support. Uncle Tom exhibited a number of qualities that endeared him to audiences. He was brave, stoic, long-suffering, hardworking, and loyal; Uncle Tom epitomized Christian forbearance.[24]

Washington's use of the faithful slave stereotype is evident throughout the first chapter of *Up From Slavery*, "A Slave among Slaves." During the Civil War and Reconstruction, as the fortunes of "their white folks" rose and fell, these "trusted slaves" showed them a genuine "tenderness and sympathy" that reflected their "kindly and generous nature." Not only would these slaves "defend and protect the women and children . . . left on the plantations when the white males went to war, the slaves would have laid down their lives." In the Atlanta address he implored whites to "Cast down your bucket among these people who have, without strikes and labour wars, tilled your fields, cleared your forests, built your railroads and cities, and brought forth treasures from the bowels of the earth." These were plainly "the most patient, faithful, law-abiding, and unresentful people that the world has seen."[25]

Popular culture, however, especially minstrelsy, turned Uncle Tom in particular into a self-absorbed caricature who fawned over whites. In modern black vernacular culture, the term has come to represent a conservative black man who kowtows to white interests. In point of fact, the extremely conciliatory quality of Washington's appeasement politics earned him, among his antagonists, the popular epithet of "Uncle Tom" in its vernacular sense. In spite of innumerable efforts to clear Washington of the charge, and cogent evidence to the contrary, the charge persists.

For an untold number, Washington has embodied and symbolized the popular yet unctuous version of Uncle Tom. Yet just as Washington was no minstrel, he was certainly no Uncle Tom. The complexity of his real life as well as that of his life narrative far outstripped the singularity and simple-mindedness of such caricatures.

Although Washington saw slavery as a "school," he also saw the slaves themselves, like himself, as agents in the making of their own history. He spoke pointedly of the strength and resilience of the slaves. By surviving slavery, and in some ways transcending its strictures, Negroes demonstrated their humanity and strength—in a measure, their equality. Slavery had obviously not destroyed African Americans psychologically, emotionally, or culturally. They were not just victims. Even more important, they were survivors; they were both survivors and victims. By projecting a view of blacks in critical ways as agents in history, not merely reactive victims, Washington crafted a historicism that has resonated among a wide spectrum of blacks and a growing number of sympathetic whites in his time and since.

This historicism also stressed the vital role of Negroes in shaping not only their history, but also that of the American nation. Consequently, Washington lobbied for greater attention to the Negro's history, especially in the education of his people. Carter G. Woodson (1875–1950), a Washington admirer in many respects and the "Father of Negro History," spearheaded efforts to publicize and support scholarship in and the teaching of Negro history. Early on, however, as shown in *The Story of the Negro* (1909), Washington, like other "New Negroes" of his time, maintained that Negro history is "likely to be both instructive and helpful, not merely to the black man but also to the white man."[26]

This perspective represented a telling and increasingly influential vision of the importance of Negro history. The corollary argument stressing that Negroes have played an active role in the construction of their own history was clearly the most empowering aspect of Washington's historicism. It was a crucial element of his own New Negro ethos. Interestingly enough, this New Negro ethos rejected the competing "tragedy of color" vision wherein "the inconveniences, the hardships and the injustices" American Negroes have endured constituted "something exceptional and tragic." Washington instead saw this pattern of development as common: "every race that has struggled up from a lower to a higher civilization has had to face these things."[27]

Typically associated with Du Bois's *The Souls of Black Folk*, the "tragedy of color" school undercut the notions of group well-being and self-help by representing Negroes as psychologically wounded and in need of therapy and a helping hand. Washington obviously dissented. So did many others. As Daryl Scott has shown, an increasingly broad and influential swath of black social scientists, artists, and intellectuals during the interwar years adopted the view that black suffering had not shattered the Negro. Speaking for his generation, Horace Mann Bond claimed to prefer the race pride associated with the Washington camp as against the "tragical self-pity of the more radical school." Rather than a "damaged group psychology" necessitating self-pity and therapeutic intervention, those like Bond and Washington saw a multifaceted group psychology more reflective of esteem and health. Echoing Washington and Bond, Zora Neale Hurston spoke for many New Negroes of the Harlem Renaissance. Hurston allowed that she did not see herself as "Tragically colored. . . . I do not belong to the sobbing school of Negrohood who hold that nature somehow has given them a lowdown dirty deal and whose feelings are all hurt about it."[28]

Washington offered his vision of the "New Negro" in a book entitled *A New Negro for a New Century* (1900). It consisted of Victorian portraits of successful Negroes and a series of appropriate historical tableaux. Rejecting images of the "old-time Negro," and "old darky," Washington provided a stunning counterimage: middle-class refinement, culture, and respectability. These Negroes were not only a powerful refutation to contemporaneous allegations of Negro inferiority and degeneracy. They were also a crucial element of the race's future. The fundamental struggle was over who would ultimately control the popular as well as the scholarly and intellectual images of the race. Historically, innumerable blacks like Washington have felt compelled, as Sundquist has noted, "to counteract the racist image of blacks as regressive, infantile, or animalistic and to restructure the race's own image of itself."[29] In particular, the Harlem Renaissance and Marcus Garvey–led generation of the 1930s and the Black Power generation of the late 1960s and early 1970s engaged in comparable racial revitalization moments.

Ellison once observed that "the motives hidden behind the mask are as numerous as the ambiguities the mask conceals."[30] This was certainly the case with Booker T. Washington. Indeed these ambiguities and hidden motives have made Washington an exceedingly difficult personality to unravel. Likewise, in concert with his life and times, these ambiguities and hidden motives have rendered his legacy not open merely to multiple interpretations, but to highly controversial ones.

In *Invisible Man*, the novel's narrator-protagonist ruminates long and hard on the Booker T. Washington–like founder's statue on the Tuskegee-like campus. His epiphany sheds powerful light on the paradoxical, multidimensional personality that was Washington. The actual and represented statues have the founders lifting the veil of ignorance from over the head of an apparently grateful Negro man. Yet as the narrator-protagonist observes: "in my mind's eye I see the bronze statue of the college Founder, the cold father symbol, his hands outstretched in the breathtaking gesture of lifting a veil that flutters in hard, metallic folds above the face of a kneeling slave: and I am standing puzzled, unable to decide whether the veil is really being lifted, or lowered more firmly in place: whether I am witnessing a revelation or a more efficient blinding."[31] Herein lies the rub.

Washington understood quite well the importance of living openly without the masks, beyond the veil of race. He observed that with emancipation the ex-slaves made explicit their formerly hidden references to freedom in the spirituals: "Now they gradually threw off the mask, and were not afraid to let it be known that the 'freedom' in their songs meant freedom of the body in this world."[32] As evidenced by his life and his autobiography, Washington himself intensely desired that same "freedom of the body in this world." From all we know, in spite of his innumerable accomplishments, he never actually satisfied that longing.

Notes

Author's note: Louise Newman, Deborah McDowell, Raymond Gavins, Patricia Sullivan, and Joshua Bloom provided comments and criticisms of earlier versions of this essay that helped in the revision process.

1. Charles M. Payne, *I've Got the Light of Freedom: The Organizing Tradition and the Mississippi Freedom Struggle* (Berkeley: University of California Press, 1995); Aldon Morris, *The Origins of the Civil Rights Movement: Black Communi-*

ties *Organizing for Change* (New York: Free Press, 1984); Leon Litwack and August Meier, eds., *Black Leaders of the Nineteenth Century* (Urbana: University of Illinois Press, 1988); John Hope Franklin and August Meier, eds., *Black Leaders of the Twentieth Century* (Urbana: University of Illinois Press, 1982).

2. Louis R. Harlan, *Booker T. Washington: The Making of a Black Leader, 1856–1901* (New York: Oxford University Press, 1972) (hereinafter cited as Harlan, *BTW*, vol. 1); Louis R. Harlan, *Booker T. Washington: The Wizard of Tuskegee, 1901–1915* (New York: Oxford University Press, 1983) (hereinafter cited as Harlan, *BTW*, vol. 2); August Meier, *Negro Thought in America, 1880–1915* (Ann Arbor: University of Michigan Press, 1963).

3. Booker T. Washington, *Up From Slavery* (New York: Doubleday, Page & Co., 1901), ed. William Andrews, Norton Critical Edition (New York: W. W. Norton, 1996), 28–29 (hereinafter referred to as the Norton edition).

4. See Waldo E. Martin Jr., *The Mind of Frederick Douglass* (Chapel Hill: University of North Carolina Press, 1984), 253–78.

5. Mary Douglas, *Purity and Danger: An Analysis of the Concepts of Pollution and Danger* (New York: Praeger, 1966). Deborah McDowell helped me to clarify my thinking on this point. Harlan, *BTW*, 2: vii.

6. Ralph Ellison, "Change the Joke and Slip the Yoke," in *The Collected Essays of Ralph Ellison*, ed. John F. Callahan (New York: Random House, 1995), 195; W.E.B. Du Bois, "Of Mr. Booker T. Washington and Others," in *The Souls of Black Folk*, ed. John Hope Franklin, *Three Negro Classics* (New York: Avon, 1965), 240; Meier, *Negro Thought in America*.

7. Booker T. Washington, *Up From Slavery*, ed. William Andrews (New York: Oxford University Press, 1995), xviii, xxii (hereinafter referred to as the Oxford edition).

8. William Andrews, in ibid., xxii.

9. Ralph Ellison, *Invisible Man* (New York: Random House, 1952).

10. Washington, *Up From Slavery*, Norton edition, 98–102.

11. Harlan, *BTW*, 1: 4; Eric J. Sundquist, *To Wake the Nations: Race in the Making of American Literature* (Cambridge: Harvard University Press, 1993), 274.

12. Washington, *Up From Slavery*, Norton edition, 112.

13. Houston Baker, *Modernism and the Harlem Renaissance* (Chicago: University of Chicago Press), 25–36; Adolph Reed, "What Are the Drums Saying, Booker? The Current Crisis of the Black Intellectual," *Village Voice*, April 11, 1995.

14. Baker, *Modernism and the Harlem Renaissance*, 36.

15. Washington, *Up From Slavery*, Norton edition, 101; Baker, *Modernism and the Harlem Renaissance*, 32.

16. Reed, "What Are the Drums Saying," 31.

17. Lawrence W. Levine, "The Concept of the New Negro and the Realities of Black Culture," in *The Unpredictable Past: Explorations in American Cultural History* (New York: Oxford University Press, 1993), 86–106.

18. Andrews, in Washington, *Up From Slavery*, Oxford edition, xii.

19. Washington, *Up From Slavery,* Norton edition, 7, 8.
20. Harlan, *BTW,* 2: viii.
21. Washington, *Up From Slavery,* Norton edition, 14, 13.
22. Ibid., 14.
23. Ibid., 145.
24. Harriet Beecher Stowe, *Uncle Tom's Cabin,* ed. Jean Fagan Yellin (New York: Oxford University Press, 1998); Eric J. Sundquist, ed., *New Essays on* Uncle Tom's Cabin (New York: Cambridge University Press, 1986); Thomas F. Gossett, Uncle Tom's Cabin *and American Culture* (Dallas: SMU Press, 1985).
25. Washington, *Up From Slavery,* Norton edition, 15, 12, 100.
26. August Meier and Elliott Rudwick, *Black History and the Historical Profession, 1915–1980* (Urbana: University of Illinois Press, 1986), 1–71; Louis R. Harlan and Raymond W. Smock, eds., *The Booker T. Washington Papers* (14 vols., Urbana: University of Illinois Press, 1972–89) (hereinafter cited as *BTW Papers*), 1: 406.
27. *BTW Papers,* ibid.
28. Horace Mann Bond and Zora Neale Hurston are both cited in Daryl Michael Scott, *Contempt and Pity: Social Policy and the Image of the Damaged Black Psyche, 1880–1996* (Chapel Hill: University of North Carolina Press, 1997), 64–65.
29. Sundquist, *To Wake the Nations,* 336–37, 448; Wilson J. Moses, *The Wings of Ethiopia: Studies in African-American Life and Letters* (Ames: Iowa State University Press, 1990), 192, 266.
30. Ellison, "Change the Joke and Slip the Yoke," 109.
31. Ellison, *Invisible Man* (New York: Vintage, 1990), 36.
32. Washington, *Up From Slavery,* Norton edition, 11.

4

Understanding the Wizard

Another Look at the Age of Booker T. Washington

ROBERT J. NORRELL

From his day to ours, Booker T. Washington has been viewed as a symbol of the age in which he lived, but he has proved to be an elastic emblem, one pulled and stretched to mean different things to different people. Washington clearly recognized his symbolic role and acted always to shape its meaning, but often he failed to persuade his audience of the object lessons he meant to teach. When Washington's autobiography *Up From Slavery* appeared in 1901, William Edward Burghardt Du Bois began to critique the Tuskegee principal as a black leader chosen by whites. Du Bois wrote that Washington had taken the idea of industrial training for blacks and "broadened it from a by-path into a veritable Way of Life." Washington thought the older black schools that offered a liberal education were "wholly failures, or worthy of ridicule," which was partly why, Du Bois claimed, other blacks had "deep suspicion and dislike" for the Tuskegeean. "Among the Negroes, Mr. Washington is still far from a popular leader." In *The Souls of Black Folk* in 1903, Du Bois perfected his critique, asserting that Washington's program "practically accepts the alleged inferiority of the Negro races." In the 1895 Atlanta Exposition speech—Du Bois dubbed it the "Atlanta Compromise," a pejorative that would prove enduring—Washington had, he insisted, accepted the denial of black citizenship rights. Washington was "striving nobly to make Negro artisans, business men, and property-owners; but it is utterly impossible, under modern competitive methods, for the workingmen and property-owners to defend their rights and exist without the right of suffrage."[1]

In the years after Washington's death in 1915, many readers of *Up From Slavery* would come to a more positive evaluation of the book and its author, and little was added to Du Bois's critique of Washington until 1951, when C. Vann Woodward's sharp irony in *Origins of the New South* seconded Du Bois's criticism of Washington's materialist values: "The businessman's gospel of free enterprise, competition, and *laissez faire* never had a more loyal exponent than the master of Tuskegee." Louis R. Harlan, a Woodward student, stepped forward as the most influential interpreter of Washington with the publication in 1972 of the first installments of both his two-volume biography of Washington and the fourteen-volume *Booker T. Washington Papers*. Professor Harlan criticized Washington's failure to protest the wrongs he witnessed against African Americans, writing that he "acquiesced in segregation," accepted "complacently" the denial of equal rights after Reconstruction, rose to power only because whites chose him to lead blacks, and offered leadership that amounted to a "setback of his race." Professor Harlan emphasized the hypocrisy of Washington's public disavowal of politics at the same time he was working constantly to influence federal appointments in the South. Precisely because Harlan drove his thesis so well and paraded a variety of vivid symbols before the readers about the "faustian" Wizard, he shaped almost all the writing on post-Reconstruction race relations published after 1972. Still, Harlan mainly put Washington in two contexts: the conflict with Du Bois, and Washington's influence in Republican politics. Placing Washington in other historical contexts, however, can yield different understandings. What follows is an attempt to broaden the contextual framework in which Washington's life and work are judged.[2]

One crucial context for understanding Booker T. Washington was the thinking of whites in the 1880s and 1890s about the future of race relations. Intellectuals and politicians writing to shape public opinion, from both North and South, had turned increasingly hostile toward African Americans. White-supremacist southerners were disproportionately represented in the pages of such current-issue magazines—all published in the North—as *Forum, North American Review, Arena, Harper's Weekly, Nation, Atlantic Monthly, Popular Science Monthly,* and *Outlook*. Intellectuals and politicians writing to shape public opinion reflected the widespread presumption that blacks would not be able to survive in freedom. A belief that African Americans were degenerating into beasts bolstered the predictions of their disappearance. By the 1880s the assertions of black bestiality pervaded both the intellectual and popular sources of opinion. Ultimately the most influential writer on the future of African Americans in the 1890s was Frederick Ludwig Hoffman, a German immigrant who made a place for himself as an actuary in the emerging life insurance business in the United States by assembling information to justify his employer's refusal to write life insurance on blacks. In 1892 Hoffman presented evidence in *Arena* to support his conclusion that "the time will come, if it has not already come, when the Negro, like the Indian, will be a vanishing race."[3]

These intensely hostile views toward African Americans found their way to the average person in the South through the white-owned newspapers in that region, which gave the suggestion of the all-encompassing nature of race trouble in the United States. In his study of small-town newspapers in the South, Thomas D. Clark found that most papers in the 1880s and 1890s clearly reflected the "Negro-as-beast" thinking of the time. The editors revealed "a general fear of the Negro," whom they often depicted as uncivilized, a "wild, ignorant animal . . . [a] black sensual fiend, whose intense hatred of the white race would cause him to strike with wild demoniacal fury at an unguarded moment." By the late 1890s the improving visual presentations that resulted from better photoengraving on web presses enabled the larger urban dailies to present more racially inflammatory visual material. Advertisements in daily newspapers began regularly to use anti-black stereotypes to sell products of all kinds. Sunday comic pages began to appear in the largest newspapers, and several strips exploited vicious stereotypes of black stupidity. Southern newspapers made great fun of African Americans in the courts, demonstrating blacks' alleged criminality while providing great hilarity to readers. Many papers featured police-court columns that were illustrated with outlandish caricatures of black men and women.[4]

American popular culture in the late nineteenth century reinforced the ideas of black criminality and moral decline, especially the minstrel show, which featured white male actors in blackface playing the stock characters of "Jim Crow" and "Zip Coon." Almost any town with a railroad station and a hall received a touring minstrel company. Near the end of the nineteenth century, the musical feature became the "coon song," which featured a bright melody and relentlessly racist lyrics. Popular titles included the perennial favorite, "All Coons Look Alike to Me." The Zip Coon and Jim Crow characters and the coon song made the transition both to burlesque and to vaudeville. During the 1890s coon songs became a main offering of the emerging sheet-music industry known popularly as "Tin Pan Alley." A million copies of "All Coons Look Alike to Me" were sold within a few years of its appearance in 1896. One could not receive American popular culture or news in the 1890s without getting constant repetition of the stereotyped African American, an image of laziness, stupidity, immorality, and criminality.[5]

In his 1895 Atlanta Exposition speech, Washington challenged the images then current in white intellectual and cultural presentations of African Americans, insisting that blacks were a people of "love and fidelity" to whites, a "faithful, law-abiding, and unresentful" people. In its larger thrust, the Atlanta speech represented Washington's attempt to counter the presumption on the part of the white South, and much of the rest of the nation, that African Americans had declined in character and morality in freedom. The overarching message that Washington intended was not acceptance of disfranchisement and segregation but rather a message of progress, of movement forward and upward. In Atlanta, Washington began to offer Americans a new point of view in order to challenge the ideology of white supremacy.

In the years after the Atlanta speech, Washington often spoke up for civil and political rights. This is contrary to Professor Harlan's contention that "his public utterances were limited to what whites approved" and that Washington's actions on behalf of civil and political rights were exclusively part of his "secret life" of arranging court challenges and organizing protests but taking no public part. In fact, in 1896 Washington told the *Washington Post* that forcing blacks "to ride in a 'Jim Crow' car that is far inferior to that used by the white people is a matter that cannot stand much longer against the increasing intelligence and prosperity of the colored people." In a speech at a Spanish-American War Peace Jubilee in Chicago before 16,000 people, Washington asserted that the United States had won all its battles but one, "the effort to conquer ourselves in the blotting out of racial prejudice.... Until we thus conquer ourselves, I make no empty statement when I say that we shall have, especially in the Southern part of our country, a cancer gnawing at the heart of the Republic, that shall one day prove as dangerous as an attack from an army without or within." In 1899, in response to the horrific Sam Hose lynching in

Newnan, Georgia, Washington wrote to the *Birmingham Age-Herald* that he opposed "mob violence under all circumstances. Those guilty of crime should be surely, swiftly and terribly punished, but by legal methods." In June of that year, he published a long article on lynching that appeared in many southern and northern newspapers in which he offered statistics to show that only a small portion of those lynched were even charged with rape. Lynching did not deter crime, Washington insisted; it degraded whites who participated, and it gave the South a bad name throughout the world.[6]

As he became recognized after 1895 as the most prominent African American—and as he consciously accepted the role as leader of his race—Washington constantly gave speeches and interviews and wrote to try to improve the image of African Americans. In practice, creating an ideology to challenge white supremacy usually amounted to influencing what the public media reported about blacks. By the late 1890s Washington frequently sent press releases to both black and white newspapers that either pointed to black achievements that contradicted the "Negro-as-beast" image by showing black success or suggesting actions that contradicted blacks' negative image. Washington seemed always to know what modern-day publicists teach public figures in a critical spotlight: Answering criticism often only fuels the public-relations crisis. He quoted Oliver Wendell Holmes: "Controversy equalizes wise men and fools, and the fools know it." Thus, whether the criticism came from whites or blacks, Washington's first instinct was to keep his response to himself.[7]

Running through all Washington's public efforts to counter the intensely anti-black feeling in the South in the late 1890s was a defense of black education. In virtually every speech, magazine article, or newspaper interview, and in many of the press releases sent out from Tuskegee, Washington dwelt on the great and growing value of African American education, and only some of his emphases promoted industrial education. Having observed the removal of blacks from politics in Mississippi and South Carolina and having fought disfranchisement in Louisiana and lost, Washington by 1900 privately doubted that anything could halt the powerful momentum of the movement to take away black suffrage. The attack on black education that intensified over the course of the 1890s, however, represented an even more fundamental assault, one that Washington had to turn back, or the purpose of his life was defeated. Senator

Benjamin R. Tillman of South Carolina constantly declared that "it is foolish to my mind to disfranchise the Negro on account of illiteracy and turn right around and compel him to become literate."[8]

Up From Slavery represented Washington's ultimate statement of black progress. "No one can come into contact with the race for twenty years as I have done in the heart of the South," he wrote, "without being convinced that the race is constantly making slow but sure progress materially, educationally, and morally." Washington had made himself, and he clearly understood that his life personified the progress that he wanted whites to believe about African Americans in general. Tuskegee Institute was to be seen as an objective demonstration of black progress. From the time that he emerged as a national figure and the leader of his race at Atlanta in 1895, through the publication of *Up From Slavery* in 1901, Washington held fast to the idea that African Americans were going up, not down.[9]

The local context in which Booker T. Washington worked always circumscribed his options. Like many Black Belt towns during Reconstruction, Tuskegee had been the scene of violent racial conflict over political power. The founding of Tuskegee Institute in 1881 represented an effort for peaceful accommodation between the dominant local whites and a defeated and unhappy black community. The white leaders mainly responsible for helping blacks obtain the initial state support for the new school had earlier helped to direct the vigilantes terrorizing Republican voters and officeholders. The message of the local history was clear: Washington's school, the object lesson of black progress, could only survive if it had the support, or at least the toleration, of the white community.[10]

Violence, threatened and real, periodically brought this reality home to Washington. In 1895 a white mob pursued a local black man, Thomas Harris, onto the Tuskegee campus to Booker T. Washington's door. Washington had had Harris taken to a safe place out of Tuskegee but apparently told the mob only that he had denied Harris sanctuary. The Thomas Harris incident also revealed the fundamental insecurity of Washington and the Institute in the always racially charged Black Belt. Black educators in the South regularly encountered violent opposition, or a threat of it that made them flee. In 1902, the principal of a black industrial school in Ramer, Alabama, forty miles from Tuskegee, had to flee that village when local whites attacked him for a perceived breach of racial etiquette. In August 1903, whites killed the principal of Point Coupee Industrial College in New Roads, Louisiana, just weeks before Washington had been scheduled to visit him and the school.[11]

Virtually from his arrival in Tuskegee, Washington faced hostile and unscrupulous competition from the heads of two other black industrial schools in Alabama. In 1903, William Paterson, the white president of a black school in Montgomery, arranged for an attack in the *Washington Post* that claimed that "Booker the Crafty" was a "shrewd darkey" forcing black political appointments on the South and teaching "soft-handed Negro dudes and loafers." William Hooper Councill, president of a state-supported agricultural and mechanical college in Huntsville, took a position that surpassed Paterson, and certainly Washington, in his efforts to curry the favor of white political power in Alabama. Councill said in 1900: "God bless the white woman! I know she wants me hung when I assault or insult her and she is right! I tell you negro men you had better let that white lady alone for she is the goddess of all virtue and purity, whose station is away up among the stars." Paterson and Councill limited Washington's room to maneuver by taking positions that pandered to white-supremacist thinking about black criminality and degeneracy.[12]

A new surge of intellectual racism at the turn of the century reduced any potential positive impact of Washington's efforts to improve the image of African Americans. In 1900, Charles Carroll published, to wide notice in the newspaper world, *The Negro a Beast*, which resurrected the old claim that African peoples were of a different biologic species from whites. The next year, William P. Calhoun offered an analysis of the "negro problem" that was captured in his title: *The Caucasian and The Negro in the United States. They Must Separate. If Not, Then Extermination. A Proposed Solution: Colonization.* In the decade after 1900, Thomas Nelson Page, various southern politicians, and various "race experts" recycled the prevailing ideas about black degeneration and criminality, the justification for lynching and disfranchisement, and the futility of black education in *North American Review, Arena, Forum,* and the *Independent.* Perhaps the most direct and effective challenge to Washington came from the pen of another black man, William Hannibal Thomas, who published, at the same time that *Up From Slavery* appeared in

1901, *The American Negro: What He Was, What He Is, and What He May Become*. Well known in northern black intellectual and religious circles in the 1880s and 1890s, Thomas was more pessimistic about black potential than Washington was optimistic. The Negro, he wrote, was "an intrinsically inferior type of humanity," his history "a record of lawless existence, led by every impulse and every passion." To Thomas, the African American's "contribution to the common treasury of American development" was "a pretentious imitation of civilization, a veneering over barbarous instincts." In 1902 the publishing world was astonished at the success of Thomas Dixon's novel, *The Leopard's Spots: A Romance of the White Man's Burden*, which, though published within months of *Up From Slavery* by the same house, sold many more copies in the ensuing years. *Leopard's Spots* offered a statement of black degeneracy, criminality, and sexual aggression within a pro-southern, melodramatic plot about the Civil War and Reconstruction. Dixon even surpassed that publishing success in 1905 with *The Clansman*, a work of similar effect.[13]

White hostility to black education was growing more intense in the South at the turn of the century. By 1903, when James K. Vardaman was elected governor of Mississippi, Booker T. Washington was alarmed about what might happen to black education, because the election had demonstrated that "the majority of white people in Mississippi oppose Negro education of any character." Industrial education was growing increasingly controversial. In 1901 the governor of Georgia expressed his view that while Washington was a "good negro . . . I am opposed to putting negroes in factories and offices. When you do that you will cause dissatisfaction between the two races and such things might lead to a race war. The field of agriculture is the proper one for the negro." In *The Leopard's Spots*, Dixon's all-knowing white minister claims that industrial education increases the Negro's danger to white society. "Industrial training gives power. If the Negro ever becomes a serious competitor of the white labourer in the industries of the South, the white man will kill him."[14]

Booker T. Washington's presence at a White House dinner in October 1901 drastically and permanently undermined his acceptance in the white South. There, he would never return to the level of popularity that he had achieved prior to the dinner. The dinner caused leading figures to erupt in outrage. "The action of President Roosevelt in entertaining that nigger," Ben Tillman announced, "will necessitate our killing a thousand niggers in the South before they will learn their place again." Governor Vardaman proclaimed that Roosevelt had insulted every white man in America: "President Roosevelt takes this nigger bastard into his home, introduces him to his family and entertains him on terms of absolute social equality." Rebecca Felton, the Georgia white-supremacist suffragist, declared that Washington "was supposed to be a level-headed, educated colored man" but at the White House he "threw off the mask" and revealed that he was a "disintegrator and disorganizer of both races. . . . He will be wise to lift his Tuskegee plant and move northward while he is basking in Presidential favor."[15]

Washington became, one historian later concluded, "a marked man in the southern press—not because of his pioneering work in Negro education but because he was 'the saddle-colored coon'"—Vardaman's favorite epithet for Washington—"who had the insolence to eat a meal in the White House." The *Atlanta Constitution* and the *Montgomery Advertiser* were mildest, fixing blame entirely on Roosevelt. The editor of the *Memphis Scimitar* represented only the extreme anger expressed in many southern newspapers: The White House dinner was the "most damnable outrage which has ever been perpetrated by any citizen of the United States," and it taught a frightening lesson: "Any Nigger who happens to have a little more than the average amount of intelligence granted by the Creator of his race, and cash enough to pay the tailor and the barber, and the perfumer for scents enough to take away the nigger smell, has a perfect right to be received by the daughter of the white man among the guests in the parlor of his home."[16]

Although threatening letters poured into Tuskegee and rumors of Washington's impending assassination circulated for years, Tuskegee's principal forged ahead with the purpose that had taken him to the White House in the first place, the naming of federal appointments in the South. Washington had already prevailed on Roosevelt to name Thomas Goode Jones, his ally and the former Democratic governor of Alabama, to the federal judiciary because Jones had, Washington wrote Roosevelt, "stood up in the constitutional convention and elsewhere for a fair election law, opposed lynching, and has been outspoken for the education of both races." In 1903 Washington began a protracted defense of Roosevelt's appointment of William Crum, a black Republican, to be collector of the port of Charleston, South Carolina, against the determined opposition of Senator Tillman. That same year, after Vardaman had ridiculed whites in Indianola, Mississippi, for "tolerating a nigger wench" as postmistress, which caused the woman in question to resign, Washington encouraged Roosevelt not to accept her resignation. All the while he was leading a vigorous, South-wide campaign against the spreading "lily-white" movement in the Republican party, an effort of southern white Republicans to become as "white" as the Democrats. From Roosevelt's entry into the White House at least through the 1908 presidential election, Washington worked constantly to get and maintain black political influence in the Republican party.[17]

Washington's determination to retain African American political influence has earned him the scorn of historians who have seen hypocrisy in his defense of black officeholding while seeming to disavow the importance of suffrage for African Americans. But it may also be understood as the resolve of a man who believed that it was only just that African Americans get some political positions. Washington believed that those few appointments encouraged blacks to feel that they were not entirely removed from American democracy. It also possibly represented the actions of a man who viewed himself as a race leader in competition with other race leaders—Tillman and Vardaman, for example—and he wanted his race to win occasionally.

Still, Washington worried about the effect of the mounting hostility to Tuskegee Institute. "I wish you would watch very carefully the tone of the Southern press, and in fact the press of the whole country for that matter, in connection with Mr. Roosevelt and colored office holders," he asked Emmett Scott in June 1902. "I want to help him and the race if I can, but at the same time I must be careful not to injure our institution." In late 1902, after an Alabama newspaper published his letter to Roosevelt recommending Jones for the judgeship, Washington felt the need to issue to all U.S. newspapers a "clarification," in which he said that he was only an educator, one still emphasizing the development of economic strength first, but that "public questions affecting our interests arise which are so fundamental and far-reaching that they transcend the domain of politics" and that "in justice to my race, I make my position known and stand for what I see to be the right." He added a lesson about progress: "We cannot elevate and make useful a race of people unless there is held out to them the hope of reward for right living."[18]

Throughout 1903 and 1904, Washington continued to push for black appointments, especially a permanent position for Dr. Crum. From 1901 to 1908, southern newspapers focused on no public issue more consistently than Roosevelt's patronage appointments, and there was virtually no support for his position from white-owned newspapers. In Alabama in 1903, Judge Jones presided over criminal trials of men charged with peonage, which occasioned condemnation of Jones, Roosevelt, and Booker T. Washington in the southern press. Time and again, editorials and articles referred back to the White House dinner, a perfect symbol of the way that black political influence led to demands for social equality. Further agitating white concerns about political participation during these years was the proposal of the Indiana congressman Edgar Crumpacker, starting in 1901, to reduce the congressional representation of the southern states that had disfranchised black voters. Booker T. Washington opposed the reduction because he thought it would validate and further encourage disfranchisement, and it was not passed in the Congress, but "Crumpackerism" provided southern politicians and editorialists with evidence of continuing northern "meddling" in whites' control of politics in the South. As such it fueled southern whites' hypersensitivity about protecting white supremacy.[19]

The rising hysteria about black political power focused the attention of white race leaders on Booker T. Washington. In early 1903 Ben Tillman included condemnations of Washington in a long and widely quoted speech on "The Race Problem" in the U.S. Senate. Vardaman, probably Washington's most persistent detractor, privately characterized him as a "fraud & liar; a smart man; training social parasites; you never heard of a student of his school who ever did anything useful except teach school." Early in 1904 in the national magazine *Leslie's Weekly*, Governor Vardaman wrote that he was "opposed to the nigger's voting, it matters not what his advertised moral and mental qualifications may be. I am just as much opposed to Booker Washington's, with all his Anglo-Saxon reenforcements, voting as I am to voting by the cocoanut-headed, chocolate-colored typical little coon, Andy Dotson, who blacks my shoes every morning. Neither one is fit to perform the supreme functions of citizenship." It was time to repeal the constitutional amendments "which gave the nigger the right to pollute politics." He returned to the issue of black education: "More than $250,000,000 has been spent since the years 1861–65 by the white people of the North and the South in a foolish endeavor to make more of the nigger than God Almighty ever intended." He had asked the Mississippi legislature to remove its state constitutional guarantee of equal education in order that funding could be spent on "the white country boys and girls who are to rule Mississippi in the future."[20]

Then, on a hot Monday morning in October 1904, the continuing jeopardy represented by the White House dinner hit close to Washington's home. J. Thomas Heflin, recently appointed to fill the congressional seat vacated when Washington's friend Charles Thompson died, was campaigning for election before a packed courtroom in the county courthouse in Tuskegee. The race had turned ugly. Fond of calling his Republican opponent, Benjamin Walker, a "Black and tan serpent hissing at the feet of honest and upright Democrats," Heflin had accosted Walker the previous afternoon at the train station in nearby Opelika, saying "you have been charging me with damned lies and you have to take it back or I will kill you right now." Even with armed Heflin supporters surrounding him, Walker refused to recant, whereupon Heflin then beat him severely with a knife handle. For some time Heflin had been using Washington as his main whipping boy, declaring that if Roosevelt was re-elected in 1904 he would appoint Washington to his cabinet. Washington "may enjoy being 'Negro Patronage Boss' of Alabama," Heflin sneered, but "he is destroying his usefullness, his head is turned, he is a changed negro and is nothing like he was five years ago. . . . If Booker Washington didn't believe in social equality, he wouldn't do as he is doing."[21]

"If the truth be told," one reporter observed about that morning, "Mr. Heflin devoted more of his remarks to Booker Washington and President Roosevelt than to all other subjects. . . . These assaults, although made almost within the hearing of the Tuskegee Institute, were received with applause and cheers." He railed against Washington's political influence with Roosevelt. "There they sat, Roosevelt and Booker," Heflin shouted sarcastically as he described the White House dinner to the constantly cheering courthouse crowd, "and if some Czolgosz . . . had thrown a bomb under the table, no great harm would have been done the country." (Here Heflin referred to Leon Czolgosz, the anarchist who had assassinated President William McKinley in 1901.) Heflin declared emphatically that Washington was secretly scheming to get Walker elected. "If Booker interferes in this thing there is a way of stopping him," he intimated to the courtroom crowd of 300, at the rear of which stood a number of African

Americans. "We have a way of influencing negroes down here when it becomes necessary." The threat of lynching was only implied, but hardly anyone hearing the congressman could have missed his message. The whites in the crowd gave the fiery congressman a standing ovation as he finished his speech.[22]

Heflin continued the attacks on Washington through his successful campaign, but in keeping with his practice, Washington said nothing publicly about them. He could not give voice to what was obvious: The threat of assassination against him, made less than a mile from his campus by a sitting United States congressman with a deserved reputation for personal violence, revealed a dangerous erosion of his public acceptance among whites. The only course was to lie low and hope the attacks passed.

But the Heflin campaign marked only a point on the downward spiral of Washington's popularity in the white South. In June 1905 Thomas E. Watson, the Georgia populist and congressman, charged in his magazine that Washington believed that "the black man is superior to the white, and he proved it . . . by statistics." After the Vardaman attack in *Leslie's*, Washington began in speeches to make an indirect counter by demonstrating the black progress through the rapid rise in literacy, comparing African Americans' lower rates of illiteracy with those in European countries. "The negro race has developed more rapidly in the thirty years of its freedom than the Latin race has in one thousand years of freedom," Watson reported Washington's saying, though it is doubtful he did express it that way. "In making up your tables of illiteracy, why didn't you include *all the Negroes,* as you included all the Italians, all the Spaniards, *all* the Russians? Why leave out your home folks in Africa, Doctor? Why omit Santo Domingo and Haiti? If you will number *all* the negroes, Doctor, your percentage of illiteracy *among the blacks* may run up among the nineties, and knock your calculation into a cocked hat. Does it not," Watson demanded of Washington, "occur to you that you may create a feeling of resentment among *all* the whites?" That, of course, was exactly what Watson was encouraging, resentment against Washington's assertion of black progress. "Whenever the North wakes up to the fact that you are teaching the blacks that they are superior to the whites," Watson warned, "you are going to feel the east wind." Watson's attack was reprinted in many southern newspapers, and according to Professor Woodward, it was more widely quoted in the South than anything he wrote.[23]

Then, two months later, in August 1905, as Washington was preoccupied with the just-created Niagara Movement, Thomas Dixon published in the *Saturday Evening Post* the most artful critique of Washington next to Du Bois's in *The Souls of Black Folk*. A man of keen public-relations skills himself, Dixon had just published *The Clansman* and was then preparing his own stage version of that novel, which would open in October and tour the South to great and continuing controversy—and big crowds. Dixon stood to benefit from a newspaper controversy with Washington. In the article, Dixon declared that Washington was not "training Negroes to take their place in any industrial system of the South in which the white man can direct or control him," or to be servants "at the beck and call of any man." Quite the contrary, "he is training them *all* to be masters of men, to be independent, to own and operate their own industries, plant their own fields, buy and sell their own goods, and in every shape and form destroy the last vestige of dependence on the white man for anything." While some people would say those were good lessons, Dixon warned that the independent black nation Washington was building within the white man's America was a great danger, something that inevitably would lead to destruction. "Every pupil who passes through Mr. Washington's hands ceases forever to work under a white man. Not only so, but he goes forth trained under an evangelist to preach the doctrine of separation and independence." Would the southern white man "allow the Negro to master his industrial system, take the bread from his mouth, crowd him to the wall and place a mortgage on his house? Competition is war. . . . What will the [southern white man] do when put to the test? He will do exactly what his white neighbor in the North does when the Negro threatens his bread—kill him!"[24]

Just as Dixon's attack appeared, Washington found himself in another firestorm. On August 14, 1905, he had dinner with John Wanamaker, a department store magnate, in a hotel at Saratoga Springs, New York. Early accounts reported that Wanamaker's daughter entered the dining room on Washington's arm. Condemnation erupted from the southern press, and newspapers that historically had supported Washington now lost all restraint in denouncing him for practicing social equality. The editor of the *Montgomery Advertiser*, a newspaper that had defended Washington for the White House dinner, wrote that "since the fateful day when Booker T. Washington sat down to the dinner table in the

White House with President Roosevelt, he has done many things to hurt the cause, of which he is regarded as the foremost man. . . . What excuse, in view of conditions, North and South, can he offer for the exhibition of himself as escort to the dinner table at Saratoga's leading hotel of the daughter of . . . Wanamaker[?]"[25]

The events of the summer of 1905 had turned so strongly against Washington that he finally answered some criticisms publicly. He flatly denied that he had escorted Miss Wanamaker to the table but admitted that he regularly dined with whites in the North. "When in the South I conform like all colored people to the customs of the South," he wrote to the *Advertiser*, "but when in the North, I have found it necessary . . . to come into contact with white people in the furtherance of my work in ways I do not in the South." But he stopped short of any direct confrontation with his detractors.[26]

The fall of 1905 was a season of defeat for Washington. Dixon's play *The Clansman* went from city to city, and audiences were wildly enthusiastic about the melodramatic staging of the Ku Klux Klan action during Reconstruction. Theodore Roosevelt also toured the South that autumn, making sycophantic overtures of sectional reconciliation to Confederate veterans. When Washington traveled that fall, he took along Pinkerton detectives to protect his life because of various assassination threats. He told a northern friend that "a large element of the South" had decided that "the education of the colored people shall go no further." He feared that whites intended to stop the progress of Tuskegee Institute as a white-supremacist object lesson: "The explanation of this is that the colored contractor or architect or carpenter or brickmason comes into competition with the white man while the Negro teacher or minister does not." To another ally he privately expressed his dismay that northern blacks did not see that when southern whites attacked him, "it is not B. T. Washington who is attacked, but the race."[27]

Although Washington correctly saw that he was a symbol on which angry white southerners could focus their racial animosity, he could not admit that he now represented something quite different from the image of the hardworking, loyal African American that he had always tried to project. By 1905 he was no longer the "good negro" to many southern whites but was instead the power-hungry and deceitful political schemer of Tuskegee. He never regained control of what he stood for, and the definition of his meaning to subsequent generations largely conformed to that given him by Du Bois and the Toms—Dixon, Watson, and Heflin.

After 1905 Washington continued on all the same lines, but his intensity waned as events relentlessly buried his optimism. Although the constitutional limits on funding black education had been defeated, Washington worried about the decimation of black primary schools as local school districts across the South discriminated against black children in the allocation of money for teachers, buildings, and books. "In the country districts I am quite sure that matters are going backward," he wrote privately in 1906. "In many cases in Alabama teachers are being paid as little as Ten dollars per month. This of course means no school." Catastrophic events in 1906 further damaged the person viewed as the leader of the race. The Atlanta riot in September and Roosevelt's wholesale dismissal of black soldiers charged with rioting at Brownsville, Texas, in November represented such injustice that African Americans and sympathetic whites in the North questioned the leadership of the man presumably in charge of protecting black rights. Roosevelt added insult to injury in a presidential address in December that grossly exaggerated black criminality and pandered to the common stereotype. Kelly Miller of Howard University wrote to Washington that Roosevelt's speech did "more to damn the Negro to everlasting infamy than all the maledictions of Tillman, Vardaman, [and] Dixon" and predicted that Washington would be held responsible for Roosevelt's behavior. "When Mr. Roosevelt requested you to act as his adviser and when you accepted that delicate responsibility, the world may be expected to believe that he is guided by the advice of his own seeking." With the symbolism of equality that the White House dinner had represented to African Americans now exploded by Roosevelt's bigotry, Washington lost authority as the leader of his race at the same time that the Niagara Movement solidified northern black opposition to him. He never recovered from these reverses, though typically he never acknowledged his defeat.[28]

The contextual evidence presented herein suggests that Booker T. Washington had great obstacles before him as he tried to lead his race in the 1890s and early twentieth century, and by no honest measure can he be seen as an overall success. His most basic goal was to demonstrate a trajectory of progress among African Americans at a time when the thoroughly white-supremacist society believed that blacks were declining into criminality and even oblivion. He faced a public discourse and a popular culture that were relentlessly set against him. He confronted personal and political enemies in the South who fought to keep him from projecting an ideology of black progress and who, starting in 1901, stirred race hate by attacking Washington for his defense of black officeholders and education. Those attacks undermined his ability to pursue his symbolic action on behalf of black progress, though he never stopped trying.

These reconsiderations of Washington's reputation should make historians think again about how this period of American history is presented. Washington often has been portrayed as the symbol of the age of segregation, he of course standing for acquiescence in Jim Crow. In light of evidence presented herein of Washington's active challenges, direct and indirect, to white supremacy, that understanding seems wrong. So do those views, including ones expressed by Professors Woodward and Harlan, which characterize Washington as "conservative." At the least they represent an unacceptably imprecise meaning for the term. Washington clearly was set against "conserving" the white-supremacist society and culture in which he lived. His purpose was to change things for African Americans. He could only be considered a conservative in his support of the capitalist system.

The designation of Washington as an "accommodationist" also has to be questioned in the light of the evidence herein. He worked too hard to resist and to overcome white supremacy to call him an accommodationist, even if some of his white-supremacist southern neighbors so construed some of his statements. Having conditions forced on him, with threat of destruction clearly the cost of resistance, does not constitute a fair definition of accommodation. The protest-versus-accommodation dichotomy has functioned as virtually a Manichaean divide in writing about African American leadership. The tendency to make protest leaders the good guys and accommodators the bad guys reflects the sentiments at large in society since the Civil Rights Movement. If Booker T. Washington has been the main historical antecedent for accommodationism as the misguided opposite of protest, and if in fact "accommodationism" misrepresents much of his real work, then writing about American race relations must be reevaluated. Indeed, there have been few if any black "leaders" in American history who were not protest leaders in some measure. It is only by comparing degrees of protest commitment, or preferring certain styles of protest to others, that distinctions are drawn (and often overdrawn). This divide has also been understood as between "idealism" and "realism," and historians have favored idealists in writing about black leaders, perhaps because of their self-identity with Washington's critics. In the early 1920s, Kelly Miller noted that "there always existed a small group of assertive Negroes . . . composed mainly of college bred men of liberal culture who were unwilling to compromise their intellectual integrity by surrendering the abstract claim of political rights. They could not tolerate the suggestion of inferiority which Washington's program implied. . . . The man with the theory always has the advantage of the man with the thing, in abstract disquisition. Since Mr. Washington's death, this group has gained the ascendancy in dominating the thought and opinion of the race, but has not been able to realize to the least degree the rights and recognition so vehemently demanded."[29]

The protest-accommodation dichotomy has obscured the fundamental similarity of the substance of Washington's action to the protests agenda put forward starting in 1909 by the National Association for the Advancement of Colored People (NAACP). Washington made public protests against discrimination on railroads, lynching, unfair voting qualifications, discriminatory funding in education, segregated housing legislation, and discrimination by labor unions—the latter two protests coming after 1910. He arranged and personally provided partial funding for lawsuits challenging disfranchisement, jury discrimination, and peonage. And he campaigned constantly against the pernicious images projected in the media and popular culture about blacks, including the 1915 protest against *Birth of a Nation*. He attempted to organize a national black newspaper. The NAACP would have the same protest concerns about segregated public accommodations, lynching, the criminal justice system, and economic discrimination, and it would bring legal challenges to protect blacks' right to vote, get an education, and have fair access to housing. It would also condemn regularly the ugly stereotypes prevalent in American life, starting with *Birth of a Nation* and continuing through *Amos 'n' Andy* on radio in the early 1930s, Hollywood films in the 1940s, and *Amos 'n' Andy* on television in the 1950s. The NAACP did, of course, establish a national publication, *Crisis*, that accomplished much of what Washington had in mind. Washington's anticipation of virtually all the

NAACP protest agenda suggests that a consensus of what needed to be done to protect black rights had been identified as early as 1900, and he and the NAACP had in turn pursued it.[30]

It seems that much common ground lay beneath the two men slugging it out for leadership of the race. Beyond the civil rights strategies that they both embraced in one way or another, they shared a similar despair at the inability of whites to see the achievement of so much decency and intelligence among African Americans. Although Du Bois held the African past in higher regard than Washington did, they both were convinced that people of African descent had been readily civilized. Both were deeply dismayed by the disjuncture between their own achievements and the awful reputation of African Americans as a group among whites. Although Washington did not voice it openly, he and Du Bois understood in similar ways the downward trajectory of black prospects between 1900 and 1908. They agreed that intelligence among African Americans had to be manifest in order to overcome the race's reputation for weakness and poor character, and they also believed that the development of a cadre of black leaders and achievers was necessary to accomplish that. To be sure, they had somewhat different ideas of how to develop African American exemplars, but the nurturing of "human capital" clearly was the first goal of each as a race leader. It is partly because each man distrusted the other so much personally and was so determined to see the other as a major obstruction to his own purposes that their similarities of thought and strategy have been overlooked.

Led by Du Bois, however, historians confused the style with the substance of Booker T. Washington. Many historians have shown a narrow-mindedness about black leaders' styles: African American leaders must always be "lions" like Frederick Douglass, Du Bois, Martin Luther King Jr., or Jesse Jackson. They cannot be "foxes" or "rabbits," else they will be accused of lacking manhood. On the level of sound logic, historians must be honest in recognizing that protest has yielded the desired results more episodically than consistently. Other strategies for change have worked better at other times, and external influences have also been the prime determinant of change at some points. It is misleading to teach that change is the result exclusively, or even predominantly, of protest.

But then Washington also misled when he taught that economic uplift would ultimately bring the return of political rights. In a hundred different ways he expressed his faith that a black person who acquired economic independence would command the respect of white neighbors and ultimately with it would come the full rights of citizenship. But he never seems to have acknowledged, not even privately, what was clear from the anti-industrial-education arguments made by Dixon and others at the turn of the century—that most whites objected fundamentally to the rise in status represented by a black skilled worker, business proprietor, or landowner. To concede that would have undermined his economic strategy. And there was no other realistic avenue for progress; certainly, neither politics nor protest would work in the South of 1901. Instead, he did what any good public-relations man does—he ignored the facts that did not fit his presentation of reality. He insisted that blacks would rise in status through education and economic success. To a certain extent, events after his death vindicated his faith: World wars, great migrations, and a vastly expanded national government did bring enough economic opportunity to free many African Americans from the South's hostility to all black economic progress. But those events also brought a greater chance for political solutions, and it would be political action in the 1960s that ended segregation and disfranchisement.

Notwithstanding the sympathetic attitude toward Booker T. Washington herein, let it be understood that he failed in his larger purpose of persuading whites that African Americans were progressing rather than degenerating. His public relations campaign simply could not overcome the intense political and cultural authority of white supremacy that mounted in the 1890s and held sway in the early twentieth century. But neither did the efforts of the NAACP in that regard succeed until World War II, when the national resolve to defeat racist enemies resulted in a commitment, some of it based in government propaganda, to the rejection of racial stereotypes in American culture. The removal of anti-black stereotypes from mass culture that began during World War II enabled the acceptance of African American equality in the 1950s and 1960s. Washington did not succeed in remaking the black image in the American mind, but he identified it as a necessary challenge that others did meet. He should be credited with anticipating the "modern" world in which image was more readily manipulated, and sometimes more important, than reality. His efforts to shape his own symbolism, and that of African Americans as a group, should be marked as a shrewd and valiant effort to lift his people.

Notes

1. Du Bois's review of *Up From Slavery* appeared in the *Dial* 31 (July 16, 1901): 53–55; Du Bois, *The Souls of Black Folk*, ed. John Hope Franklin, *Three Negro Classics* (New York: Avon, 1965), 241, 246–47.

2. C. Vann Woodward, *Origins of the New South* (Baton Rouge: Louisiana State University Press, 1951), 218; Louis R. Harlan, *Booker T. Washington: The Making of a Black Leader, 1856–1901* (New York: Oxford University Press, 1972) (hereinafter cited as Harlan, *BTW*, vol. 1), 157, 160, 227, 228, 324; Louis R. Harlan, *Booker T. Washington: The Wizard of Tuskegee, 1901–1915* (New York: Oxford University Press, 1983); Louis R. Harlan [and others], *The Booker T. Washington Papers*, 14 vols. (Urbana: University of Illinois Press, 1972–87) (hereinafter cited as *BTW Papers*).

3. This discussion is based in part on George M. Fredrickson's *The Black Image in the White Mind: The Debate on Afro-American Character and Destiny, 1817–1914* (1971; reprint, Middletown, Conn.: Wesleyan University Press, 1987); Frederick L. Hoffman, "Vital Statistics of the Negro," *Arena*, April 1892, 529–42.

4. Thomas D. Clark, *The Southern Country Editor* (Indianapolis: Bobbs-Merrill, 1948), 195–207. Examples of the preoccupation with ugly black stereotypes can be found in the *Atlanta Constitution* and the *Birmingham Age-Herald* starting in the late 1890s, but consistent portrayals are also in the newspapers of Chattanooga, Nashville, Knoxville, Memphis, and Montgomery.

5. David A. Jasen and Gene Jones, *Spreadin' Rhythm Around: Black Popular Songwriters, 1880–1930* (New York: Schirmer Books, 1998), 1–10; Robert C. Toll, *Blacking Up: The Minstrel Show in Nineteenth-Century America* (New York: Oxford University Press, 1974).

6. Louis R. Harlan, "The Secret Life of Booker T. Washington," *Journal of Southern History* 37 (August 1971): 393–416; Washington, "An Address at the National Peace Jubilee, October 16, 1898," *BTW Papers*, 4: 490–93; Washington, "A Statement on Lynching in the *Birmingham Age-Herald*," *BTW Papers*, 5: 91; Washington to Emmett Jay Scott, ca. June 5, 1899, *BTW Papers*, 5: 125. The article "Lynching in the South" was included in Washington's *The Story of My Life and Work*, reprinted in *BTW Papers*, 1: 149–54.

7. For examples of Washington's speeches that emphasized black progress, see "An Address before the National Educational Association, July 10, 1896," *BTW Papers*, 4: 188–99; "A Speech at the Institute of Arts and Sciences, September 30, 1896," *BTW Papers*, 4: 211–23; "An Address before the Christian Endeavor Society, July 7, 1898," *BTW Papers*, 4: 438–41, 5: 278–79; Washington to Randall O. Simpson, October 22, 1903, *BTW Papers*, 7: 302–4; and Washington to Louis G. Gregory, January 19, 1904, *BTW Papers*, 7: 401.

8. Washington to Timothy Thomas Fortune, November 7, 1899, *BTW Papers*, 5: 256–57; Stephen Kantrowitz, *Ben Tillman and the Reconstruction of White Supremacy* (Chapel Hill: University of North Carolina Press, 2000), 217–21.

9. Washington, *Up From Slavery*, in *BTW Papers*, 1: 347.

10. For a discussion of Tuskegee race and politics during Reconstruction, see Robert J. Norrell, *Reaping the Whirlwind: The Civil Rights Movement in Tuskegee* (New York: Knopf, 1985), 3–18.

11. Harlan, in *BTW Papers*, 1: 171–73; see "A Sunday Evening Talk, May 6, 1900," *BTW Papers*, 5: 504n.1; *New Orleans Times Democrat*, August 31, 1903.

12. Gordon Macdonald to the editor of the *Washington Post*, ca. April 28, 1903, *BTW Papers*, 7: 132–35; *Atlanta Constitution*, September 3, 1899, and July 29, 1900.

13. Charles Carroll, *The Negro a Beast* . . . (St. Louis: American Book and Bible House, 1900); William P. Calhoun, *The Caucasian and The Negro in the United States. They Must Separate. If Not, Then Extermination. A Proposed Solution: Colonization* (Columbia, S.C.: R. L. Bryan Co., 1902). For example, see, in the *North American Review*, Marion L. Dawson, "The South and the Negro" (February 1902); Clarence H. Poe, "Suffrage Restriction in the South: Its Causes and Consequences" (October 1902); Henderson M. Somerville, "Some Co-operating Causes of Negro Lynching" (October 1903); Thomas Nelson Page, "The Lynching of Negroes—Its Cause and Its Prevention" (January 1904); and William Garrott Brown, "The White Peril: The Immediate Danger of the Negro" (October 1904). See also Alfred Holt Stone, *Studies in the American Race Problem* (New York: Doubleday, Page & Company, 1908). Thomas was quoted in John David Smith, *Black Judas: William Hannibal Thomas and the American Negro* (Athens: University of Georgia Press, 2000), 175–76; see also 191–95. Thomas Dixon, *The Leopard's Spots: A Romance of the White Man's Burden* (New York: Doubleday, Page & Co., 1902); Harlan discusses publishing figures on *Up From Slavery* and *Leopard's Spots* in *BTW Papers*, 1: xxxiv.

14. Washington to Oswald Garrison Villard, August 31, 1903, *BTW Papers*, 7: 273; the governor of Georgia was quoted in the *Atlanta Constitution*, April 25, 1901; Dixon, *Leopard's Spots*, 338.

15. Dewey W. Grantham Jr., "Dinner at the White House: Theodore Roosevelt, Booker T. Washington, and the South," *Tennessee Historical Quarterly* 18 (June 1958): 117; William F. Holmes, *The White Chief: James Kimble Vardaman* (Baton Rouge: Louisiana State University Press, 1970), 99; newspaper clipping, citation unclear, in the Papers of Booker T. Washington, reel 718, Library of Congress.

16. Grantham, "Dinner," 116–18, 125.

17. Washington to Theodore Roosevelt, October 2, 1901, *BTW Papers*, 6: 221. For a sample of evidence of Washington's commitment to combating lily white-ism, see Washington to Theodore Roosevelt, September 27, 1902, *BTW Papers*, 6: 527; Washington draft letter to *Montgomery Advertiser*, ca. September 1901, *BTW Papers*, 6: 536–39; Washington to Francis Jackson Garrison, October 14, 1902, *BTW Papers*, 6: 547; and Washington to Thomas Ruffin Roulhac, October 29, 1902, *BTW Papers*, 6: 561–62.

18. Washington to Emmett Jay Scott, June 23, 1902, *BTW Papers*, 6: 487; Washington letter to *Birmingham Age-Herald*, November 24, 1902, *BTW Papers*, 6: 590–92.

19. See Michael Perman, *Struggle for Mastery: Disfranchisement in the South, 1888–1908* (Chapel Hill: University of North Carolina Press, 2001), 224–44.

20. Tillman, *The Race Problem*, speech in the U.S. Senate, February 23–24, 1903; Vardaman quoted in Harlan, *BTW*, 1: 307; and *Leslie's Weekly*, February 4, 1904.

21. *Lafayette (Alabama) Sun*, October 5, 1904; unidentified newspaper clippings, Heflin Scrapbook 6, Box 848, J. Thomas Heflin Papers, Gorgas Library, University of Alabama.

22. Unidentified newspaper clippings, ibid.; undated Tuskegee *News* article reprinted in *Nashville American*, October 19, 1904.

23. *Tom Watson's Magazine*, June 1905, 392–93; C. Vann Woodward, *Tom Watson: Agrarian Rebel* (New York: Macmillan, 1938), 380.

24. Thomas Dixon Jr., "Booker T. Washington and the Negro: Some Dangerous Aspects of the Work of Tuskegee," *Saturday Evening Post*, August 19, 1905.

25. Editorial in the *Montgomery Advertiser*, August 16, 1905, *BTW Papers*, 8: 341–43.

26. Washington, letter to the editor, *Montgomery Advertiser*, August 20, 1905, *BTW Papers*, 8: 343–44.

27. Washington to Charles William Anderson, September 13, 1905, *BTW Papers*, 8: 356–57; Three Reports of Pinkerton Detectives, October 22, 1905, *BTW Papers*, 8: 418–21; Washington to Francis Jackson Garrison, October 5, 1905, *BTW Papers*, 8: 394–96. Garrison replied that he too feared violence: "I have long felt, as I have told you, the possibility of the torch being applied even to Tuskegee in some sudden whirlwind of passion" (Garrison to Washington, October 12, 1905, *BTW Papers*, 8: 402–3). Garrison's nephew Oswald Garrison Villard wrote at about the same time to his uncle that he pitied Washington, "for he is in a desperate position and may yet prove a martyr to his cause" (ibid.); see also Washington to George H. Woodson, September 13, 1905, *BTW Papers*, 8: 358.

28. Washington to Hollis Burke Frissell, July 18, 1906, *BTW Papers*, 9:43; Kelly Miller to Washington, November 16, 1906, *BTW Papers*, 9: 129–31. Washington and Miller had seen Roosevelt's address prior to his public delivery. Washington tried mightily to get Roosevelt to change the speech but to little effect.

29. Kelly Miller, *The Everlasting Stain* (Washington: Associated Publishers, 1924), 267.

30. Washington's ownership of the *New York Age*, and his alleged ownership of other newspapers, was a main preoccupation of Du Bois, and so it has been of Professor Harlan. It is important to recognize that white race leaders like Vardaman and Watson owned newspapers and that many influential white supremacists, such as Tillman, Dixon, and Felton, also had ready access to the pages of one or more papers. Du Bois and Trotter certainly used the *Boston Guardian* and other newspapers to vie with Washington for leadership of African Americans. To condemn Washington for ownership of newspaper(s), whether secret or not, is applying a double standard.

5

What Made Booker Wash(ington)?
The Wizard of Tuskegee in Economic Context

PETER A. COCLANIS

> You can have an affection for a murderer or a sodomite, but you cannot have an affection for a man whose breath stinks—habitually stinks, I mean."[1]
>
> George Orwell, *The Road to Wigan Pier*

> In all my teaching I have watched carefully the influence of the tooth-brush, and I am convinced that there are few single agencies of civilization that are more far-reaching."[2]
>
> Booker T. Washington, *Up From Slavery*

As every schoolboy (homeboy?) knows, in *Up From Slavery* Booker T. Washington was all over cleanliness and personal hygiene. Indeed, Washington was lucky that Freud, writing around the same time, never weighed in on the 1901 autobiography. All that talk of cleaning, sweeping, dusting, washing, and brushing, and all that talk of dirt, grime, and filth would have fascinated the Austrian as it has fascinated and either angered or amused historians over the years. Fetish, anyone?

Not that Booker Taliaferro Washington didn't have scrubbin' on his mind in *Up From Slavery*. Now that the book has been digitalized, one can easily perform content analysis on the text, and the results of such analysis are instructive, if not surprising: twenty-two references to cleaning and cleanliness, eight to dirt, eight to sweeping, seven to washing, five to soiled persons or property, five to laundering, four to filth, and on and on.[3] At the outset of a period of virulent racism and horrific race relations, a period scholars have tried to capture and encapsulate by employing terms such as *crucible*, *nadir*, and *betrayal*, and, more recently, calling it a "dark journey" and "trouble in mind," there was ol' Booker blathering about "the use and value of the bath" and pontificating about the purpose of the top sheet.[4]

And that's just the first bill against Booker. "Don't start me to talkin', cause I'll tell you everythin' I know," as the great bluesman Sonny Boy Williamson famously sang.[5] Critics point out, for example, that in those rare moments in *Up From Slavery* when Washington isn't scrubbin', he's either waxing on about the wonders of industrial education or is on his knees up North beggin' and money grubbin'. Moreover, these same critics never tire of asking why Washington never got himself similarly worked up (at least publicly) about such turn-of-the-century incidentals and divertissements as segregation, disfranchisement, and lynching. As a result of Washington's, shall we say, misplaced priorities, many anti-Bookerites would like nothing more, figuratively speaking (I think), than to cast down a bucket on Washington's head or to apply that closed fist upside the same, such actions being "essential to ... progress" in the eyes of members of certain interpretive communities.[6]

I'm intentionally being a bit sardonic here, but only for purposes of scholarly purchase. What I hope to do in this essay is to make a case for looking more sympathetically both at Washington and at Washingtonian priorities. To be sure, in recent years a few writers—Adam Fairclough comes immediately to mind—have begun to revisit and in some ways to rehabilitate Washington, but many scholars are still frustrated and even a bit embarrassed by the Wizard of Tuskegee.[7] Indeed, some of Washington's earlier defenders, most notably Houston Baker, have recently had second thoughts about him.[8] The case I'll make will be an economic or, perhaps more accurately, a socioeconomic one, but in so doing I hope to help us to understand and interpret certain cultural phenomena as well, including the possible links between all that scrubbin' in *Up From Slavery* and the fact that in 1996 Bijan's Michael Jordan Cologne was the best-selling fragrance in the world.[9]

Since this essay will proceed at the social rather than psychoanalytical level, Washington's concern with, if not fixation upon matters hygienic in *Up From Slavery* will be analyzed not as a personality quirk, but in the context of his larger social goals. Along with his views on education, values, and economic development, Washington's position on personal and social hygiene constitutes or at least retrospectively can be made to constitute part of a relatively consistent and coherent worldview.[10] In this regard it is perhaps apropos to highlight a point Milton Friedman made long ago about analyzing human economic behavior. Just as a billiards player need not have studied geometry and physics in a formal way to become expert in the game, a human being—in this case Booker T. Washington—need not self-consciously and explicitly articulate, or, for that matter, even be totally cognizant of formal economic theory in order to promote developmental policies that, *ceteris paribus*, make a good deal of sense.[11]

Washington wrote no formal treatises on economics. Nonetheless, one can piece together the rudiments of an implicit theory of economic development from Washington's various writings, speeches, actions, and affinities. Indeed, maybe from his economic behavior, too: according to Louis Harlan, Booker was a pretty good businessman/entrepreneur in his own right.[12] In any case, Washington's views on most matters are well known, and those treated below are often discussed under another rubric—social philosophy. What I hope to do is to reconfigure his views, and, in so doing, tease out the developmental implications of matters economic, social, moral, and philosophical.

Clearly, if ironically, Washington's "social philosophy" centered around the values and behaviors of discrete individuals. To Washington, the historical legacy of slavery had left most rural African Americans without the tools, skills, and mind-sets required for economic growth. Life for most freedmen and freedwomen (as well as their progeny) in the late-nineteenth-century South was Hobbesian in nature—nasty, brutish, and short. Given the circumscribed role, developmental priorities, and class and racial preferences of the American state, governmental remedies, in the form of allocations or reallocations of public goods and/or social transfers of one type or another, were unlikely. It was thus up to individuals or, at most, communities of individuals to help themselves.

Washington believed, first and foremost, that the "values" of African Americans would have to change before such self-help was forthcoming. Actually, the word *values* is at once a misnomer and somewhat anachronistic, for what Washington, a Victorian man in the truest sense, was calling for was a turn to Victorian *virtues*. Indeed, there is not much to distinguish Washingtonian virtues—hard work, sobriety, thrift, self-help, and self-discipline—from those promoted by the great moralists of the Victorian age, people such as Thomas Carlyle and, to a lesser extent, Samuel Smiles.[13]

Once such virtues or values were inculcated, adopted, and sufficiently diffused among the African American population in the South, the process of self-sustaining economic growth could begin. Washington was confident that this would be the case despite the fact that the growth scenario he envisioned would unfold without the help or necessarily even the blessing of the state. For according to Washington, even without state support, the above virtues would manifest themselves over time in the slow, incremental accumulation of economic assets of one type or another, most importantly, real property. Once property holding became widespread among African Americans in the rural South, greater independence, enhanced autonomy, and more "degrees of freedom" would be possible, for Washington believed that even white America, however racist at the turn of the century, viewed property rights, even among blacks, with considerable respect, if not with total sacrosanctity.

The transubstantiation process described above—of virtue into property, as it were—would be mediated and facilitated through the development of black human capital, particularly via greater access to education. Not just any kind of education either, but basic education, manual training, and the diffusion of useful, practical knowledge through "industrial" institutions along the lines of the Hampton and Tuskegee models.[14] Washington's faith in industrial education was such that he was willing to go to great lengths to cultivate financial support for the same from assorted (sordid?) benefactors (and malefactors) of great wealth. Why? Because in his view such "industrial-training" schools would help moral, purposive African American men and women gain the agricultural, artisanal, and domestic skills needed to acquire small farms and to start small businesses, to manage households, to amass property, and gradually to make themselves central, even "indispensable" to the southern economy. Slowly but surely, they would thence *earn* both the respect, however grudging, of white southerners and, more important, true citizenship with the rights, privileges, and immunities attending thereto.

∞

It didn't take opponents long to carp at Washington's developmental views. Although both contemporary and latter-day critics generally took greater umbrage at his unwillingness to fight publicly or immediately for political and civil rights for African Americans, Washington's positions on economic and educational matters also came under sharp attack. Indeed, no part of Washington's developmental program escaped criticism.[15] For example, many critics over the years have judged Washington's economic views to be not merely antimodern, but truly atavistic. At precisely the time that the United States was urbanizing and industrializing at a frenetic clip, there was ol' Booker exhorting African Americans to stay down on the farm. In more sophisticated versions of this critique, it is pointed out that one of the most severe economic problems the New South faced was an overabundance of poor, low-productivity farmers, black and white alike. Accordingly, it is argued or at least alleged that Washington's program, even if successful on its own terms, was too limited and too small in scale to do much to alleviate the truly massive problems of redundant labor and misallocated resources in the southern economy. Better to get those dirt farmers out of agriculture and into higher-value-added mining or manufacturing activities, whether in the South or in the North.[16] Moreover, Washington's economic assumptions—his "priors," as economists say—often came under fire as well. Some liberals and critics on the left, most notably C. Vann Woodward, attacked Washington for what they considered to be an anticollectivist bias in his approach to growth, and they were particularly critical of Washington's emphasis on thrift, individual responsibility, and self-help, as well as his low regard for unions.[17] Finally, even friendly critics—Charles W. Chesnutt, for example—as well as ardent foes such as W.E.B. Du Bois believed that Washington's dogged defense of industrial training and resistance to other educational models ultimately served procrustean ends, boxing African Americans of varying abilities and inclinations into a limited range of physically demanding, intellectually stultifying, low-prestige vocations.[18] In recent times, some African American scholars, figurative descendants of the "Talented Tenth," have taken their critiques of Washington's educational views even further, sensing conspiratorial overtones, and linking industrial training to black poverty, various social pathologies, and even the prison-industrial complex.[19] That's a lot of heavy lifting. One reason

Booker may have washed, it seems, was because of the critical weight he was made to bear.

Not that Washington's critics didn't have some—okay, *many*—valid points. I'm not interested in any scorched-earth defense of Washington, then, but merely in taking his views on development more seriously than they have generally been taken in the last thirty years or so (another legacy of the sixties?).[20] In so doing, I'll make the case that there were a number of positive elements in his program, particularly when considered in the context of recent research in microeconomics and in the field of economic development. First, however, a few words about the genealogy of Washington's views, how and whence they came about.

As Louis Harlan pointed out long ago, Booker T. Washington was a man of action, not a man of ideas.[21] However, even his critics recognized that he was observant, smart, and canny, and he seems to have had a knack for absorbing, processing, and disseminating certain powerful "covering" ideas or (not to put too fine a point on this) "covering" *themes,* to which he was exposed. In some ways, what I'm suggesting is a turn-of-the-century version of "talking points," which allowed Washington (admittedly with the help of the Samuel Chapman Armstrongs, Max Thrashers, and Lyman Abbotts of the world) successfully to articulate that "vision thing."[22]

This said, one shouldn't minimize the role of Washington's own instincts, lived experiences, and temperament in shaping his worldview. Born a slave—the son of a female slave and a still unidentified white man—and raised in hardscrabble circumstances in the salt-mining town of Malden (Kanawha Salines), West Virginia, Washington knew a thing or two about, shall we say, the materiality of poverty, and he seems to have developed rather quickly certain psychosocial mechanisms—maybe even algorithms—for inuring himself to, coping with, and even overcoming the same. All of this is quite evident in *Up From Slavery,* part bildungsroman, part Carnegie-esque (Andrew and Dale!) manual for self-improvement. Either way, Washington's rise, following Victorian tropes, can be attributed to talent, hard work, pluck, and luck.[23]

Thirsting for education and self-improvement, Washington learned what he could in the Negro school in Malden and on his own, while pulling shifts in the town's salt furnaces and coal mines. In 1871, Washington, then fifteen, took a job that in many ways would reshape his life, going to work as a live-in houseboy with the family of General Lewis Ruffner, owner of the Malden mines. Ever ambitious and eager to please, Washington got on well, after a rocky start, with Ruffner's wife, Viola, a "hyperstrict Yankee woman," who both encouraged the youth's intellectual development, and taught the ex-slave (or at least reinforced within the ex-slave) "the gospel of thrift, propriety, cleanliness, and hard work."[24] This may or may not have been Washington's first brush with Yankee values or virtues; it certainly was not his last. After a year and a half with the Ruffners, Washington, having heard vague rumblings about the recently established Hampton Institute in Hampton, Virginia, made his famous "long march" east, where he was to meet another New Englander (by way of Hawaii), General Armstrong, who, of course, was to be his inspiration/role model/surrogate father, and so on, for the rest of his life.[25]

This is not the place and I am not the historian to reconstruct in detail the relationship between Armstrong and Washington. Such reconstruction is hardly essential to my purpose here in any case. Suffice it to say that Armstrong was nothing if not a true champion of the Victorian virtues mentioned earlier, and Hampton the institutional embodiment, indeed, the avatar of the same. Washington spent three years at Hampton—approximately two of them sweeping, scrubbing, combing, and brushing, or so it seems. More seriously, though, the Hampton way—which is to say, industrial and moral training *cum* moral and industrial training—left an indelible imprint on Washington. Armstrong's educational philosophy—the multivalent focus on head, heart, and hand, as it were—came naturally to him, growing, seemingly organically, out of his Puritan/Presbyterian background, his parents' missionary work in Hawaii, Armstrong's familiarity with the curricular design of the Hilo Manual Labor School (for native boys) in Hawaii, his close relationship with the illustrious nineteenth-century moralist Mark Hopkins while a student at Williams College, and his Civil War experience leading Negro troops into Virginia.[26] Head, heart, and hand, industrial and moral training, sweeping, cleaning, brushing, over and over, day after day. This is what Armstrong brought to his African American charges at Hampton, and this is precisely what Booker T. Washington took away.

It was thus with the Hampton template in mind that Washington became principal of the Tuskegee Institute in 1881. Washington had learned his lessons well under the tutelage of Armstrong and another strongly moralistic New Englander, Mary Mackie, the assistant principal at Hampton. He completed the three-year course of study there in 1875, and, after bouncing around a bit, returned to the school as a member of the staff in 1879. The rest is history, as they say. Two years later, he was off to east-central Alabama to attempt to establish and build a Hampton "knock-off" at Tuskegee, almost as a franchise.

Over the next two decades, as we are reminded again and again in *Up From Slavery*, Washington, and his talented team of dedicated staffers and teachers, rendered Tuskegee highly successful. Moreover, the school succeeded in a number of ways, not only as a discrete site for industrial education, for example, but also as a platform for northern philanthropy, and as a widely publicized, relatively comprehensive, and highly regarded model of (or at least set of stylized ideas about) economic development and race relations. Tus-ke-gee. Here was a faraway place that molded or at least purported to mold impecunious African Americans from the rural South into sober, thrifty, disciplined producers. My wording is cautious here because, although I believe there is a good deal of truth to the Tuskegee foundation story, I am unaware of any systematic longitudinal study of the mobility outcomes of early Tuskegee graduates, let alone of the far greater number of students who merely passed through.[27] If we give the official Tuskegee story the benefit of the doubt, however, the school provided its students with the vocational skills, moral training, and support networks needed to build small farms and businesses, to nourish and sustain households, and, in so doing, gradually to acquire property and its presumptive concomitants and correlates: greater economic independence, enhanced self-respect and social standing, and eventually perhaps even basic civil and political rights. Up from slavery! Up with Booker T.!

After discounting the hype and cutting through the self-aggrandizement and the spin, what remains of the message of *Up From Slavery*? From the vantage point of 2002, is there a there there, to appropriate Gertrude Stein's phrase? In a word, yes. Whatever else Washington may have been doing in his autobiography, he succeeded in articulating, consciously or not, both a value orientation and a development vision that made a good deal of sense, given the position of rural African Americans and economic conditions in the late-nineteenth-century South.

Harkening back to the title of this paper, why, then, did Booker wash?

One can certainly find all kinds of evidence in *Up From Slavery* suggesting that Washington washed because he was so often surrounded by dirt and filth as a youth. Whether one points to the earthen kitchen floor he slept on as a slave boy or his squalid Malden house, the stench and filth of the salt furnaces and coal mines, or his legendary night under the sidewalk in Richmond, Booker was one with dirt. Viola Ruffner tried her best, but Washington's social circumstances were such that filth and stench engulfed him. Nor did things change much, at least initially, at Hampton, though over time, under the tutelage of General Armstrong and Mrs. Mackie, dirt was gradually transformed into a vehicle for personal redemption. And verily I say unto you, the "gospel of the toothbrush" was begat.

But one might counter this straightforward approach—the Willie Sutton approach, as it were—by looking for something at once deeper, more abstract, and ostensibly more profound; something from social theory, in other words. Here, we can do no better than to trot out the heavy artillery on cleanliness behaviors: Norbert Elias and Mary Douglas. Both theorists, in their own ways, interpret the pursuit of cleanliness in structural terms as a kind of cultural marker, as an attempt to organize and order the environment, and as a means invidiously to separate, classify, and distinguish certain behaviors, individuals or groups from others. In this way, "clean" and "dirty" become arbitrary, conditional cultural constructs that need not and often do not have much to do with anything so mundane as, let us say, antisepsis or disease.[28]

Other writers also see powerful cultural dimensions to various cleanliness behaviors, but focus rather more on the desire or even need among some to project gentility and refinement. In the nineteenth century, cleanliness behaviors associated with such desires and needs became more and more prevalent among the middle classes in Europe and the United States, and are often viewed as (if not reduced to?) anxious manifestations in the bourgeois search for order.[29]

Then, too, there is the approach recently taken by Houston Baker, who emphasizes the "performative" aspects of Washington's obsessive cleaning, particularly its sexual overtones. Indeed, in Baker's imaginative reading, Booker's sweeping and dusting—especially when conducted with or under the auspices of older white women such as Viola Ruffner and Mary Mackie—should be read as ritualized acts of sexualized intimacy. He points out, for example, that in Italy today, the verb *scopare* ("to sweep") is used colloquially as a synonym for copulation, and, Baker, seemingly inevitably, makes his own ritualized reference to bluesman Robert Johnson's signature song, "I Believe I'll Dust My Broom" in support of his case.[30]

The critic Terry Eagleton once wrote that he was sure that Shakespeare had read Freud, and at times Washington, similarly, seems familiar with both Elias and Douglas.[31] Moreover, I'm sure that Washington's singular attachment to the ideology of the broom owed something to his desire to render poor rural African Americans a bit more refined, if not genteel. There may even be something to Baker's sexualized reading of Booker's purifying *pas de eux*. This said, I'm equally convinced that Washington's personal fixation with cleanliness and his zealous promotion of cleanliness behaviors of one type or another among African Americans were both closely related to, if not direct functions of his "lived experience" in the highly morbid and mortal disease environment of the late-nineteenth-century South.

It is appropriate at this time, perhaps, to quit the realm of cultural theory for a dose or two of material reality. Following the conventions of the U.S. Bureau of the Census, let us label reality the "South Atlantic" and the "East South Central" regions, regions wherein Booker T. Washington was born, flourished, and died. Let us note that these two areas were the poorest parts of the poorest aggregate census region (the "South") in the United States according to every decennial census from 1860 through 1940.[32] Let us note too that the rural population generally—and the African American portion of the rural population specifically—constituted the poorest groups in the two poorest parts of the poorest aggregate census region in the United States over this same period.

And let us try to get a sense of what poverty on this scale, poverty of this scope really meant. Let us vivify deprivation so that readers might begin to recognize the existence of, if not necessarily start to praise some unknown women and men. Simply put, the African American population in the South Atlantic and East South Central states lived lives of (mostly) quiet desperation in the decades after the Civil War. The abysmally low levels of income and wealth achieved (endured?) by this population are only the beginning, offering the merest hints of its plight. Indeed, when considered in broader developmental terms, the base and rank economic position of rural African Americans in these regions seems, if anything, even more appalling, even more degraded and vitiated, and, ultimately, vicious. Heavily burdened, when not imprisoned by debt, rural African Americans, by and large, were, to use the language of President Franklin Delano Roosevelt's Second Inaugural speech, "ill-housed, ill-clad, ill-nourished." They were ill-educated, ill-served politically, and often simply ill, when not subject to premature death.

To be sure, the populations in these regions, black and white alike, had suffered from high levels of morbidity and mortality for centuries before Washington was even born.[33] Indeed, in terms of developmental measures such as the PQLI (Physical Quality of Life Index) and the HDI (Human Development Index), which go beyond income and wealth in assessing the well-being of populations, the South—with its low levels of literacy, high levels of infant mortality, and relatively low life expectancy—had fared far below levels "predicted" by income/wealth even during the antebellum period.[34] During the postbellum period, though, the South became an unmitigated economic, epidemiological, and developmental disaster area. It's not surprising, of course, that a region devastated by four years of combat, shocked by emancipation and the ensuing transformation of social relations, pinched by decades of economic hardship, and enervated by a severe lack of capital would find itself in difficult straits. With poverty and illiteracy widespread, with much of the population bereft of social "capabilities" of the sort discussed by Nobelist Amartya Sen, and with minimal state commitment to matters of public health and welfare, we see, for example, increased incidence and levels of morbidity and mortality attributable to the region's traditional diseases—malaria, typhus, diphtheria, smallpox, and so on—and "newer" diseases such as tuberculosis surging as well.[35]

Moreover, these diseases led not only to higher levels of mortality in the region, but also, in many cases, to chronic health problems among those fortunate enough to survive them. Such problems, in turn, were often compounded by the dietary regime characteristic of most parts of the South in the late nineteenth century. This regime was dominated by the "three *Ms*"—meat, meal, and molasses—which meant a diet very high in fats and carbohydrates, but low in minerals, vitamins, and (because of the poor quality of pork, the South's principal meat) proteins. In combination, the epidemiological environment, characteristic dietary practices, and economic and social conditions—and, as we shall see, practices—prevailing in the late-nineteenth-century South led as well to a variety of deficiency and wasting diseases—malaria, hookworm, pellagra, and rickets in particular—among a sizeable proportion of the southern population. Thus, the roots of one of the most troubling findings unearthed in recent years by practitioners of the new field of anthropometric history: diminished physical stature, as measured by height, weight, and BMI (body mass index) for various segments of the southern population in the late nineteenth century.[36]

One could go on and on, of course. The biopathologies discussed above had their social and moral analogues as well. It was, I believe, the way in which things linked up—the economic, the biological, the social, and the moral—that provides a key to Booker's scrubbin' and sweepin,' a key, in other words, to his worldview. As James C. Riley has recently demonstrated, the "filth theory of disease"—which, as the name implies, drew a correlation between filth and disease—was widely held in the nineteenth century. The more rigorous germ theory was also becoming widely known and accepted in both Europe and America by the time Washington wrote *Up From Slavery*. The germ theory, one recalls, was widely known and pretty much accepted in both Europe and America by the time Washington wrote *Up From Slavery*.[37] It is not at all a stretch to suggest that Washington—as meticulous and fastidious as Louis Pasteur—believed that by changing their cleanliness behaviors, rural African Americans would not only improve their physical environment and enhance their physical health, but also gradually acquire, internalize, and routinize the virtues that would at once stabilize their social situations and set them on the path to the slow accumulation of modest amounts of wealth.[38]

Don't laugh. In recent years, a number of economists have challenged traditional assumptions about the direction of the relationship between health, particularly ill health, and economic growth. Whereas the conventional view has long been that low socioeconomic status correlated with, and arguably "caused" ill health, James P. Smith, Jeffrey Sachs, and others, picking up on insights noted a half century ago by the iconoclastic "tropicopolitan" Pierre Gourou, have not denied the existence of said relationship, but have argued that at times causal lines are, in fact, reversed; thus, they argue that ill health can be and often is an independent variable helping to bring about and explain low socioeconomic status, particularly in tropical and subtropical climes (including the American South).[39]

Which brings us logically to matters economic, and, more precisely, to the efficacy of Booker's views on the same. Here, we must perforce be illustrative rather than exhaustive, but, hopefully, sufficiently illustrative to make the basic point. For example, recent research on labor markets in underdeveloped areas at once complicates the already complex relationship among ill health, cleanliness behaviors, nutrition, climate, and low socioeconomic status, and suggests, again, that in economic terms Washington was about more that platitudes and pieties. Economists studying (and estimating) so-called capacity curves in Less Developed Countries have repeatedly found that work intensity is severely affected by health and nutrition, or rather, by ill health and undernutrition.[40] In light of these studies, can there be any serious doubt that, if followed, Washington's admonitions regarding greater self-sufficiency (and ipso facto food security) and better rural sanitation and hygiene could have helped to break or at least ameliorate African American poverty?

Pursuing this line a bit further, sickly, malnourished populations, generally speaking, will be less productive, may require greater labor monitoring, and because of health-related absences—through flare-ups or recurrences of malaria, for example—will benefit less from "learning by doing" than would healthier, and, hence, more regular and reliable workers. As a result, they will typically earn less, and, for reasons of both ill health and poverty, be seen as poor credit risks, and thus subject to higher interest rates when entering credit markets.[41] Talk about a tough row to hoe.

What else, though, other than soap, a toothbrush, and a broom did Washington have to offer in economic terms? Plenty. New developments in microeconomics as well as work written in the so-called new institutional tradition suggest that a rethinking, or, to be more direct, an upward revision of Washington's economic views is long overdue. Similarly, numerous scholars and practitioners in the field of development are returning to the view that values and ideology are in fact important to the process of economic growth: recent, highly publicized volumes such as Francis Fukuyama's *Trust: Social Virtues and the Creation of Prosperity* and *Culture Matters: How Values Shape Human Progress*, edited by Lawrence E. Harrison and Samuel P. Huntington, offer evidence thereto.[42]

Can anyone any longer doubt that property and secure (and transferable) rights to property are central to growth? Over the past thirty years, a hugely influential school of economics has grown up around the idea that such property rights were indispensable to the "rise of the West," and, increasingly, around the parallel idea that the absence of such rights is largely responsible for many of the problems in the Less Developed Countries.[43] Regarding the latter claim, solid empirical work has demonstrated that even a tiny amount of landed property markedly improves the life chances of people in the so-called periphery today, a conclusion with which Washington, if he were still alive, would agree.[44]

Washington's efforts throughout his career to stabilize African American families in the rural South and to enhance the ability of African American women both to manage households and to contribute to family income should not be brushed aside, either. However quotidian classes in cooking, sewing, and cleaning may seem today, however prosaic lessons on gardening and poultry keeping, we know from comparative work done on other parts of the United States and on other parts of the world just how important such lessons can be.[45]

And what of savings, thrift, and self-help? Certainly, the poor, *ceteris paribus*, have the potential gradually to become less poor if they can manage to withhold some part of income from consumption. Indeed, in development circles today both microsaving and microlending (à la Muhammad Yunus, Grameen Banks, the so-called *Nayakrishi* or New Agriculture movement, and so on) are now quite the rage.[46]

Nor does Washington's fondness for industrial training seem wrongheaded, much less foolhardy from the standpoint of today. Studies conducted by Richard Easterlin and, more recently, by the World Bank, have found that perhaps the best predictor of, or at least correlate with early phases of economic development is the proportion of the population with an eighth-grade education.[47] Washington may have exaggerated for effect when he lampooned African Americans in the late nineteenth century for learning their Latin demonstrative pronouns and conjugating their Greek verbs, but, clearly, rural African Americans benefited more by learning better tillage practices, how to lay bricks, and how to draw mechanically. To the idea of a Talented Tenth, then, *hic, haec, hoc* is about all I can say!

Mentioning the World Bank reminds me of another Booker thing: cannot his courting of northern philanthropists—the Rockefellers, Rosenwalds, and Carnegies—be seen as the late-nineteenth-century analogue of Less Developed Countries seeking grants from funding authorities and agencies such as the IMF, the UNDP, the ADB, or the World Bank today? This is not the whole answer, obviously, but the strategy wasn't all bad for either Washington or his students at Tuskegee.

To square the circle, as it were, we need to get back to values and virtues, if only for a moment or two. In the great scheme of things, individual behaviors such as cleanliness, thrift, hard work, discipline, and self-help might not seem like much. That is to say, given the monumental *structural* problems plaguing southern society in the postbellum period and the gross inequities and injustices perpetrated on rural African Americans in this society, appeals to values and virtues appear a mere palliative or topical salve. We don't prescribe VapoRub or Tiger Balm for lung cancer, do we? Touché, point well taken, whatever—but I can't help but think, nonetheless, that even within the narrowly circumscribed bounds of African American life in the rural South in the late nineteenth century, such values and virtues were worth something, and, when sufficiently present, did at least some individuals some good. And it's not just me, Gertrude Himmelfarb, and other Victorians who would be inclined to feel this way. A few years ago, for example, I coauthored a piece on Goh Keng Swee, a London School of Economics–trained (and thus Fabian-influenced) economist who, according to most observers, was the leading architect of Singapore's so-called economic miracle, that is, the process that led the island nation from underdeveloped status to the very highest level of socioeconomic development in thirty-odd years. In a number of pieces over the years, both formal and occasional, Goh laid out his views on economic growth and development, and his views, those of a thoughtful applied economist and public policy professional, are well worth noting. To be sure, in these writings Goh acknowledges the role of capital, macrofundamentals, and the like, but he also stresses—repeatedly—the importance in economic development of peoples' values and virtues, particularly those values and virtues associated with one Samuel Smiles, who preached the same gospel in Victorian Britain that Booker T. Washington preached at Tuskegee.[48] Go, Keng Swee!

So where does that leave us? How do we conclude? What I have tried to do in this essay is to suggest that we revisit Booker T. Washington and rethink some of the Wizard of Tuskegee's economic and social views. Although Washington has for the most part been the object of scholarly disapproval, if not derision over the past thirty or forty years, some eminent intellectuals—Eugene Genovese, most notably, but at the end of his life even Du Bois, apparently—have viewed Washington's positions more charitably.[49] A good deal of recent work in the social sciences has convinced me that Booker washed for a reason, as it were, and such washing worked at least to some degree. Whereas some scholars continue to disparage Washington as an opportunist, I would prefer to associate another, similar sounding adjective with Washington and his views: *opportune*—"suitable or appropriate for a particular occurrence or moment." If you want a turn-of the-century African American *opportunist*, I'll give you a turn-of the-century African American *opportunist*—William Hannibal Thomas—whose 1901 racist screed *The American Negro* Washington attacked vigorously in the *Outlook* in an (unsigned) review.[50] I say Washington was *opportune* rather than opportunist, for, as Adam Fairclough has recently reminded those that still need reminding, we're talking about the South a hundred-odd years ago. What else would critics have had Washington do? In preaching the gospel of the toothbrush, the breviary of the broom, Washington bought time and provided shelter for people who had "been in the storm" for a very long time, as it were. In so doing, he pushed a program that was not going to make the world anew, but that would do some people some good. Ultimately, things would change and new leaders pushing different programs would emerge. But it was the fastidious, heavily starched Booker Man who helped rural African Americans down a path that ultimately would lead to a degree of black economic empowerment (in part through the rise of a black petite bourgeoisie) and to at least a semblance of substantive civil rights and legal equality. All that scrubbin' may have had other, psychosocial effects as well, particularly by demonstrating to *some* white, middle-class Americans that *many* African Americans aspired to the same norms and championed the same values and virtues as did they. In this regard, Washington's assumption of the role of "race spokesman" upon the death of the handsome but feral-looking and sometimes threatening-sounding Frederick Douglass in 1895 was arguably of considerable importance.[51] Given the racialized nature of the much-remarked-upon psychosexual dramas of the early twentieth century, however, open recognition of "norm convergence" didn't come quickly among whites, but only gradually. Few white males of any class, I submit, wished to smell like Jack Johnson, for example, or, for that matter, like Jackie Robinson, or even like Muhammad Ali.[52] But by the mid-nineties, everyone wanted to be like Mike and smell like Mike—as both Gatorade and Bijan realized—and for some clues about the roots of Michael Jordan's crossover cultural power and authority, one could do worse than to look back to the Wizard of Tuskegee.[53]

Notes

Author's note: The author would like to thank Fitz Brundage and the other participants in the symposium on *Up From Slavery* held at the University of Florida in October 2001. Three participants deserve special thanks: Louis Harlan, Louise Newman, and David Leverenz. The author would also like to thank John Kasson for several excellent suggestions, and Leah Potter for some help with research.

1. George Orwell, *The Road to Wigan Pier* (1937; reprint, New York: Berkeley Medallion, 1961), 112.

2. Booker T. Washington, *Up From Slavery: An Autobiography* (New York: Doubleday, Page, and Co., 1901), 75.

3. The content analysis was done via the electronic version of the 1901 edition of *Up From Slavery* published by Doubleday and digitalized for the "Documenting the American South" project of the University of North Carolina at Chapel Hill Libraries. The electronic version is located in the project's Library of Southern Literature: Collection of Electronic Texts. The collection is located at http://docsouth.unc.edu/index.html.

4. The references in the text are to the following: Joel Williamson, *The Crucible of Race: Black/White: Relations in the American South Since Emancipation* (New York: Oxford University Press, 1984); Rayford W. Logan, *The Negro in American Life and Thought: The Nadir, 1877–1901* (New York: Dial Press, 1954); Rayford W. Logan, *The Betrayal of the Negro, from Rutherford B. Hayes to Woodrow Wilson* (New York: Collier Books, 1965); Neil R. McMillen, *Dark Journey: Black Mississippians in the Age of Jim Crow* (Urbana: University of Illinois Press, 1989); Leon F. Litwack, *Trouble in Mind: Black Southerners in the Age of Jim Crow* (New York: Knopf, 1998). For Washington's comments on the value of the bath and the purpose of the top sheet, see *Up From Slavery*, 58 (quote), 60–61, 175–76.

5. I'm referring to the song "Don't Start Me To Talkin'" by the great blues harpist Sonny Boy Williamson. As blues aficionados know, there were two famous blues harpists who used the name Sonny Boy Williamson. Here, I'm referring to the man known alternatively as Rice Miller, born Aleck or Alex Ford. On the two Sonny Boys, see Peter A. Coclanis, "'I Don't Know': Sonny Boy(s) Williamson, Elusive Identity, and the Pre-Postmodern South," *The Griot* 19 (fall 2000): 62–64.

6. The references are taken from the address that Washington delivered at the opening of the Atlanta Cotton States and International Exposition in Atlanta on

September 18, 1895. The speech is reprinted in Washington, *Up From Slavery*, 218–25. For the manuscript and standard versions of the speech, see Louis R. Harlan and Raymond W. Smock, eds., *The Booker T. Washington Papers*, 14 vols. (Urbana: University of Illinois Press, 1972–89), 3: 578–87 (hereinafter cited as *BTW Papers*).

7. Adam Fairclough, *Better Day Coming: Blacks and Equality, 1890–2000* (New York: Viking, 2001), 41–65. For a short but interesting and insightful defense of Washington, see Glenn C. Loury, "Two Paths to Black Progress," in Loury, *One by One from the Inside Out: Essays and Reviews on Race and Responsibility in America* (New York: Free Press, 1995), 63–82. Another scholar, Heather Cox Richardson, has recently offered a fresh (and respectful) reinterpretation of Washington's social philosophy, arguing that in *Up From Slavery* and elsewhere, Washington was attempting (unsuccessfully as it turned out) to reclaim for African Americans the individualistic, free-labor ideology associated with mid-nineteenth-century Republicanism. See Richardson, *The Death of Reconstruction: Race, Labor, and Politics in the Post–Civil War North, 1865–1901* (Cambridge: Harvard University Press, 2001), 1–5, 225–45.

8. See Houston A. Baker Jr., "Men and Institutions: Booker T. Washington's *Up From Slavery*," in Baker, *Long Black Song: Essays in Black Literature and Culture* (Charlottesville: University Press of Virginia, 1972), 84–95; Baker, *Modernism and the Harlem Renaissance* (Chicago: University of Chicago Press, 1987), 15–41. Baker's recent reappraisal of Washington appears in *Turning South Again: Rethinking Modernism/Re-reading Booker T.* (Durham: Duke University Press, 2001). Note that Baker's early praise of Washington was rather more formal and aesthetic than economic or political in nature.

9. See the promotional material about Michael Jordan Cologne by Bijan Fragrances at www.prismaweb.com. As stated in the text, my argument pertains mainly to economic and socioeconomic concerns. This being the case, I shall not be discussing explicitly the large body of work by literary scholars on *Up From Slavery* as autobiography, exercise in self-representation, identity creation, and so on. I would, however, like to point interested readers to an excellent piece on such matters by James M. Cox: "Autobiography and Washington," *Sewanee Review* 85 (spring 1977): 235–61. Many of the textual points made by Cox are consistent with and supportive of my socioeconomic argument.

10. It should be obvious that I am taking Washington's ideas and positions more seriously than do many other scholars, including Washington's most important biographer, Louis R. Harlan. In 1972, for example, Harlan wrote: "Those who try to understand Washington in ideological terms, as the realistic black philosopher of the age of Jim Crow, or as the intellectual opposite of W.E.B. Du Bois, miss the essential character of the man. He was not an intellectual, but a man of action. Ideas he cared little for. Power was his game, and he used ideas simply as instruments to gain power. Washington's mind as revealed in formal public utterance was a bag of clichés." With all due respect, I disagree. For the quote above, see Harlan, *Booker T. Washington:*

The Making of a Black Leader, 1856–1901 (New York: Oxford University Press, 1972), ii (hereinafter cited as Harlan, *BTW*, vol. 1). For similar sentiments, see Harlan, *Booker T. Washington: The Wizard of Tuskegee, 1901–1915* (New York: Oxford University Press, 1983), ix (hereinafter cited as Harlan, *BTW*, vol. 2).

11. Milton Friedman, "The Methodology of Positive Economics," in Friedman, *Essays in Positive Economics* (Chicago: University of Chicago Press, 1953), 14. For an earlier iteration of this theme, see Milton Friedman and L. J. Savage, "The Utility Analysis of Choices Involving Risk," *Journal of Political Economy* 56 (August 1948): 279–304, especially 298.

12. Louis R. Harlan, "Booker T. Washington and the National Negro Business League," in *Booker T. Washington in Perspective: Essays of Louis R. Harlan*, ed. Raymond W. Smock (Jackson: University Press of Mississippi, 1988), 98–109, especially 102–3.

13. See Gertrude Himmelfarb, *The De-Moralization of Society: From Victorian Virtues to Modern Values* (New York: Knopf, 1995), 3–52. Note that such virtues were consonant with the presuppositions of mid-nineteenth-century republican ideology as well. The *Booker T. Washington Papers* are, of course, replete with evidence demonstrating Washington's belief in and support for the Victorian virtues mentioned above; see, for example: "An Address before the Alabama State Teachers' Association," Birmingham, Alabama, June 8, 1892, *BTW Papers*, 3: 234–36; "A Sunday Evening Talk," Tuskegee, Alabama, February 10, 1895, *BTW Papers*, 3: 508–15; "Extracts from an Address in Birmingham," Birmingham, Alabama, January 1, 1900, *BTW Papers*, 5: 393–94; "A Sunday Evening Talk," Tuskegee, Alabama, January 13, 1901, *BTW Papers*, 6: 7–11; and "A Sunday Evening Talk," Tuskegee, Alabama, January 27, 1907, *BTW Papers*, 9: 201–3.

14. For succinct statements of Washington's views of industrial education, see, for example, "A Speech at the Institute of Arts and Sciences," Brooklyn, New York, September 30, 1896, *BTW Papers*, 4: 211–23; "An Article in the *Tuskegee Student*," [Industrial Training for Southern Women], Tuskegee, Alabama, May 24, 1902, *BTW Papers*, 6: 469–72; and "The Fruits of Industrial Training," *Atlantic Monthly* 92 (October 1903): 453–62. One should note that industrial education for African Americans meant different things to different constituencies in the late nineteenth century, and Washington's views on industrial education were not the only ones out there. On this point, see, for example, August Meier, *Negro Thought in America, 1880–1915* (Ann Arbor: University of Michigan Press, 1963), 85–99. Note, too, that some scholars, including economist Robert Margo, contend that industrial education "has received more attention in the history books than it ever did in real life." See Margo, *Race and Schooling in the South, 1880–1915* (Chicago: University of Chicago Press, 1990), 48. Gunnar Myrdal made much the same point more than a half century ago. See Myrdal, *An American Dilemma: The Negro Problem and Modern Democracy* (New York: Harper, 1944), 879–907.

15. The classic early critique is, of course, that of Du Bois; see "Of Mr. Booker T.

Washington and Others," in W.E.B. Du Bois, *The Souls of Black Folk* (Chicago: A. C. McClurg & Co., 1903), 41–59. William Monroe Trotter and Ida B. Wells-Barnett would also be included on any short list of early anti-Washingtonians.

16. See, for example, Jay R. Mandle, *The Roots of Black Poverty: The Southern Plantation Economy after the Civil War* (Durham: Duke University Press, 1978), 107–14, and Mandle, *Not Slave, Not Free: The African American Economic Experience since the Civil War* (Durham: Duke University Press, 1992), 17–19, 70, 72–74. This seems to be Louis Harlan's general orientation as well; see Harlan, *BTW*, 1: viii–x, 202–37.

17. C. Vann Woodward, *Origins of the New South, 1877–1913* (Baton Rouge: Louisiana State University Press, 1951), 356–68. One should note that Woodward's views on these matters were similar to the views articulated by Gunnar Myrdal; see Myrdal, *An American Dilemma*, 786–88. For a more nuanced interpretation of Washington's views on African Americans, unions, and the U.S. labor movement, see Meier, *Negro Thought in America*, 100–118.

18. See, for example, Charles W. Chesnutt, "A Plea for the American Negro," *Critic* 36 (February 1900): 160–63; Du Bois, "Of Mr. Booker T. Washington and Others."

19. See, for example, James D. Anderson, "Education as a Vehicle for the Manipulation of Black Workers," in Walter Feinberg and Henry Rosemont Jr., eds., *Work, Technology, and Education: Dissenting Essays in the Intellectual Foundations of American Education* (Urbana: University of Illinois Press, 1975), 15–40, especially 37–38; James D. Anderson, *The Education of Blacks in the South, 1860–1935* (Chapel Hill: University of North Carolina Press, 1988), 33–109; Donald S. Spivey, *Schooling for the New Slavery: Black Industrial Education, 1868–1915* (Westport, Conn.: Greenwood Press, 1978), 45–70; and Baker, *Turning South Again*, 79–98.

20. Other than Adam Fairclough and Glenn Loury (and, to some extent, Heather Cox Richardson), few authors since the 1960s have defended Washington's economic ideas. Among the authors writing in the 1950s and 1960s who did treat parts of Washington's "program" in positive terms were Samuel R. Spencer Jr., August Meier, and Eugene D. Genovese Jr. It should be pointed out as well that at times Louis Harlan seems positively disposed toward parts of Washington's economic "program," though in Harlan's view Washington's opportunism and the monumental nature of the South's economic problems doomed the "program" to failure. See Spencer, *Booker T. Washington and the Negro's Place in American Life* (Boston: Little, Brown, 1955); Meier, *Negro Thought in America*, 85–118; Genovese, "The Legacy of Slavery and the Roots of Black Nationalism," in Genovese, *In Red and Black: Marxian Explorations in Southern and Afro-American History* (New York: Oxford University Press, 1972), 129–57; and Harlan, *BTW*, 2: viii–x, and especially 202–37.

21. Harlan, *BTW*, 1: ii.

22. On Armstrong's role in Washington's life, see Washington, *Up From Slavery*,

54–58; Harlan, *BTW*, 1: 52–77 and passim. On the editorial roles of Thrasher and Abbott in the crafting of *Up From Slavery*, see Harlan, *BTW*, 1: 246–48.

23. The biographical details that follow are standard and can be found in any of the leading sources on Washington's life. See, for example, Spencer, *Booker T. Washington and the Negro's Place in American Life;* and Harlan, *BTW*, vol. 1.

24. The quoted passages are from Spencer, *Booker T. Washington and the Negro's Place in American Life*, 24, 25.

25. On Armstrong and his influence on Washington, see the works cited in note 22. Also see the sketch on Armstrong by Samuel Atkins Eliot in the *Dictionary of American Biography*, 22 vols. (New York: Scribner, 1928–58), 1: 359–60.

26. On Hopkins and his influence on Armstrong, see the essay on Hopkins by William W. Fenn in *Dictionary of American Biography*, 5: 215–17; the *Dictionary of American Biography*, 1: 359–60; Mark A. DeWolfe Howe, *Classic Shades: Five Leaders of Learning and Their Colleges* (Boston: Little, Brown, 1928), 81–120; and Frederick Rudolph, *Mark Hopkins and the Log: Williams College, 1836–1872* (New Haven: Yale University Press, 1956). For illuminating visual corroboration of the points made in the text, see Frances Benjamin Johnston, *The Hampton Album: 44 Photographs from an Album of Hampton Institute* (New York: Doubleday, 1966). The photographs included were selected from an album originally made for the Paris Exposition of 1900.

27. For some limited information on student outcomes, see Harlan, *BTW*, 2:170–73; and Spivey, *Schooling for the New Slavery*, 95–96.

28. Norbert Elias, *The Civilizing Process: The Development of Manners*, trans. Edmund Jephcott (1939; reprint, New York: Urizen Books, 1978); Mary Douglas, *Purity and Danger: An Analysis of Pollution and Taboo* (London: Praeger, 1966).

29. See, for example, Richard L. Bushman, *The Refinement of America: Persons, Houses, Cities* (New York: Knopf, 1992), and John F. Kasson, *Rudeness and Civility: Manners in Nineteenth-Century Urban America* (New York: Hill and Wang, 1990).

30. Baker, *Turning South Again*, 40–49.

31. Terry Eagleton, *William Shakespeare* (Oxford: Oxford University Press, 1986), ix–x.

32. See Richard A. Easterlin, "Interregional Differences in Per Capita Income, Population, and Total Income, 1840–1950," in National Bureau of Economic Research, Conference on Research in Income and Wealth, Studies in Income and Wealth, vol. 24, *Trends in the American Economy in the Nineteenth Century* (Princeton: Princeton University Press, 1960), 73–140, especially 85–89, 97–104, and 137–40, and Easterlin, "Regional Income Trends," in Seymour E. Harris, ed., *American Economic History* (New York: McGraw-Hill, 1961), 525–47, especially 528.

33. For a good, succinct overview of the epidemiological history of the South, see James O. Breeden, "Disease as a Factor in Southern Distinctiveness," in Todd L. Savitt and James Harvey Young, eds., *Disease and Distinctiveness in the American South* (Knoxville: University of Tennessee Press, 1988), 1–28.

34. All good texts in economic development devote attention to these measures and approaches. See, for example, Michael P. Todaro, *Economic Development*, 7th ed. (Reading, Mass.: Addison-Wesley, 2000).

35. For fuller, technical discussions of many of these problems, see John Komlos and Peter A. Coclanis, "Nutrition and Economic Development in Post-Reconstruction South Carolina: An Anthropometric Approach," *Social Science History* 19 (spring 1995): 91–115, and Komlos and Coclanis, "On the Puzzling Cycle in the Biological Standard of Living: The Case of Antebellum Georgia," *Explorations in Economic History* 34 (October 1997): 433–59. On Sen's "capabilities" approach, see, for example, Amartya K. Sen, *Resources, Values, and Development* (Oxford: Oxford University Press, 1984); Sen, *Development as Freedom* (New York: Knopf, 1999); and Martha C. Nussbaum, *Women and Human Development: The Capabilities Approach* (Cambridge: Cambridge University Press, 2000).

36. See the works by Komlos and Coclanis mentioned in note 35. For an excellent overview of the field of anthropometric history, see Richard H. Steckel, "Stature and the Standard of Living," *Journal of Economic Literature* 33 (December 1995): 1903–40. Washington spoke and wrote frequently regarding the importance of proper diet and nutrition. See, for example, "A Sunday Evening Talk," Tuskegee, Alabama, October 6, 1907, *BTW Papers*, 9: 366–71; "A Sunday Evening Talk" [The Resurrection Season], Tuskegee, Alabama, March 27, 1910, *BTW Papers*, 10: 298–303; and "A Sunday Evening Talk" [Our Death Rate], Tuskegee, Alabama, December 10, 1911, *BTW Papers*, 11: 407–10.

37. On the filth theory, see James C. Riley, *Rising Life Expectancy: A Global History* (New York and Cambridge: Cambridge University Press, 2001), 61–68, 187–89. On the dissemination and acceptance of the germ theory, see Nancy Tomes, *Gospel of Germs: Men, Women, and the Microbe in American Life* (Cambridge: Harvard University Press, 1998), 23–47.

38. On Pasteur's personal meticulousness, see Tomes, *Gospel of Germs*, 47. Note that a recent econometric study has demonstrated that, after adjusting for socioeconomic status, education, and a host of other variables, the "cleanliness of one's home" is predictive of one's earnings, one's children's educational attainment, and one's children's earnings measured twenty-five years hence. See Rachel Dunifon, Greg J. Duncan, and Jeanne Brooks-Gunn, "As Ye Sweep, So Shall Ye Reap," *American Economic Review* 91 (May 2001): 150–54. For Washington's views on such matters, see, for example, "A Sunday Evening Talk" [The Years of Concentration], Tuskegee, Alabama, November 1, 1908, *BTW Papers*, 9: 681–84, and "Extracts from Three Addresses Delivered in Louisiana," April 13–16 [1915], *BTW Papers*, 13: 268–70. For a somewhat negative view of actual health conditions at Tuskegee, see Jno. A. Kenney [John Andrew Kenney] to the Tuskegee Institute Executive Council, Tuskegee, Alabama, May 26, 1903, *BTW Papers*, 7: 159–65. Kenney, resident physician at Tuskegee for many years, later helped Washington to establish National Negro Health Week in the United States. Finally, one should note that Jacob Riis seems to have shared some of the same views as did Washington regarding the

relationship between cleanliness and virtue. Referring to immigrant families in late-nineteenth-century New York, for example, Riis wrote, "The true line to be drawn between pauperism and honest poverty is the clothes-line. With it begins the effort to be clean that is the first and best evidence of a desire to be honest." See Riis, *How the Other Half Lives: Studies among the Tenements of New York* (1890; reprint, Boston: Bedford Books, 1996), 90.

39. James P. Smith, "Healthy Bodies and Thick Wallets: The Dual Relationship between Health and Economic Status," *Journal of Economic Perspectives* 13 (spring 1999): 145–66; Jeffrey Sachs, "Helping the World's Poorest," *Economist,* August 14, 1999, 17–20; "Tropics of Poverty," *Business Week,* September 3, 2001, 28; David E. Bloom, David Canning, and Jaypee Sevilla, "The Effect of Health on Economic Growth: Theory and Evidence," National Bureau of Economic Research Working Paper Series, Working Paper 8587, November 2001. See also Pierre Gourou, *The Tropical World: Its Social and Economic Conditions and Its Future Status,* trans. S. H. Beaver and E. D. Laborde, 4th ed. (New York: Wiley, 1966). For a recent attempt to apply some of these concepts to the late-nineteenth-century American South, see Peter A. Coclanis, "In Retrospect: Ransom and Sutch's *One Kind of Freedom,*" *Reviews in American History* 28 (September 2000): 478–89. The word *tropicopolitan* is borrowed from Srinivas Aravamudan; see his *Tropicopolitans: Colonialism and Agency, 1688–1804* (Durham: Duke University Press, 1999). In taking dirt seriously, I have benefited significantly from Tomes's *Gospel of Germs.* On the truly astounding degree of dirt and filth Americans lived with in past times, see, for example, Suellen Hoy, *Chasing Dirt: The American Pursuit of Cleanliness* (New York: Oxford University Press, 1995).

40. See, for example, Debraj Ray, *Development Economics* (Princeton: Princeton University Press, 1998), 272–79.

41. Ibid., 272–79, 483–527.

42. Francis Fukuyama, *Trust: Social Virtues and the Creation of Prosperity* (New York: Free Press, 1995); Lawrence E. Harrison and Samuel P. Huntington, eds., *Culture Matters: How Values Shape Human Progress* (New York: Basic Books, 2000).

43. See, for example, Douglass C. North and Robert P. Thomas, *The Rise of the Western World: A New Economic History* (Cambridge: Cambridge University Press, 1973); North, *Institutions, Institutional Change, and Economic Performance* (Cambridge: Cambridge University Press, 1990); and Hernando de Soto, *The Mystery of Capital: Why Capitalism Triumphs in the West and Fails Everywhere Else* (New York: Basic Books, 2000). For a review of the so-called new institutional approach and its recent contributions to economics, see Eirik G. Furubotn and Rudolph Richter, *Institutions and Economic Theory: The Contribution of the New Institutional Economics* (Ann Arbor: University of Michigan Press, 2000).

44. See, for example, Ray, *Development Economics,* 259–61; and De Soto, *Mystery of Capital.* No one at the turn of the century pushed landownership as much as did Washington. See, for example, "An Address before the National Negro Business League," Philadelphia, August 20, 1913, *BTW Papers,* 12: 259–65.

45. On the importance of "industrial education" for women, see, for example, "An Article in the *Tuskegee Student*" [Industrial Training for Southern Women], Tuskegee, Alabama, May 24, 1902, *BTW Papers*, 6: 469–72, and "A Sunday Evening Talk" [The Resurrection Season], Tuskegee, Alabama, March 27, 1910, *BTW Papers*, 10: 298–303. The literature on the crucial economic role(s) played by rural women is vast. On such role(s) in the United States, see, for example, Joan Jensen, *Loosening the Bonds: Mid-Atlantic Farm Women, 1750–1850* (New Haven: Yale University Press, 1986); Nancy Grey Osterud, *Bonds of Community: The Lives of Farm Women in Nineteenth-Century New York* (Ithaca: Cornell University Press, 1991); Deborah Fink, *Agrarian Women: Wives and Mothers in Rural Nebraska, 1880–1940* (Chapel Hill: University of North Carolina Press, 1992); Katherine Jellison, *Entitled to Power: Farm Women and Technology, 1913–1963* (Chapel Hill: University of North Carolina Press, 1993); Jane Adams, *The Transformation of Rural Life: Southern Illinois, 1890–1990* (Chapel Hill: University of North Carolina Press, 1994); Lu Ann Jones, *Mama Learned Us to Work: Farm Women in the New South* (Chapel Hill: University of North Carolina Press, 2002); Sally Ann McMurry, *Transforming Rural Life: Dairying Families and Agricultural Change, 1820–1885* (Baltimore: Johns Hopkins University Press, 1995); and Melissa Walker, *All We Knew Was to Farm: Rural Women in the Upcountry South, 1919–1941* (Baltimore: Johns Hopkins University Press, 2000).

46. See Ray, *Development Economics*, 529–89, especially 578–84; Alex Counts, *Give Us Credit* (New York: Times Books, 1996); Muhammad Yunus (with Alan Jolis), *Banker to the Poor: The Autobiography of Muhammad Yunus, Founder of the Grameen Bank* (London: Aurum Press, 1998). On the Nayakrishi movement, see Craig Cox, "Hope for Bangladesh," *Utne Reader* 107 (September–October 2001): 18–19, or access "Nayakrishi Andolon" via the website www.south-asian-initiative.org. Nowhere are the credit problems of rural African Americans in the late-nineteenth-century South covered more completely than in Roger L. Ransom and Richard Sutch's *One Kind of Freedom: The Economic Consequences of Emancipation* (Cambridge: Cambridge University Press, 1977). For an assessment of the findings, achievements, and problems of this work, see Coclanis, "In Retrospect: Ransom and Sutch's *One Kind of Freedom*."

47. Richard A. Easterlin, "Why Isn't the Whole World Developed?" *Journal of Economic History* 41 (March 1981): 1–19; World Bank, *The East Asian Miracle: Economic Growth and Public Policy* (New York: Oxford University Press, 1993), 43–54, especially 52; Ray, *Development Economics*, 119–23. Note that in some ways the differences between Washington and Du Bois over industrial education and "classical" education can be overstated. Du Bois was never totally against industrial education, and Washington saw a place for humane learning. Even in his 1895 "Atlanta Compromise" address, it is worth noting that Washington exhorted African Americans to cast down their buckets "in agriculture, mechanics, in commerce, in domestic service, *and in the professions*" (italics mine).

48. See Goh Keng Swee, *The Economics of Modernisation and Other Essays*

(Singapore: Asia Pacific Press, 1972), 31–41 (especially 40), 42–46; Goh, *The Practice of Economic Growth* (Singapore: Federal Publications, 1977), 44–46, 238–40. On Smiles, see *Dictionary of National Biography*, ed. Leslie Stephen et al., 66 vols. and ongoing supplements (London: Smith, Elder, and Co., 1885–), Supplement, 1901–1911 (1920), 322–25 (sketch by Sidney Lee); and Adrian Jarvis, *Samuel Smiles and the Construction of Victorian Values* (Gloucestershire: Sutton, 1997). In a 1966 speech before the Malayan Economic Society, Goh stated that "If I may be so presumptuous as to give advice to others (having been freed from the burdens of the Finance Ministry, I can look at this problem with a detachment that was not possible before), I would ask them to throw away all the books published on economic growth since World War II. I would advise them instead to read the essays of Samuel Smiles—his exhortations to thrift, industry, ambition, honesty, perseverance, etc. No doubt, to people who have been brought up in the sophisticated twentieth century—an era which has grown to accept Beatles and beatniks—this may be an intolerable imposition, for Smiles must appear a singularly odious character. Yet what else is there to do? The economic planners have manifestly failed in their job simply because, I suspect, they have not realized that at the stage of development of their country, the injunctions of Samuel Smiles, however offensively sanctimonious they may be, are more in keeping with the needs of their times and their countries than all the stuff that the econometricians are producing." See Goh, *The Economics of Modernisation*, 40–41. On Goh, see Tilak Doshi and Peter Coclanis, "The Economic Architect: Goh Keng Swee," in Lam Peng Er and Kevin Y. L. Tan, eds., *Lee's Lieutenants: Singapore's Old Guard* (London: Allen & Unwin, 1999), 24–44, 206–14.

49. In a postscript to his essay "The Legacy of Slavery and the Roots of Black Nationalism," Genovese reproduces a letter to him from Conor Cruise O'Brien, wherein O'Brien recounts a conversation he had with Du Bois in Ghana shortly before Du Bois's death. According to O'Brien, Du Bois told him that "he had in his youth spoken slightingly of Booker T. Washington and had been memorably reprimanded by his aunts, who told him that it ill became one who had been born free to speak disrespectfully of a man whose back bore the marks of the lash. He went on to say that in the circumstances of the South in Washington's day, he could not have been effective in any other way. He—Du Bois—with his Northern and relatively privileged background, had been able to take a different stance and had been obliged to enter into public controversy with Washington. He did not want that controversy to obscure the merits of what Washington had achieved." See Genovese, "The Legacy of Slavery and the Roots of Black Nationalism," 154. David Levering Lewis also reports the story, but with less detail; see Lewis, *W. E. B. Du Bois: The Fight for Equality and the American Century, 1919–1963* (New York: Holt, 2000), 569.

50. William Hannibal Thomas, *The American Negro: What He Was, What He Is, and What He May Become* (New York: Macmillan, 1901). On Thomas, see John David Smith, *Black Judas: William Hannibal Thomas and* The American Negro (Athens: University of Georgia Press, 2000). For Washington's review, see "The American Negro," *Outlook* 67 (March 30, 1901): 736. Although the review is un-

signed, Smith argues convincingly that the piece was written by Washington; see *Black Judas,* 347n.42.

51. Even a quick comparison—from extant photographs—of the miens and cultural styles of Douglass and Washington illustrates what I have in mind here. On style as cultural marker among African Americans, see Shane White and Graham White, "Slave Hair and African American Culture in the Eighteenth and Nineteenth Centuries," *Journal of Southern History* 61 (February 1995): 45–76.

52. On the white male response to Jack Johnson's success against white boxers (and with white women), see, for example, Gail Bederman, *Manliness and Civilization: A Cultural History of Gender and Race in the United States, 1880–1917* (Chicago: University of Chicago Press, 1995), 1–44. In this regard, too, let me point readers to Alain Corbin, *The Foul and the Fragrant: Odor and the French Social Imagination,* trans. Miriam L. Kochan et al. (New York: Berg, 1986), especially chapter 9 ("The Stench of the Poor"), and to Orwell, *The Road to Wigan Pier,* 112–19.

53. On the marketing of Jordan as nonracial, bourgeois symbol, see Mary G. McDonald, "Safe Sex Symbol? Michael Jordan and the Politics of Representation," in *Michael Jordan, Inc.: Corporate Sport, Media Culture, and Late Modern America,* ed. David L. Andrews (Albany: State University of New York Press, 2001), 153–74.

6

More Than an Artichoke

The Pragmatic Religion of Booker T. Washington

WILSON J. MOSES

In a classic Hollywood film from the forties, a little colored kid is stymied by his first encounter with a fresh artichoke. The action streaks into fast-forward as he peels away leaf after leaf, until there is nothing left. "Well," he says, "it may have choked Artie, but it sho' ain't gonna choke me!" Booker T. Washington is sometimes seen as an intellectual artichoke, a man who neither had, nor recognized a need for an ideological position, whose dreams were embarrassingly pedestrian, a "pragmatist," but merely in the vernacular sense.[1] His critics say that the Tuskegeean's industrial programs were hopelessly outdated, that he sabotaged the careers of critics, that he ignored the rising tide of white racism, that he told embarrassing stories about stealing chickens.[2] His defenders say that Washington was foolishly maligned, that Tuskegee offered necessary ingredients for meeting "the needs of those times," and that its program would have been more successful with better support from the so-called Talented Tenth.[3]

Washington survives in college textbooks as analogous to a shrewd, but uncomplicated ward boss, whose main goal was to keep Tuskegee running smoothly. If it had been invented as a means of black uplift, the purpose of the Tuskegee Machine ultimately became nothing more than supplying power to itself. Academic folklore presents Washington as a benevolent despot, whose programs were helpful, if somewhat narrow, who made attempts to counter the most egregious instances of discrimination, who spoke out against lynching, who worked quietly "behind the scenes" to oppose Jim Crow, and who denounced European colonialism in Africa—when he could do so without damaging Tuskegee's interests. My impression is that in most college courses, he is presented as an intelligent but unimaginative *padrone*, capable of munificence, dangerous if crossed, fearful of situations he could not control, and possessed of a Nixon-like defensiveness.[4]

The central idea of this essay is that it is possible for us to reconcile the contradictions of the foregoing interpretations, and at the same time credit Washington with an ideology that was clearly conceived, consistently maintained, and imaginatively expressed. It is true that he seldom alluded to "great books" or their authors, rarely defended his positions, and never explicated the metaphysical foundations of his ideology. This, however, need not be seen as evidence of intellectual narrowness. More likely, Washington, like his namesake George Washington, understood that one of the most effective means of maintaining power was to give the impression of not seeking it, and to appear unexcitable—at least in public.

In 1866, around the time that little Booker T. Washington was conducting his celebrated experiments on the relativity of space and time by making fine adjustments on the clock in his place of work, Horatio Alger was putting the finishing touches on his first novel, *Ragged Dick*, which made his name synonymous with the gospel of the self-made man. In 1867, the year in which Booker T. went to work for Viola Ruffner, Alger began to serialize the chapters in which we find an extended reference to the antecedent legend of Dick Whittington, that earlier "ragged Dick," a poor orphan, who migrated to London and began his career by picking up pins and needles with the intention of selling them. The merchant for whom he worked, pleased with his saving disposition, allowed him to invest his only possession, a cat, in an expedition to foreign parts, and the ship eventually reached an island infested with rats and mice. The cat was sold, Dick's fortune was made, and he eventually became Lord Mayor of London.[5]

Many are rightly suspicious that the legend really had anything to do with the historical Richard Whittington. The story of the cat antedates him by at least 160 years, and he began life as the son of a respectable country knight.[6] Nonetheless, Whittington is enshrined in the mythology of the English-speaking world as a representative of the idea of upward mobility in a free market. Just as the cream always rises to the top, so too does the worthy individual rise, according to merit, and despite all apparent obstacles. Horatio Alger's novels offer more than one literary antecedent to *Up From Slavery*, for there are other types of Alger hero, notably Luke Larkin, who is more of a goody-goody and has a widowed mother.[7] The hero of *Up From Slavery* has another literary analogue in Benjamin Franklin's Poor Richard, the acknowledged inspiration for Max Weber's imaginative and controversial thesis in *The Protestant Ethic and the Spirit of Capitalism*.

Ralph Ellison grasped the obvious literary connection between Booker T. and the Alger myth when he created The Founder in *Invisible Man*. It is well known that Ellison always forcefully insisted that neither The Founder nor anyone else in his powerful novel was intended to represent any real historical figure. The reader may decide whether Ellison's creation has any mythic significance within the contours of American literary or intellectual history, and whether Ellison is merely playing with words when he refers to "the black rite of Horatio Alger . . . performed to God's own acting script." Whatever the answer, Ellison was obviously aware that Booker T. Washington's appeal to the reading audience depended on an intuitive grasp of the same myths that inspired Horatio Alger.

Like Alger, Washington was endowed with the genius to manipulate contrasting archetypes—that of the adventurous ragamuffin, like Ragged Dick, sleeping under sidewalks and practicing clever deceits, and that of the prim and proper Luke Larkin, the devoted son of a long-suffering mother. The successes of both are realistic and realizable, for the Alger hero never represents any ideal so impossible or dramatic as a progression from "rags to riches." The quest of the Alger hero is not for wealth, but for respectability. The promise of Hampton and Tuskegee is not to make their trainees wealthy, but to make them respectable, productive, solid citizens, and "useful" in the communities they are destined to serve. This idea of service is fundamental to the American concept of Republican virtue. The American hero struggles to the same ends as Benjamin Franklin, Andrew Carnegie, or William James, claiming that his goal is to "give back to the community," something in return for the fulfilled promises of American life.

Up From Slavery was published four years before Max Weber's *The Protestant Ethic and the Spirit of Capitalism* appeared in the original

German edition. It is remarkable to note how thoroughly Washington grasped the formula for American success that was later to be codified in Weber's thesis. But where Weber's approach was formalist, Washington's was instrumentalist.[8] His utilitarian attitude to American protestantism anticipates the central ideas that Weber later developed. In recollecting his childhood, Washington attributed a this-worldly and materialistic element to the religion of the slaves. The lyrics of their songs referred to a practical desire for "freedom of the body in this world." And thus, we are to assume, that Washington was early introduced to the idea that practical religion was inextricably related to the demands of daily life, that it must be related intrinsically to politics and economics.[9]

A practical, muscular, cold-water Christianity was firmly planted in Booker T.'s mind from those early days of hearing the utilitarian slave songs. From the beginning, religion was seen to have its social and political uses. To his tremendous advantage, he encountered in early youth those influences that led him to conceive of religion in terms of struggle and duty, rather than comfortable and fatalistic contentment. He was apparently never tempted to view religion in terms of an ecstatic conversion experience—at least nothing of the sort is mentioned in *Up From Slavery*. He does not seem obsessed with the personality of Jesus, but addresses his prayers, so he tells us, to a God who providentially blesses peoples and individuals with a series of trials along the road to a material salvation in a material world, as well as in the next.

Washington received his puritan indoctrination at an impressionable age, and there were enduring effects on his practical religiosity and utilitarian ethic, his constant emphasis on work, cleanliness, and thrift. He came under those influences at around ten years of age, according to his own self-conscious narrative, upon going to work for Viola Ruffner. She was a Yankee woman, he recounted, who "had a reputation all through the vicinity for being very strict with her servants [who] wanted all things done promptly [and] wanted absolute honesty and frankness." The experience with Viola Ruffner prepared him for his encounter with Mary F. Mackie, the head teacher at Hampton, who later became "one of his strongest and most helpful friends." What these women taught him, and the lesson he seems to have valued most strongly, was the New England Protestant ethic, which lay at the basis of Washington's later economic and industrial theory.[10]

Washington's brilliance in *Up From Slavery* is in his ability to blend the seemingly contradictory themes of self-interest and self-sacrifice, an interesting conundrum, clearly not confined to Bookerite religion. American "civil religion," on the whole, reinforces the traditions of republican virtue and civic humanism that have received so much attention from Douglass Adair, J.G.A. Pocock, and others. Within this interpretation of American Christianity, General Samuel C. Armstrong is memorialized as a "type of that Christlike body of men and women who went into the Negro schools at the close of the war by the hundreds to assist in lifting up my race." His Christianity is the civil religion of disinterested republican humanism, a reinvigorated communitarianism in the Reconstruction South that would rehabilitate the emancipated masses without recourse to the Hamiltonian leviathan of federal government.

But Washington had simultaneously tied his program to the alternative tradition of Lockean liberalism, consistent with a directly self-interested interpretation of Christian doctrine, in which self-love inspires the Christian to practical Christianity. His preachments reflected what Robert Bellah has called the doctrine of "Salvation of Success in America."[11] Washington certainly never claimed that God and Mammon were in league. He sought rather to exploit the traditional puritan belief that religiosity need not imply impracticality. He realized, as Weber would later realize, that American values could be interpreted as an elaboration on Franklin's secularization of the Protestant ethic. Washington understood, in addition, that the enlightened self-interest of Adam Smith was an essential ingredient of the spirit of capitalism.

Adam Smith, interestingly, does not play an important part in Weber's construction of the Protestant ethic, nor, for that matter, have I been able to find a reference to Adam Smith in Washington's writings. The only reference in the index to the *Booker T. Washington Papers* is an incidental reference in a letter from Andrew Carnegie, referring to Smith's having preceded him in addressing the Philosophical Society of Edinburgh. Whether Carnegie had reason to assume that Washington would recognize the name of his distinguished predecessor is unclear. Carnegie was clearly inspired by the tradition of civic humanism, patterning his own life after that of Benjamin Franklin, who, after accumulating a fortune, devoted his life to community service. As Robert Bellah has observed, there is a level of the problematic in George Washington's adage "honesty is the best policy." Presumably Bellah means that while Washington's adage has become a reflexive commonplace, his eighteenth-century diction contains an often overlooked irony. The word *policy*, in his time, could imply a subordination of honesty to convenience, and there is a persistent craftiness throughout Franklin's writing.

Weber contends that Poor Richard's morality is pragmatic and displays no kinship to the doctrine that virtue is its own reward. This contention is dubious; Franklin is ironic but not cynical, and his economic maxims are theologically sustainable by the emerging Scottish common sense doctrine of self-love. Alexander Pope, a Roman Catholic, penned the maxim that "self and social interest are the same." The Protestant version of enlightened self-interest, which appears in Adam Smith's *Wealth of Nations*, is somehow minimized by Weber, although it dominates Poor Richard's ideals. Franklin's refusal to have beer with his noon meal was neither prissy nor purely calculating. The young Franklin was given to dietary experiments, and his temperance met a need that was both practical and moral—remaining alert and able to discharge his responsibilities to himself and his employer. Booker T. preached the same practical behavior that Franklin endorsed. These preachments were not hypocrisy, as charged by the novelist D. H. Lawrence and other vulgar Freudians and gullible post-Victorians. Lawrence's famous attack on Franklin fails to grasp the tricky relationship between Poor Richard's microeconomics and his macroeconomics. More troubling is the failure of literary imagination in addressing an elaborate personal mythology that took a half-century to construct.

It seems almost inevitable that whenever Booker T. is discussed, we either encounter, or are tempted to employ the word *pragmatic*. Some scholars will allow that he was "a pragmatist in the colloquial sense," but this seems to be little more than an embarrassed recognition of his "accommodations" to southern "realities." If there are cognates between Washington's thinking and that of John Dewey or William James, these are seen as casual or unsophisticated. The similarity of Washington's praxis to that of Dewey is almost too obvious, but Louis Harlan—after seriously considering the possibility of an analogy—in the end figuratively shakes his head and says, in effect, "Naw, it can't be."[12] With apparent ease, scholars have seemingly dismissed the fact that Washington shared with James a belief that the ultimate test of an idea's truth was to apply the question, "What difference does it make?" Likewise, parallels between Washington's missionary ideals and the form of social gospel presented in some of James's later works seem to have impressed very few.[13]

Washington was not a follower of James, and his importance would not be enhanced if he had been. Nor would Washington have had anything to gain by claiming any such ideological influence. The spontaneous appearance of pragmatism in Washington should not seem remarkable, if it is, as some scholars seem to think, a peculiar product of the American environment. Pragmatism seems consistent with the supposedly distinctive American characteristic of shaping ideology around practice. It would seem to be stimulated by that "fluidity of American life," and "antipathy to control," ascribed by Frederick Jackson Turner to the influences of a frontier.[14] Pragmatism, as an American ideology, does not spring full-blown from the head of Pierce, James, or Dewey. Its lineaments are visible in the "policy" of Benjamin Franklin, the opportunism of Thomas Jefferson, and the circumspection of Abraham Lincoln. Washington adopted Lincoln as a hero and patron saint, claiming to have read "nearly every book and magazine article that has ever been written about Abraham Lincoln." Washington also cites Lincoln's "Speeches and Addresses," politically safe, maybe, but neither shallow nor uncomplicated.[15] And if Washington quoted Ralph Waldo Emerson only once, it was with a telling degree of sensitivity.[16]

The common impression of Washington, which isolates him from the realm of intellectualism, grows out of W.E.B. Du Bois's *The Souls of Black Folk*. In two remarkable chapters, Du Bois presented two contrasting examples of African American leadership. The better known is, of course, chapter 3, "Of Mr. Booker T. Washington and Others," which is remarkable for its frankness, if not its candor. The other is chapter 12, "Of Alexander Crummell," an exercise in evasive sentimentality. Not surprisingly, many people who have read *The Souls of Black Folk* cannot remember the chapter on Crummell. In both of these essays, Du Bois displays a lack of interest in intellectual biography, which is equally apparent in his reminiscences on William James. He makes one fleeting reference to James's work on pragmatism in his *Autobiography*, but he focuses almost exclusively on the man's character and spares not a line to express his own understanding of pragmatism, or any specific influences it had on him. Du Bois never published an essay comparable to Bertrand Russell's explication of James's ideas, although he was better equipped than Russell to perform the work.[17]

Du Bois simply was not interested in the "Men and Ideas" approach to history, which was associated with his almost exact contemporary, John Huizinga, and one almost suspects that he held such methods in contempt.[18] He passes over several intriguing figures in his chapter on Washington, including Frederick Douglass, Elliot, Bruce, and John Mercer Langston, without any discussion of their ideas. His most frustrating reference is to J. C. Price, who unfortunately did not provide much of a legacy, but Du Bois is no help. We suspect that Du Bois must have known much more about Crummell than he cared to reveal. He never addressed the complicated intellectual evolution of Frederick Douglass, to whom he attributed the goal of "ultimate assimilation," a contestable proposition, for Douglass expressed contradictory ideas on cultural assimilation. Furthermore, Douglass's presumed advocacy of biological assimilation may be inferred, but not precisely documented, as Waldo Martin has pointed out.[19] Du Bois's omission cannot be attributed to the unavailability of relevant sources, as some of these authors' published writings were readily available.

Du Bois's 1956 pamphlet on Benjamin Franklin likewise is a disappointment, and this is a surprise, given his ties to and sometime collaboration with Max Weber, who based his theory of the Protestant ethic on quotations from Franklin.[20] Booker T. Washington is often discussed in terms of the "Protestant ethic," popularly and simplistically misconceived as merely hard work and thrift. It is again surprising that Du Bois never yielded to any temptation to mention similarities between Washington's program and Weber's theories. *The Protestant Ethic and the Theory of Capitalism* was published almost simultaneously with *The Souls of Black Folk*, perhaps in obedience to the law that prevailing historical conditions spontaneously generate ideas, so that similar theories condense independently but simultaneously in the minds of, say, Isaac Newton and G.V.F. Leibniz, or Charles Darwin and Alfred Wallace. It is not surprising that Du Bois's portrait of Washington has some of the same strengths and weaknesses as Weber's portrait of Franklin.

The Washington created by Du Bois is as much a caricature as the Franklin created by Weber. Du Bois and Weber were less concerned with subtle portraiture than they were with using a historical personality as a vehicle for expressing their discomfort with capitalism and the rising tide of commercialism. It is therefore not surprising that Du Bois's analysis should contain the following description of Washington: "by singular insight he intuitively grasped the spirit of the age which was dominating the North. And so thoroughly did he learn the speech and thought of triumphant commercialism, and the ideals of material prosperity, that the picture of a lone black boy poring over a French grammar amid the weeds and dirt of a neglected home soon seemed to him the acme of absurdities. One wonders what Socrates and St. Francis of Assisi would say to this."[21] Washington expressed opinions on the likes of Francis of Assisi and other Italian mystics during his 1910–11 tour of Europe, as we shall presently witness.[22] More to the point, while Washington self-evidently understood "the speech and thought of triumphant commercialism," he was ambivalent regarding some of its manifestations and decidedly hostile to others. Despite his complexity of vision and intuitive grasp of the contradictions within American thought, he allowed the intentionally obtuse Du Bois to think he endorsed a commercialism that he often disparaged. Respecting commercialism, Washington's ideas were comparable to those of Thorstein Veblen, who satirized commercialism in *The Theory of Business Enterprise*, while at the same time recognizing the privateering resourcefulness of its functionaries. And here Du Bois's superficial commentary on Washington is almost deceitful, for where Washington's thinking is most analytical and complex is exactly where Du Bois accuses him of a singleness of vision.

"It is as though Nature must needs make men narrow in order to give them force," Du Bois wrote, with a serpentine subtlety that is best described as Machiavellian.[23] It would have been more forthright to have admitted that in order to make Washington into a forceful symbol, *he* found it necessary to make him narrow. Du Bois's brilliant operation on Washington—so ingenious and withal so disingenuous—is comparable to the scalpel work that Thomas Jefferson did on George Washington. Minds as surgically keen as those of Jefferson and Du Bois are careful to avoid the accusation of intellectual butchery; therefore each attributed intellectual power and singular insight to his respective Washington. Jefferson never said that Washington was dull-witted, only that he lacked the creativity of an Isaac Newton, and that he seemed in danger of backsliding into royalism.[24] Similarly, Du Bois never said that Washington was dull-witted, only that he lacked the imagination of a Socrates, and that he seemed in danger of encouraging white supremacy. People like Jefferson and Du Bois are brilliant wielders of the poisoned pen. Their interpretations of events endure long after their passing, to become gospel for the credulous, who often have no conception of their source.

Both Booker T. Washington and George Washington were more intellectually complicated and imaginative than the stolid, granite heads sculpted by their accomplished detractors. Booker T. anticipated—and he was not alone—the very ideas whose provenance Max Weber so inventively (but inaccurately) traced, and he was not a naive or uncritical advocate of the Protestant ethic that he hoped to appropriate and manipulate. His goal was to instrumentalize a concept that he and others had synchronically discovered and that Weber, on a level of abstract idealism, disparaged. Washington fully understood the world-historical implications of "Protestant ethic," and he pragmatically sought to implement religion as a tool of black uplift.

Where Weber's purpose was to explain behavior as the product of religious ideals and practices, Washington's was "instrumentalist." He viewed religious ideals not only as forces driving social realities, but also as plans for social action; also, in his view, religious practices and beliefs were utilitarian instruments for producing desired behavior. Thus, Washington's theory of capitalism was pragmatic, rather than formalistic; it had little usefulness independent of its desired application. While both he and Weber attributed great importance to religion as a foundation of material prosperity, Weber devoted his efforts to demonstrating an assumption that Washington held to be primary and self-evident. Having begun where Weber would later conclude, Washington's goal was not descriptive but prescriptive sociology.

By the time Weber's ideas were in print, Washington had published two versions of his autobiography and another book called *Character Building*, a collection of sermons delivered in Tuskegee Chapel, with many links to religion and industry. The crusading journalists T. Thomas Fortune and Victoria Earle Matthews had compiled a little book of his occasional remarks, called *Black Belt Diamonds*, practically a success manual in the tradition of Franklin's best-sellers.[25] The book was hardly a model of political honesty, and it caused the more militant journalist William Monroe Trotter to blow a gasket, but despite its simplistic nostrums, it was not an example of racial treason.[26] Beneath its studied pedestrianism was a program of indoctrination, a veritable catechism for Tuskegee's missionaries to the masses. It was a guidebook for those dedicated to effecting material change by reshaping black religion in accord with the gospel of capital accumulation. Washington's efforts to tamper with the black church represented an attempt to create propaganda that would work simultaneously on the body, the emotions, and the mind, to create mental attitudes that would produce desired material results. Washington hoped that his preachments could inspire his pupils with a missionary zeal that they would carry beyond the Tuskegee Chapel. With the aid of well-connected ministers like Daniel Alexander Payne and Francis J. Grimké, he could foster basic reforms in African American mass religion.

I have said elsewhere that Washington was a materialist, an economic determinist, but now I am convinced that he approached the problem of determinism—Calvinistic or economic—in a completely pragmatic fashion.[27] Washington said that he believed until the age of eleven "that nobody but a Baptist could get to heaven," but there is no evidence of his having retained any commitment to Calvinism beyond that age. The "instrumentalist" version of Protestant ethic that he applied to the black masses of the South was more pragmatic than the imaginative but spurious theories of Weber. Washington had observed black-belt antinomianism, the extreme of Calvinistic fatalism, in which people believe themselves to be saved by irresistible grace alone. At its most extreme, this attitude led to an almost complete indifference to the law of Moses—a point Washington illustrated with the following anecdote. "An old brother came into meeting one night and said: 'I have had a bad time since I was here a week ago. I have been sometimes up and sometimes down, I have gnawed hard bones and swallowed bitter pills, and I believe I have broken all the Commandments; but, thank the Lord, I haven't yet lost my religion.'"[28]

In Washington's experience, Calvinistic fatalism did not lead to a Protestant ethic; just the contrary, it led to antinomianism. Because it relied not on works but on a "conversion experience" for salvation, it often failed to draw any connection between religion and practical morality. The Christianity that Washington preached placed little emphasis on the evangelical notion of "friendship with Jesus," but much emphasis on the "imitation of Christ." Washington sought to tap a grassroots Arminianism—the belief that people are saved by their behavior, and that salvation or damnation, in this world and in the next, resulted from works and deeds. He believed that religious ideas could determine mass behavior in the material world: "If you once make a colored man believe that he will be punished hereafter for drinking whiskey, he will never touch another drop. Moreover, the Negro believes what he reads, and takes the most that he can see in print for gospel truth. Put temperance tracts and primers into the hands of colored people and you will soon see temperance spread all over the South."[29]

Washington did not claim to be either a social scientist or a theologian, and he refused to debate the question of whether mind or matter was the driving force of history. Seemingly, he believed that mind was the dominant factor, but he had no aversion to making contradictory statements. One day he might argue that religion produced thrifty, industrious workers; another day he might argue that thrift and industry produced good Christians. Washington routinely attributed a missionary or even a messianic role to Hampton and Tuskegee, but he did not have to solve the problem of whether economics or ideas—capitalism or religion—would determine the "Future of the American Negro." He obviously viewed economic and religious uplift as collateral agencies.

This idea of collateral agency was not original to him. It had long been preached by Alexander Crummell, even at the Atlanta Exposition, several weeks after Washington delivered his more famous oration. Crummell offered a theological compromise in his address, in which he affirmed that civilization, in the material sense, was a "Collateral and Indispensable Instrumentality" for the Christianizing of African people.[30] Throughout all his work, Crummell argued that it would be impossible to Christianize black people anywhere without civilizing them, and impossible to civilize without Christianizing. Ideas were fundamental, but material factors were "indispensable." Washington ultimately preached that same principle, unperturbed by the question of whether religion would determine economics or vice versa.

Crummell, despite his suspicions concerning Washington, shared ideas with him, notably a belief in "industrial education." He had been exposed as a youth to industrial education, during his studies at Beriah Greene's Oneida Institute, which interspersed studies in biblical languages with training in practical trades. He had attempted to transport this combination of literary learning and industrial training to Liberia, where he tutored ministerial candidates in Greek and experimented with an industrial school of his own during the 1860s. He continued to support industrial training after his return to America in 1872, as he revealed in his 1880 testimony before Congress. Crummell never reversed himself on this position, nor was he tempted to do so, as his theory of education recognized and attempted to reconcile the commonly presumed, but merely apparent, conflict between manual training and the Greek testament. Where Crummell and Washington overlapped in terms of religious doctrine was in their condemnation of enthusiastic religion.

Washington was convinced that shouting and ring dancing until the wee hours were not much better than some of the more deleterious secular practices in gambling halls and bawdy houses.[31] "Many of our people without knowing it are Christian heathen," he said to an audience of New England women, "and demand as much missionary effort as the heathen of foreign fields." Washington was not the only leader of his time to accept such pejorative notions of the surviving plantation religion. Daniel Alexander Payne warned that the ring shout could not lead to true conversions, and worked to purge his church of "Africanisms." Alexander Crummell also condemned emotional conversions but had an entirely different view of their origins. He did not blame enthusiastic practices on Africa, but saw them as a disease generated in the United States by slave religion. On one occasion he declared that the "benighted pagans" of Africa were better off than American Negroes, who had been corrupted by the travesty of Christianity that infected the Plantation South.[32]

Washington intimated that frenzied worship on an empty stomach could easily awaken the midnight hunger for stolen chicken. "No matter how much our people 'get happy' and 'shout' in church, if they go home at night from church hungry, they are tempted to find something to eat before morning."[33] Thus, Washington observed, it was "hard to make a good Christian of a hungry man," but in discussing the relationship between economic progress and Protestant ethic, there always was the constantly recurring question of which came first, the chicken or the egg?[34] He did not mean to imply that everyone must be fat and prosperous before Christianity could take effect. There was simply a reciprocal relationship between the world and the church, civilization and Christianity, as Crummell had long maintained.

Washington made the point more precisely elsewhere: "The Negro needs not only that religion that is going to fill his heart, but that kind which is going to fill his stomach, clothe and shelter his body, and employ his hands." To this end, Washington insisted that the old type of religious leader, who hoped to win conversions by inflaming semipagan enthusiasms, must be replaced. "What are some of the problems that the ministry is to help us work out? Our religion must not alone be the concern of the emotions, but must be woven into the warp and woof or our everyday life. Besides, the ministry, the church, must help the educators bring about such a change in the education of the black man that there will be a more vital and practical connection between the Negro's educated brain and his means of earning a living."[35]

A contemporary racial joke illustrated the widespread belief that black churchmen were oblivious to any relationship between religion and morality. One old deacon was supposed to have said, "If I prays for chicken, sometimes I gets it an' sometimes I don't. But if I prays the Lawd to send me aftah a chicken, I always gets one."[36] Washington had his own "darky story," as we have seen, about the old man who had broken all the commandments, but hadn't lost his "religion." This variety of religion was not peculiar to the Black Belt. During his European tour of 1910, Washington "heard the same criticism of the people in Sicily." Superstition, otherworldliness, and the inability to relate religion to morality were widespread. He transmitted the prevailing opinion that "for the average Sicilian, religion has no connection with moral life," and that a peasant bent on robbing his landlord's field or flock would pray to a graven image for success before starting out. This was "pragmatism," grafted on "antinomianism," and an attitude that Washington, along with Crummell, Grimké, and Payne, was determined to exterminate, root and branch.[37]

Before the rise of Washington, Crummell had argued the necessity of race-conscious social institutions for the enactment of economic and industrial programs. This was the basis of a clash with Frederick Douglass at the commencement of Storer College at Harper's Ferry in 1885. Douglass—speaking with characteristically incautious bravado—had on another occasion said that the best policy for emancipation was "free the Negro and leave him alone." In other words, Douglass advocated that very attitude of laissez-faire that a youthful Du Bois later condemned at the organizational meeting of the American Negro Academy, where he was attempting to prove himself to Crummell. Crummell, at Harper's Ferry, assailed two pillars of Douglass's philosophy—laissez-faire and the "constant recollection" of slavery. He anticipated Washington by calling for abandonment of the old abolitionist strategy of relying on moral appeals to whites and advocated the formation of black institutions, in order to pursue "new ideas and new aims for a new era."[38]

Under the slavery system, argued Crummell, a social structure and an organization of labor had existed. The problems created by this social structure—and even more by its disappearance—were not to be understood in purely moral terms. The evil of slavery did not exist purely in the moral sphere; it existed in the economic sphere. With almost Taylorite rhetoric, Crummell described slavery as an industrial institution that had made black labor into one vast, evil, but nonetheless efficient machine.[39] His exact words were, "The Race was one great machine, every member in his place; working with severest regularity, and producing vast and valuable results. Within a range of both narrow and material interests, but alas, with a constant muzzling of our personal wills, the whole world saw the physical value of the Negro Race. Every man was made to stand in his own place; every man to do his own work; every man to yield a distinct and telling product! Out of this came labour; industrial order; servile systematized energy and activity."[40] The problem, in economic terms, was that all this organization and industrial efficiency did not benefit the mass of black people whose labor made the system profitable—it benefited only their exploiters. Nonetheless, the abolition of slavery signaled not only the decline of a moral evil, but the disappearance of an industrially effective form of social and economic organization.

Booker T. Washington was forced to recognize the same bitter truth on the question of the economic and industrial efficiency of slavery as was Crummell. He shared, by the way, Du Bois's cultural nostalgia for the presumed gentility of the antebellum South. In the late nineteenth century, there were many contradictions among deep-thinking African Americans, which rose out of the contradictions within the system they sought to analyze to their benefit. Washington's pronouncements on the effects of slavery on the industrial habits of African Americans oscillated between clichés. At times slavery was characterized as a school for industrious habits; at other times slavery was said to undermine the work ethos. Washington reveals his unreconciled contradictions regarding this economic conundrum in the opening pages of *Up From Slavery:* "The whole machinery of slavery was so constructed as to be looked on as a badge of degradation, of inferiority. Hence labour on the plantation was something that the slave plantation sought to escape.... On the other hand, the slaves, in many cases, had mastered some handicraft, and none were ashamed, and few unwilling to work."[41]

Both Crummell and Washington refer to the entire slavery *system* as one extended "machine." Crummell recognized the cruelty but also the industrial precision of the antebellum southern "machine process." Like Washington, he believed that slavery was morally wrong; nonetheless, he viewed the plantation as economically efficient—an issue on which Washington was ambivalent. Crummell took a strong stand on another issue where Washington vacillated, denying one of the themes of *Black Belt Diamonds*, that slavery had inculcated Christian morality. Crummell and Washington did, however, agree on another point—the need for new social institutions, once slavery had been destroyed. Laissez-faire would not work. A program for uplift must include a socializing element and a regulatory mechanism. Washington's "Tuskegee machine," aptly named by his detractors, was designed to replace the torturous machinery of slavery with a progressive engine that would function to the advantage of black folk.

Thorstein Veblen, in his much-neglected book *The Theory of Business Enterprise*, made a distinction between business and industry. This distinction he related to a more fundamental dichotomy that appears in his better known *Theory of the Leisure Class*. He explained human behavior and class formation in terms of two universal and congenital human traits—the instinct of sportsmanship and the instinct of workmanship. Sportsmanship in primitive societies gave birth to the leisure class, as it was tied to the masculine arts of hunting, warfare, and other "exploits" of derring-do, activities that were sporadic in nature. Workmanship involved the constant drudgery of industrial pursuits and was therefore relegated to women and slaves. The inevitable result was that leisure came to have higher status than work in primitive societies. In advanced societies, leisure retained its status-conferring essence, as upper-class males continued to strive for status in games, rather than in work—on the playing fields of Eton, or at Waterloo, or in the exploits of business.

Washington was given to a preference for industry over business, and a hostility to conspicuous consumption, albeit, unlike Veblen, he did not disparage business. Veblen respected the activities of the workman, the mechanic, and the engineer rather than the gamesmanship and buccaneering attitudes of the business world. Compare this to Washington's expressed dislike for games, and his belief that the planter classes were lazy as well as exploitative. It was the industrious roundheads of the North, rather than the swashbuckling cavaliers of the South, who captured his progressive imagination. Identical sympathies pervade the works of William James and Veblen, with their inclinations towards social engineering and their distaste for the atavistic exploits of the military and business classes. Veblen, in particular, expressed an amused and supercilious irony in his descriptions of wastefulness and "conspicuous consumption." Veblen, like Washington, admired workmanship and the "machine process"; he disparaged gamesmanship and commercialism.[42]

Washington was not the first black leader to attack conspicuous consumption. In an essay on "Right Mindedness," Crummell had called for some modification of the aesthetic instincts that led African Americans to be consumers rather than producers. In another essay, "Common Sense in Common Schooling," he called for practical education and studies that would toughen the minds of the elite and meet the material needs of the masses. Crummell shared such ideas with Washington, although in private correspondence he expressed vague suspicions regarding Washington's position. What he opposed was Washington's accommodating rhetoric.[43] He criticized Washington's gospel of materialism and panacea of wealth in his opening addresses at the first convention of the American Negro Academy, but he never disparaged the idea that accumulation of wealth was a good thing. This was, in effect, why he advocated practical education in his Congressional testimony. "I went in 1872, in the city of New York, into the kitchen of the Union League Club, and there I saw a young man with a copy of Euripedes and Tacitus, in the originals, sitting there with his apron upon him awaiting his turn, as a servant, to stand as a waiter behind the table. I have seen young men who have graduated from college as lawyers and doctors, who have been forced at last to gain a livelihood as servants."

The above is the basis for Washington's "saddest-thing-I-ever-saw" stories, in *Up From Slavery* and elsewhere. Washington's caricature of Alexander Crummell as a miseducated colored minister is oblique and inaccurate but unmistakable. "Only a few days ago, I saw a colored minister preparing his Sunday sermon just as a New England minister prepares his sermon. But this colored minister was in a broken down, leaky, rented log cabin, with weeds in the yard, surrounded by evidences of poverty, filth, and the want of thrift. This minister had spent some time in school studying theology. How much better it would have been to have had this minister taught the dignity of labor, theoretical and practical farming in connection with his theology, so that he could have added to his meager salary, and set an example to his people in the matter of living in a decent house, and correct farming."[44] It is more than likely that

Washington stole the anecdotal formula for this story from Crummell, whose testimony before Congress was publicized well enough. Washington used the purloined blueprint many times in subsequent years, notably in *Up From Slavery*, where, to the affected astonishment and dismay of Du Bois, he described the feckless young man studying a French grammar. The story was once adapted to ridicule a pantless native African reading Cicero's orations.

The following variation, which belittles an improvident young African American woman, provides the additional element of Washington's opposition to one aspect of "triumphant commercialism," that is, conspicuous consumption.[45] "One of the saddest sights I ever saw in the South was a colored girl, recently returned from college, sitting in a rented one-room log cabin attempting day by day to extract some music from a second-hand piano, when all about her indicated want of thrift and cleanliness."[46] Despite their obvious distaste for dirt and disorder, the liberal-artsy Crummell, and social-scientific Du Bois were inclined—within reason, of course—to smile indulgently on undeveloped artistic tendencies. The aesthetic, the emotional, the love of colorful adornment seemed to be aspects of the "Negro genius" worth retaining and transforming, in much the way that Mozart and Brahms had transformed country dances into masterpieces of sophistication. They had an irrational fear that Washington might replace the folksy charm of the black belt with a bleak, colorless Puritanism, all to the end of accumulating capital. Crummell expressed it as, "constantly dogmatizing theories of sense and matter . . . declaring now that property is the source of power; and then that money is the real thing which commands respect."[47]

In addition to lamenting bad piano music, Washington disparaged conspicuous consumption of sewing machines, which, despite their industrial potential, he observed standing idle in southern cabins. In another lecture Washington had encouraged black washerwomen to acquire washing machines. Why then should he attack the purchase of a sewing machine? They were overpriced and bought on installment plans. Besides, a sewing machine was useless without some industrial training, whereas a washing machine could profitably be employed without any special knowledge or skill.[48] More likely, it was simply that Washington went into conniptions at any signs of improvidence or impracticality. This was no time for idly wasting money or incurring debt. The utilitarianism that Du Bois had attributed to him was a shrewdly spoken half-truth, but far from swallowing the doctrine of "triumphant commercialism," Washington questioned the doctrine's most garish manifestation, conspicuous consumption.

Washington's mother gave him his first lesson in the Protestant ethic, which is diametrically opposed to conspicuous consumption. It was she who prepared him for his successful associations with Viola Ruffner and Mary F. Mackie. There is no necessity for doubt or skepticism when Washington tells us of his mother's sending him to school in a cap made by her lovingly industrious hands, instead of a "store hat," like those of his school chums. The anticommercialism that had helped him up the ladder of success ought to work for anyone smart enough to listen. Thus he failed to appreciate the harmlessness of window shopping on Saturdays and Sundays in isolated southern towns, or cruising the boulevards of Washington, D.C., in flashy rented carriages.[49]

Ross Posnock has said that Booker T. Washington was the forerunner of the modern black public intellectual, but a pragmatist only in the colloquial sense.[50] I would suggest that there is more of vulgar pragmatism in the modern public intellectual than in Booker T. Washington. While, as in prior works, I continue to recognize the persistent expressions of materialism in his philosophy and even some signs of economic or materialistic determinism, it is now my position that Washington addressed the idealism-versus-materialism controversy in a spirit of pragmatism, asking himself, "What difference does it make?" If he could create black capitalism by preaching Arminian Christianity, he had the means to make the attempt. If he could create a model Christian citizen by laying an economic foundation, that too was worth the effort.

Washington undeniably vacillated between economic and ideological determinism. At times he claimed that economic development was prerequisite to religion, and at others he insisted that it was hard to make a Christian of a hungry man; on occasion, he followed Crummell's doctrine that Christianity and civilization were reciprocal codeterminants of black progress. The Tuskegee philosophy asserted the primacy of ideas but the indispensability of economics. This indicates both a "pragmatist" and an "instrumentalist" sociology of religion, aimed at effecting social change through the manipulation of ideas. Weber's subsequent sociology of the Protestant ethic was "formalistic" and purely descriptive.

Washington's Christianity followed Crummell's in preaching an imitation of Christ, rather than a friendship with Jesus, and the Tuskegee machine attempted to manipulate church and clergy in order to assert justification by works, instead of justification by faith—or by shouting. The underground wiring of the Tuskegee machine intruded no less into the church than into politics, and Washington, whether addressing his pupils in chapel or publishing in popular magazines, had a thorough appreciation of religion as a means of affecting social behavior. Thus his opposition to the religious vernacular that was expressed in frenzied conversions and ring shouts; thus his pragmatic and unsentimental support for those religious doctrines that he associated with capital accumulation and Protestant ethic, useful countermeasures to the insinuating serpents of mail-order commercialism and conspicuous consumption.[51]

Notes

1. Louis Harlan said of Booker T. Washington, "If we could remove those layers of secrecy as one peels an onion," we might find, "as in the case of the onion, nothing—a personality that had vanished into the roles it played." See Louis Harlan, *Booker T. Washington: The Making of a Black Leader, 1856–1901* (New York: Oxford University Press, 1972), ix. Ross Posnock, in *Color and Culture: Black Writers and the Making of the Modern Intellectual* (Cambridge: Harvard University Press, 1998), 36–37, sees Washington as a pragmatist "in the colloquial sense but the virtual antithesis of a philosophical pragmatist." Since he proceeds to define the "very imprint of philosophical pragmatism [as] esteem for experimental action," one of Washington's most distinguishing traits, I find the statement puzzling.

2. Ida B. Wells—never given to diplomatic niceties—once embarrassed the philanthropist Julius Rosenwald, Sears & Roebuck's chairman of the board, for retelling one of Washington's chicken jokes. See Ida B. Wells-Barnett, *The Autobiography of Ida B. Wells* (Chicago: University of Chicago Press, 1970), 331.

3. Typical folklore is Dudley Randall's poem, "Booker T. and W. E. B.," in Arthur P. Davis and J. Saunders Redding, eds., *Cavalcade*, 774–75. My impressions derive from over fifty years of interaction with relatives and friends, and thirty-six years with students. My father, a highly skilled plasterer, apprenticed in his father's trade, was a graduate of Morehouse College but was a qualified supporter of Washington, unlike Redding, his freshman English teacher, whose anti-Bookerism is evident in *They Came in Chains* (New York: Lippincott, 1950). I interviewed the anti-Bookerite Rayford Logan in 1972, author of *The Betrayal of the Negro* (New York: Collier, 1965), an influence cited by Lerone Bennett in *Before the Mayflower* (Chicago: Johnson, 1962), 226–29, 274–79. See also August Meier, "Booker T. Wash-

ington and the Talented Tenth," in his *Negro Thought in America, 1880–1915* (Ann Arbor: University of Michigan Press, 1963), 207–47.

4. For examples in recent American history survey texts, see John A. Garraty and Mark C. Carnes, *The American Nation* (New York: Longman, 2000), 2: 474–75; Gary B. Nash et al., *The American People* (New York: Longman, 2001), 553; Robert A. Divine et al., *America, Past and Present* (New York: Longman, 1999), 602; John M. Murrin et al., *Liberty, Equality, Power,* 2d ed. (New York, Harcourt, 2001), 563–64; and George Brown Tindall and David Shi, *America: A Narrative History* (New York: Norton, 1999), 851–55.

5. Horatio Alger, *Ragged Dick* (New York: A. K. Loring, 1868).

6. H. J. Rose, *A Handbook of Greek Mythology* (New York: E. P. Dutton, 1959), 5, provides these details and dismisses amateur mythography of Dick Whittington "with proud disdayn and cruele despite."

7. Horatio Alger, *Struggling Upward, or Luke Larkin's Luck* (New York: Porter and Coates, 1890; reprint, with introduction by Carl Bode, New York: Penguin, 1985).

8. Morton White, *Social Thought in America: The Revolt against Formalism* (Boston: Beacon, 1957), 7, defines *instrumentalism* as "Dewey's doctrine which holds that ideas are plans of action."

9. Washington asserts the worldly religiosity of "Freedom" songs in *Up From Slavery*, in Louis R. Harlan and Raymond W. Smock, eds., *The Booker T. Washington Papers*, 14 vols. (Urbana: University of Illinois Press, 1972–89), 1: 224 (hereinafter cited as BTW Papers). Future citations to *Up From Slavery* are to this edition. The "Sorrow Songs" are given a more complicated interpretation in W.E.B. Du Bois, *The Souls of Black Folk* (Chicago: McClurg, 1903), 250–64.

10. BTW Papers, 1: 236–37, 242.

11. Robert Bellah, *The Broken Covenant* (New York: Seabury Press, 1975), 70.

12. See Louis Harlan, *Booker T. Washington: The Wizard of Tuskegee* (New York: Oxford, 1983), 144, 151.

13. Bertrand Russell praises James's philosophy and personality in *A History of Western Philosophy* (New York: Simon and Schuster, 1945), 811–19. Du Bois makes several brief allusions to James in his *Autobiography* (New York: International, 1968). His most extended comment includes, "I became a devoted follower of James" (132), but caution is advised; on page 126, referring to his Fisk commencement, he says, "Bismarck was my hero," but his handwritten draft of the address lambastes Bismarck as a symbol of Germany's intrinsic flaws.

14. "The Significance of the Frontier in American History," in George Rogers Taylor, *The Turner Thesis* (New York: D. C. Heath, 1972), 4, 22.

15. Washington makes his claim in *Up From Slavery*, 355; Lincoln is referred to as Washington's patron saint in BTW Papers, 6: 365, and is heroized by Washington in BTW Papers, 10: 26–27, 33–39, and 12: 188.

16. Washington once told the story in which friends noticed Emerson gazing out

a window and asked him, "What are you looking for, Mr. Emerson?" The answer was, "I am trying to find Ralph Waldo Emerson"; see *BTW Papers*, 3:154. This suggests that artichokes may have self-awareness, as well as the awareness that they are artichokes.

17. Russell, however, agreed with Du Bois that James was a nice guy in *History of Western Philosophy*.

18. John Huizinga, in *Men and Ideas* (New York: Free Press, 1959), relates the thought of Erasmus, Abelard, and others to what he calls "cultural history." Du Bois's "progressive" ideology may have led to a historiography in which socioeconomic forces are the determinants of ideas, although works such as *Souls of Black Folk* and *Darkwater* are replete with Hegelian idealism. See Joel Williamson, "Du Bois as Hegelian," in his *New People* (New York: Free Press, 1980). Without adopting Huizinga's ideological biases, Du Bois might effectively have analyzed Crummell's or James's thought as the socialist Russell did that of James. Crummell had published three volumes of writings by the time of his death.

19. On Joseph Charles Price, see Jessie Corey Smith, ed., *Notable Black American Men* (Detroit: Gate, 1999), 963–66. Douglass believed that the question of interracial intermarriage was moot, since he was convinced that it was inevitable and that even without amalgamation, environmental influences would ultimately whiten the Negro. See "Claims of the Negro Ethnologically Considered" (1854), reprinted in John Blassingame et al., *Frederick Douglass Papers* (New Haven: Yale University Press, 1982), 2: 522–23. Note particularly Douglass's remarks on the effects of climate and environment on the physiognomy of the Jewish people, white Americans, and native Africans. He implicitly advocated biogenetic assimilation, but Waldo Martin discusses his twists and turns on the subject in *The Mind of Frederick Douglass* (Chapel Hill: University of North Carolina Press, 1984), 220–21.

20. W.E.B. Du Bois, *The Story of Benjamin Franklin* (Vienna: Secretariat for World Peace, 1956), reprinted in *Pamphlets and Leaflets by W. E. B. Du Bois* (White Plains, N.Y.: Kraus-Thomson Organization, 1986).

21. Du Bois, *Souls of Black Folk*, 43.

22. Washington's views on the ethics and superstitions of nineteenth-century Italian peasants are elaborated in his work *The Man Farthest Down*, written with the "collaboration" of Robert E. Park (New York: Doubleday, Page, 1912), 166–91. I discuss these views and the contribution of Park in greater detail in a forthcoming work on the contradictions and conflicts in black leadership ideology.

23. W.E.B. Du Bois, "The Evolution of Negro Leadership," *Dial* 81 (July 16, 1901): 55.

24. Thomas Jefferson to Walter Jones, January 2, 1814, in *Thomas Jefferson: Writings*, ed. Merrill Peterson (New York: Library of America, 1984), 1317.

25. Washington, *Black Belt Diamonds: Gems from the Speeches, Addresses, and Talks to Students of Booker T. Washington, Selected and Arranged by Victoria Earle Matthews, Introduction by T. Thomas Fortune* (New York: Fortune and Scott, 1898). Fortune's introduction mentioned Henry W. Grady and Washington as the "only

two men" produced in the South since the Civil War who had achieved "national reputation." Du Bois pushed the idea further, saying that Washington was "the most distinguished Southerner since Jefferson Davis" (43).

26. With reference to the subtitle of *Black Belt Diamonds*, Trotter published "Some Real Tuskegee Gems," taken from Washington's Boston 1903 speech, in his newspaper, *The Guardian*, April 4, 1903, reprinted in August Meier, Elliot Rudwick, and Frances L. Broderick, eds., *Black Protest Thought in the Twentieth Century* (Indianapolis: Bobbs-Merrill, 1971), 35–36.

27. Wilson J. Moses, *Black Messiahs and Uncle Toms* (University Park: Penn State Press, 1982), 90.

28. Washington, *Black Belt Diamonds*, 39.

29. Ibid., 34–35.

30. Washington was not the only black person to speak at the Cotton States Exposition. Alexander Crummell's address at that event was entitled "Civilization as a Collateral and Indispensable Instrumentality in Planting the Christian Church in Africa"; see J.E.E. Bowen, ed., *Africa and the American Negro* (Atlanta: Gammon Theological Seminary, 1896).

31. Ross Phares, *Bible in Pocket, Gun in Hand* (New York: Doubleday, 1962), 86–89, describes the emotionalism and particularly the sexual excitement associated with camp meetings and great revivals among white and black participants.

32. For the most scholarly and meticulous study of the ring shout, see Sterling Stuckey, *Slave Culture: Nationalist Theory and the Foundations of Black America* (New York: Oxford University Press, 1987).

33. Washington, *The Future of the American Negro* (Boston: Small, Maynard & Co., 1899), reprinted in *BTW Papers*, 5: 347; see also Washington, "Speech before the National Unitarian Association," in *BTW Papers*, 3: 477.

34. Washington, *Black Belt Diamonds*, 93.

35. Ibid., 59, 73–74.

36. Joke reprinted in Phares, *Bible in Pocket, Gun in Hand*, 28. Phares also cited his "personal recollection," which leads me to assume the joke was an "old one."

37. When Washington condemned defects of the Negro clergy in an article in *Outlook*, AME Bishop Daniel Alexander Payne came to his defense; see *BTW Papers*, 1: 203, 2: 97–98. Payne's hostility to "praying and singing bands" is discussed by Stuckey, in *Slave Culture*, 92–93. For Washington on Sicilian peasants, see *Man Farthest Down*, 171.

38. "The Need for New Ideas and New Aims for a New Era," (1885), in Crummell, *Africa and America* (Springfield, Mass.: Willey & Co., 1891); see also the introduction to that volume.

39. Frederick Winslow Taylor developed the industrial efficiency system (Taylorism), widely adopted in the late nineteenth century, that forced human beings to adapt to the rhythms of industrial production. In 1912, in testimony before Congress, Taylor denied that his system was dehumanizing.

40. Alexander Crummell, "The Discipline of Freedom," M.S.C. 16, first published

in Wilson J. Moses, ed., *Destiny and Race: Selected Writings, 1840–1898* (Amherst: University of Massachusetts Press, 1992), 246.

41. Washington, *Up From Slavery*, 223–24.

42. Washington does not make Veblen's distinction between business and industry and is therefore unequivocal in his advocacy of business; see Washington, *Black Belt Diamonds*, 61–62.

43. Wilson J. Moses, *Alexander Crummell: A Study of Civilization and Discontent* (New York: Oxford University Press, 1989), 292.

44. The relationship between Washington and Crummell is treated more extensively in ibid., 266.

45. For Crummell's congressional testimony, see ibid., 233–34. For more on Washington's "saddest sight stories," see ibid., 266–67, 271.

46. Washington, *Black Belt Diamonds*, 25.

47. Alexander Crummell, "Civilization: The Primal Need of the Race," and "The Attitude of the American Mind toward the Negro Intellect," in *American Negro Academy Occasional Papers No. 3* (Washington, D.C.: The American Negro Academy, 1898), 5.

48. Washington ridicules sewing machines in *Up From Slavery*, 274–75. He advocates washing machines in *Black Belt Diamonds*, 13.

49. For Du Bois's contrasting views on Saturday pastimes of the peasantry, see *Souls of Black Folk*, 114.

50. I assume Posnock was thinking of Cornell West, whose self-definition as public or "organic" intellectual is notorious and whose essay on Du Bois as a Jamesian pragmatist excites his interest. Thulani Davis delivered a withering attack on West, along with Henry Louis Gates's Harvard syndicate, in the *Village Voice*, as the present-day manifestation of the Tuskegee machine which, in her view, has limited freedom of expression and damaged employment opportunities for African Americans.

51. An irony discussed in my forthcoming book, *Dynamic Tension*, is that Julius Rosenwald, head of the Sears and Roebuck mail order department, was a major Tuskegee benefactor.

7

"Curious Silence"?

African American Women in *Up From Slavery*

PATRICIA A. SCHECHTER

It would seem hard to miss the African American women characters in Booker T. Washington's *Up From Slavery*. His mother, Jane Ferguson, figures distinctly in the first four chapters of the narrative and receives praise and gratitude from her son. Olivia A. Davidson, Washington's second wife, is cited as a cofounder of Tuskegee Institute and is the most clearly defined of his three spouses. The activities and accomplishments of Washington's third wife, Margaret Murray, receive considerable attention toward the end of the narrative. Washington also takes a strong stand in defense of black womanhood in general, decrying the "base falsehood" propagated by whites that "Negro women are not virtuous."[1] Given these and other details about African American women in *Up From Slavery*, it was interesting for me to note our conference's "Overview," which lists among its themes "Washington's curious silence about his wives and his omission of black women in his autobiography."[2]

"Silence" measured by what standard? "Curious" to whom, and why? Reticence about love and romance are not new to me as a student of African American literature; Washington's contemporary Ida B. Wells-Barnett, someone gifted with written and spoken language, provides few details in her autobiography, *Crusade for Justice*, about her courtship with Ferdinand Barnett or the emotional content of their marriage.[3] What historian Darlene Clark Hine calls a "culture of dissemblance"—a kind of tactical nondisclosure—on matters of sexuality in African American writing and speech registers in some scholarly arenas not as a defect or "curiosity" but rather as a self-conscious choice and a vital resistance strategy in Washington's day, especially for black women.[4] In such a context, it does not seem particularly "curious" that Washington would describe his marriages in few words, and these only the most decorous and chaste. And so he does, at the end of his narrative, when he mentions favorite family pastimes like reading together or a pleasant tramp in the woods, "where no one can disturb or vex us" (187). The lack of further details about married life—if such can be called "silence"—is, in any case, never a blank void, but a space portending multiple meanings, among them, protection, privacy, or an unwillingness to participate in oppressive discourses.[5]

Reflection upon our conference's notion of "silence"—which I learned at our meeting included the critical dimensions mentioned above—prepared me well to tackle the secondary literature on *Up From Slavery*. In most treatments written in the 1960s through the 1990s, the silence around black women in the narrative is deafening. Most readers of *Up From Slavery* situate Washington in relation to white audiences and potential patrons or juxtapose him to other "great men" in U.S. history—mainly Frederick Douglass and Benjamin Franklin.[6] Both strategies privilege a mostly white and male-centered vision of historical succession, political struggle, or literary anxiety/influence rather than place Washington among the African Americans, to whom, for example, he dedicates the narrative—Margaret Murray or his brother, John H. Washington.[7]

One scholar of *Up From Slavery* notes that matters of "sexual desire" are necessarily "suppressed by racial mythology" dominant in the time that the narrative was written, but even this comment is made in the context of black men's attitudes toward white masters and mistresses and not, primarily, toward black women—a structure of observation that retains the polarization of "black man–white woman" with its erasure of black women.[8] An excellent essay by James Olney treats the Washington-Douglass-Franklin nexus with great insight. To this essay, written in 1989, Olney appends a coda in which he worries out loud about his construction of historical influence to the exclusion of the "Founding Mothers of another Afro-American literary tradition." I agree with Olney that restoring Washington's narrative to a fuller context of intellectual production by African Americans in his day must include texts by and about black women, but it might be worth observing that even Olney's coda still leaves the actual women in Washington's text invisible.[9]

The construction of *Up From Slavery* as "silent" on black women seems to draw upon a number of crosscurrents around Washington's legacy in U.S. culture. First is the recent scholarly promotion of Washington from a disparaged "Uncle Tom" to that of a man who did the best he could under terrible circumstances.[10] In this context of general critical rapprochement, it seems important to ask new questions about his life, including pointed questions about women and gender, especially given the wonderful flowering of scholarship on African American women produced by black feminist scholars in the last decade. Indeed, raising the specter of "possible sexism," to quote David Levering Lewis in his recent biography of Du Bois, is important, because acknowledging male privilege in the lives of heroic black men humanizes and historicizes them and wards off hagiography.[11] The opportunity to probe gender politics in the interest of liberated scholarship is, I think, part of my assignment as a feminist historian in this conference, and I will return to it shortly. But I want to reflect further on the basis for the construction of *Up From Slavery* as "silent" on black women because it rests, however casually or uneasily, on a long-standing critical pattern in the academy. Here I propose to interrogate not Washington's silence—which is something of a myth—but the silence of the critics and historians who sometimes speak louder than the historical actors. Who benefits by the excision, the forgetting of, and the talking-past the black women who inhabit *Up From Slavery*? Who has the right to be "curious" about Booker T. Washington's marital affairs, and what is at stake with this kind of access? What kinds of narratives about slavery and its legacy in U.S "race relations" are sustained by the marginalization of black women in the critical literature—or conversely, by demanding access to their connection to Washington?[12]

Treatments of Washington in isolation from any black community in general, and from black women specifically, reflect a "shrink to fit" tendency in many writers' preconceptions of a "race leader" or "great man." In everyday discourse, such "famous people" are sui generis types, the product of quirks of fate or genetic inheritance rather than of complex social processes and interactions. I use the taxonomic metaphor deliberately, for the legacy of whites' perception of Washington's mixed "racial" ancestry—like that of Frederick Douglass and Ida B. Wells-Barnett—has certainly influenced commentators from the beginning of Washington's career, as in early appraisals by Hampton Institute's Samuel Armstrong's of his student as "a very competent and capable mulatto" and "no ordinary darkey."[13] Erasure of black women also enables a particular reading of U.S. "race relations" as a problem among men, fixable by men. When constructed as a question of structural inequity between groups of men, racism becomes tractable within liberal politics. An example of this remedy in law is "leveling the playing field," a metaphor for social reform whose legitimacy inheres in part through an appeal to historically male spheres of utopian striving and projection, namely engineering and sports. A classic legal example of this remedy is, of course, the Fourteenth Amendment, which, by fully enfranchising "male citizens," excluded all women, citizens and noncitizens, as well as the Asian immigrant and Native American men excluded from citizenship eligibility.[14]

Another contributing factor to the erasure of black women in the scholarly literature on *Up From Slavery* is that critics seem to take for granted rather than analyze the fact that Booker T. Washington was married through most of his adult life. The legal fact of marriage cancels the need to discuss it; once Washington's heterosexual bona fides are established, the existence and lives of real wives need no analysis. The fact of marriage triggers cultural permission to rest on the cliché: "Behind every great man ..." Had Washington remained single, his marital status might have drawn more attention, as it would have been outside the norm of his time. Furthermore, unmarried black women have historically been a flashpoint of racist attention—a negative "controlling image," as Patricia Hill Collins has theorized. In this context, marriage, especially Victorian middle-class marriage, can sometimes serve to veil black women from the dominant culture's frame or "gaze." Washington's reticence about them might be read as part of such a protective strategy. As Collins and numerous scholars have extensively documented, black women in U.S. culture are usually invisible, or visible only in the negative.[15] In this sense, Booker T. Washington's wives are not sharply in focus for the critics; they are the wallpaper. As for the other black female characters in the text—Tuskegee students, young working women, neighborhood mothers and grandmothers who supported the school—they also quickly fade into the background. Ignoring black women is both an example of and a cover for the racist sexism in U.S. culture.

A good example of this negating framework in an analysis of *Up From Slavery* can be found in William L. Andrews's 1991 essay "Booker T. Washington, Belle Kearney, and the Southern Patriarchy." As the title suggests, Andrews reads Washington's narrative not alongside one of the black women's slave narratives that he himself has made a focus of scholarly attention for many years, but Belle Kearney's memoir, *A Slave Holder's Daughter* (1900). Andrews edited the Schomburg collection's volume, *Six Women's Slave Narratives* (1988), which includes texts by three of Washington's contemporaries, Lucy A. Delaney, Kate Drumgoold, and Annie L. Burton. Andrews compares Washington and Kearney because they are both "reformers," and he wants to say something about southern-style progressivism. While Andrews's introduction notes that an in-depth analysis of the "New Woman" and the "New Negro" in the South should include the work of Anna Julia Cooper (and Du Bois), he nonetheless moves on to take those "New" terms at face value, that is, as white and male, respectively. "The idea of a *black* southern reformer or a *woman* southern reformer was not just oxymoronic," writes Andrews, "it was just plain moronic, from a patriarchal point of view" (emphasis in original). Andrews then further justifies the comparison, actually dubbing Kearney's narrative, in his words, "a kind of slave narrative," because the title of her book "makes the daughter the object of the slaveholding father's possession." This bizarre construction of Kearney as "black/slave" jostles most uncomfortably against Andrews's contention that she wrote her autobiography to establish a "liberating standard . . . for white womanhood."[16] Thus Andrews's frame triply erases black women: first, in bypassing Cooper, second, by dubbing Kearney a "black/slave," and finally, by ignoring the black women characters in *Up From Slavery*.[17]

A few scholars have begun the work of uncovering the women of Tuskegee in Washington's lifetime. Jacqueline Anne Rouse's 1996 article on Margaret Murray; Adele Logan Alexander's research into the career of her grandmother, Adella Hunt Logan, a longtime teacher and administrator at Tuskegee; and Carolyn A. Dorsey's ongoing work on Olivia Davidson, all promise to restore a fuller cast of characters to Tuskegee's landscape.[18] The silence in the critical literature around Davidson's life makes Dorsey's complaint that Davidson is still the "unacknowledged cofounder of Tuskegee Institute" understandable, despite Washington's direct testimony in *Up From Slavery*. In a related vein, Rouse notes that most of the "public discourse" around Murray has "limited her voice to the language of her husband," and her essay challenges that frame. She argues that Murray's work of female-centered community outreach was critical to encouraging poor and rural African Americans to take the risks necessary to change their lives and labor under Jim Crow. The work of Rouse, Alexander, and Dorsey documents what others have ignored and what Washington himself noted plainly in *Up From Slavery:* that Margaret Murray relieved her husband of "many burdens and perplexities" (189) in running Tuskegee and that Olivia Davidson's contributions to the school in the 1880s were utterly vital to its success.

African American Women in *Up From Slavery*

The representation of Washington's wives in *Up From Slavery* is not "curious" as in "odd" or "silent" in the sense of a blank gap. But it might be fair to say that their integration into the narrative could be a bit confusing to the reader, at least initially. Their lives are confusing because they do not neatly fit into the linear "upward" sweep of history implied by the autobiography's title. There are unexpected and untimely deaths; debilitating illnesses; the seesaw of child-rearing; the chosen or fated childlessness of his third marriage—and a detailed representation of all of this complexity could destabilize the "simple, straightforward story" promised in the narrative's preface, as they nearly threatened the march of the life. As biographer Louis Harlan notes, Davidson's death pressed the reality upon Washington that "course of life was clearly not a straight line" as he had imagined for himself or projected in his prose.[19] We are conditioned by our contemporary culture's "tell-all" mentality, and Washington's restraint might seem excessive or, from another angle, even complicit with his contemporary culture's devaluation and silencing of black women. But a closer look at the components of Washington's restraint reveals *Up From Slavery*'s kinship with the literary conventions of his day.

Booker T. Washington married Fannie Smith, a Hampton graduate and his "sweetheart" from his hometown, Malden, Virginia, in 1882; she died in 1884 after the birth of a daughter, Portia. Washington then wed Olivia A. Davidson, also a Hampton graduate, in 1885, and two sons, Booker and Earnest, were born. Davidson died in 1889. In 1893, Washington married Margaret Murray, after meeting her at her graduation ceremony at Fisk University, at which he gave the commencement address. Washington obviously met Fannie Smith chronologically first among these three women, but *Up From Slavery* introduces Olivia Davidson first, in chapter 8, in a paragraph in which Washington also mentions that she "later became my wife" (87). Davidson arrived at Tuskegee in 1881, the year before Washington wed Smith. Davidson's dedication to Tuskegee and her talents and success at fund-raising are discussed in two places in chapter 8 and again in chapter 9. Fannie Smith is introduced and then quickly exits in the space of two unembellished paragraphs at the very end of chapter 9. The briefness of the marriage, as represented here and in the extant written record, has been taken by Louis Harlan to be a fair imprint of Smith on her husband and on Tuskegee. "Her death was as unobtrusive as her life had been" he notes.[20]

The structure of the narrative locates Davidson at the emotional center of Washington's adult married life. He notes her "new and rare face" upon her arrival at Tuskegee, a fleeting hint, perhaps, at her attractiveness to him. He directly praises her integrity and good judgment. Davidson was light-skinned enough to pass for white, but Washington notes that "under no circumstances and for no considerations would she consent to deceive any one in regard to her racial identity" (88). Davidson brought an up-to-date education and a "rare moral character and a life of unselfishness" to her work at Tuskegee. "No single individual did more toward laying the foundations of the Tuskegee Institution as to insure the successful work that has been done there than Olivia A. Davidson" (88). The reader learns of Davidson's advocacy in the North on behalf of Tuskegee as she moves, with the help of her patron, Mrs. Mary Hemenway of Boston, through an exhausting fund-raising circuit. Davidson epitomizes the type of womanhood valued by Washington and Tuskegee: self-sacrificing, efficient, hardworking, dedicated. Davidson expends herself to the point where she is too tired to undress for bed at night; while traveling up north, she falls asleep when given a moment's rest while waiting for an appointment. Later, in chapter 8, Washington again praises her work for Tuskegee, crediting her as "largely responsible for the success of the school during its early history" (140).

These terse details and others in *Up From Slavery* hint at the emotional quality of both the woman and the marriage. "In 1889 she died, after four years of happy married life and eight years of hard and happy work for the school" (140). Washington surely projects his conservative temperament and values when he characterizes Davidson as a woman who worked herself to death for her race, a worshipful but far from liberated view.[21] "She literally wore herself out in her never ceasing efforts in behalf of the work that she so dearly loved" (140). The idea that a woman can and should be selfless to the point of losing her life for a cause is a very old idea, underwritten by Christian mythology, and one that contemporary black feminist theologians have recently begun to critique as historically ill-suited for African American women's survival.[22] Samuel Armstrong, for his part, apparently thought rather little of Davidson's potential, noting in a letter to Washington in 1887, "You lack strong supporting help, especially on the woman side."[23]

Washington's critical stance toward everyday racist sexism directed at black women is evident in the treatment of his mother, Jane Ferguson. Ferguson receives consistent high regard in *Up From Slavery*. The reader learns of her ingenuity as a provisioner and protector of her family. She "somehow" procures extra food, like a chicken, for her hungry children (3), and she conveys the family safely during a weeks-long trek from Virginia to West Virginia after the Civil War, to rejoin her husband (17). Ferguson also gave emotional and practical support to her son's intellectual ambition. Washington explains that she "sympathized with me and aided me in every way that she could," including procuring "in some way" his first book, an old copy of Webster's "blue-back" spelling book (19). She held a relatively high-status job on the plantation as cook, and her responsibility, integrity, and resourcefulness are consistently acknowledged by her son. Washington "never . . . felt so proud" of an article of clothing than he was of the first cap his mother sewed him from homespun cloth for his first day of school (23). Rather than fall into racist humor or the "mammy" stereotype—as Washington certainly indulged in his written and verbal statements about black male preachers and chicken thieves—Washington's treatment of his mother strikes me as respectful and admiring. "Though she was totally ignorant, so far as mere book knowledge was concerned, she had high ambitions for her children, and a large fund of good, hard, common sense which seemed to enable her to meet and master every situation. If I have done anything in life worth attention, I feel sure that I inherited the disposition from my mother" (19). Read alongside Washington's dismissive description of his father—merely that he "was a white man who lived on one of the near-by plantations" (2)—his statement about inheriting his disposition for success from his mother cuts subtly against the racist evolutionist thought that ran deep in his day.

In an African American literary context, Washington worked in a highly articulated tradition of homage to mothers, especially slave mothers. As practiced in literary narratives by black women, mothers often inhabit the emotional center of the author's life and often are dynamic actors in the story, partners in their struggle for freedom.[24] In Lucy Delaney's narrative, her mother "never spared an opportunity to impress it upon us, that we must get our freedom whenever the chance offered" (16). When Kate Drumgoold's mother was sold away early in the Civil War, there was a "clear place in the sky" for her daughter—a literal tear in the universe—which remained until her mother returned to Drumgoold at the end of the war (5). For black men of this generation, mothers also figure prominently, though in my reading, more often as inspiration than as coconspirator in life's struggles. The founder and publisher of the *Chicago Defender* newspaper, Robert S. Abbott, was born on the Georgia Sea Island of St. Simons and credited his mother as his main supporter and influence in his life, the "delight of his heart," according to his biographer Roi Ottley. Freeborn Ohioan Reverdy C. Ransom, an AME bishop, anchored his life story around his mother. *The Pilgrimage of Harriet Ransom's Son* (1949) contains a memorable scene in which Harriet approaches the dais in tears to embrace her son at his graduation from Oberlin College, in fulfillment of her lifelong dream to see her son educated.[25]

Up From Slavery records Jane Ferguson's similar hopes, her "wish that she might be permitted to live to see her children educated and started out in the world" (49). Not only did her death deprive her of that wish but of her son's also; one of Washington's "chief ambitions" was "to get to be in a position in which I could better make my mother comfortable and happy" (49). The narrative describes Jane Ferguson's death in measured but emphatic terms. "This seemed to me the saddest and blankest moment in my life" (49), language that echoes Drumgoold's metaphor of a torn, emptied universe without her mother.[26] As do the mothers in black women's narratives, Jane Ferguson actually functions as a coconspirator in the achievement of her son's education in *Up From Slavery*; Washington notes that he "induced" his mother to "get hold of a book" for him. "How or where she got it I do not know, but in some way she procured" the volume—perhaps much in the same way she secured extra food for her family, of which Washington similarly notes "how or where she got it I do not know" (3, 19). Washington could never "believe that my mother was guilty of thieving," given the conditions of slavery.

While he was well aware that she—and almost everyone around him growing up—was in some degree "a victim of slavery," the overall portrait of Jane Ferguson is substantial, dignified, and in Washingtonian terms, heartfelt.[27] Rather than "silence," *Up From Slavery* offers portraits of the women in Washington's life in terms ideologically consistent with portrayals of slave mothers and spouses produced by his male and female literary peers.

In this essay, I refer to Washington's mother as Jane Ferguson. My text names Washington's mother, while *Up From Slavery* does not. Why?[28] My intervention around this silence relies on Louis Harlan's research for the fact of her name. It also relies on black feminist theory and allied critical discourses that affirm the centrality of naming to restoring the historical agency of actors who have been silenced or ignored in the practice of history.[29] But what about Washington? My assessment is mixed. *Up From Slavery* appeared at a historical moment in which African American women's claims for protection and the right to protection for their children—the kind of claims that held great persuasive power in antislavery discourse—was losing ground. Part of the work of the National Association of Colored Women, organized in 1896, was to reaffirm black women's power and authority over the integrity of their homes and family members—and Washington mentions the organization by name at the end of the narrative (189–90).[30] In this context, Washington's discussion of his mother, yet his not-naming of Jane Ferguson, could be read as a universalizing gesture, creating an archetype for every slave mother who dreamed her child's dreams and acted as best she could in their interest.

And yet I am left wondering about Washington's choice here, well aware as he was of the power and importance of naming in his own life. He memorably recounts his school-days episode of self-naming in *Up From Slavery*: "[W]hen the teacher asked me what my full name was, I calmly told him 'Booker Washington,' as if I have been called by that name all my life; and by that name I have since been known" (24). In the next breath, he draws attention to and affirms his mother's agency and, perhaps, too, her sense of history and family: "Later in life I found that my mother had given me the name of 'Booker Taliaferro' soon after I was born, but in some way that part of my name seemed to disappear, and for a long while was forgotten, but as soon as I found out about it, I revived it, and made my full name 'Booker Taliaferro Washington'" (24).

His final comment—"I think there are not many men in our country who have had the privilege of naming themselves in the way that I have"—leaves me with a provocatively ambiguous mixture of irony and pride, as well as subtle anger. In this rendering, names are provisional; the claims and protections of family are fraught and fragile, and the details of Jane Ferguson's life, like her name, "seem to disappear" from the text, to paraphrase her son.

What of other African American women described in the text? For the purposes of this essay, I will only note that these sketches are notably absent of negative stereotype. At the end of chapter 8, while describing the first year of Tuskegee's operation (1881), Washington shares two anecdotes about the surrounding African American community's support for the school, especially praising the "gifts of the older coloured people, most of whom had spent their best days in slavery" (92). In the first anecdote, Washington tries to convince an "old coloured man who lived near and sometimes helped me" to assist him in cleaning out the chicken coop which was to be converted into school use. "What you mean boss?" Washington recalls this man saying. "You sholy ain't gwine to clean out de hen-house in de *day*-time?" (91). I sense a double entendre here, not just a chicken-thief joke but possibly some sexual innuendo as well—an innuendo Ida B. Wells-Barnett might justifiably have found unforgivable, given the context of lynching. Yet it might be worth noting that Washington adopts a much more restrained tone when he relates the offering of an "old coloured woman, who was about seventy years of age" two pages later. He quotes her as saying: "Mr. Washington, God knows I spent de bes' days of my life in slavery. God knows I's ignorant an' poor; but . . . I knows what you an' Miss Davidson is tryin' to do. I knows you is tryin' to make better men and better women for de coloured race. I ain't got no money, but I wants you to take dese six eggs, what I's been savin' up, an' I wants you to put dese six eggs into de eddication of dese boys an' gals." Washington concludes the story and the chapter by stating that of all the gifts Tuskegee has ever received, none "touched me so deeply as this one" (93). The passage is certainly open to a sentimental, racist reading, with the old woman representing the kindly old face of slavery, a comforting image for whites looking for a "mammy" figure. Yet juxtaposed to the spirited work of Miss Davidson, her story has the weight of reality. This "old coloured woman" functions as a noble archetype rather than a negative stereotype.[31]

In an extended discussion that touches on the theme of mothers and generational relations, *Up From Slavery* describes the author's visit to Washington, D.C., in 1878. Washington is both impressed and dismayed by the development of the African American community there, noting that young men and women are underemployed and underpaid. Rather than criticize racist wage scales, however, he decries the attraction of young people for expensive entertainment and consumer goods. *Up From Slavery* describes "girls whose mothers were earning their living by laundrying," who, after "six or eight years" in the public schools, wanted "more costly dresses, more costly hats and shoes" (63). The passage is susceptible to a racist reading in which, in Washington's words, "book education" has "weaned them away" from subordinate, domestic labor. Yet another reading is also possible, that is, the idea that moving too far from "the occupations of their mothers" made the daughters vulnerable: "The result of this was in too many cases that the girls went to the bad." The answer, of course, in this promotional tract for Tuskegee, is that industrial-style education would offer them "mental training" but at the "same time . . . give them the most thorough training in the latest and best methods of laundrying and other kindred occupations" (63), providing a recipe for community protection and perhaps self-protection.

Much has been written about Washington's innovations as an educator, particularly the concepts of adult education and night school. Few if any have commented on coeducation, still a notable modernization of higher education in the early 1880s when Tuskegee was founded.[32] *Up From Slavery* makes plain that Washington valued the ideal of the self-sacrificing and capable "Christian helpmate" when it came to girls' education, and the Tuskegee curriculum was replete with a gender division of labor.[33] These ideals Olivia Davidson taught and enacted and Margaret Murray put into full force in her club and educational work in and around Tuskegee. Washington prized stability, order, and hierarchy as a significant part of the answer to the "Negro Question," and similar values infused his comments on women, girls, and gender in *Up From Slavery*. Girls would be trained and strengthened, but also protected—again a conservative idea but one with critical implications for black-white relations at a time when black women were considered the legitimate sexual prey for white men and the presumptive servants for white households.

When the "boarding department" at Tuskegee opened, girl students were given priority for indoor rooms—though it seems that both boys and girls initially bunked in tents, rented cabins, or "shanties" (118). As the need for housing grew, some boys boarded in town, but Washington notes that this arrangement would not be acceptable for girl students whom "we did not care to expose in this way" (126). Well aware of the vulnerabilities of African American women and girls, Tuskegee countered racist sexism by protection—a strategy that Anna Julia Cooper strongly endorsed alongside her feminist clarion call to black women.[34] *Up From Slavery* further refutes the racist sexism that underwrote lynching, rape, and other abuse of black people by whites. After a lecture and research tour with Margaret Murray for the Slater Fund in 1897, Washington reports the following: "I have seen the statement made lately, by one who claims to know what he is talking about, that, taking the whole Negro race into account, ninety per cent of the Negro women are not virtuous. There never was a baser falsehood uttered concerning a race or a statement made that was less capable of being proved by actual fact" (176). This rebuttal of racism underscores Washington's commitment to fact and rationality as essential to easing the "race problem" in the United States. The racist sexism directed against African American women is simply untrue and not provable, and therefore it should dissolve in the pure light of reason and fact. That Washington himself would be the victim of racial violence, despite his lifetime of service and accomplishment, finally moved him to more direct protest rather than the "usual weasel words" he used when discussing white racism in *Up From Slavery* and elsewhere.[35] Yet it seems to this reader that he used few, if any, "weasel words" when describing African American women in his autobiography.

Conclusion

Booker T. Washington has been criticized for appeasing white racism in speech and print in his autobiography (and beyond), but in the case of the African American women characters in *Up From Slavery*, Washington demonstrates values and a style consistent with the standard of treatment for women of all ages within African American communities: respect to elders, homage to mothers, credit to wives, and protection to girls. At the same time, Washington was not "silent" about his wives, nor did he "omit" black women in *Up From Slavery*. Instead, the echo of this myth in the present day, however inquiring, is rooted in the legacy of the academic scholarship that has consistently ignored the black women who figure in Washington's text and who worked as thinkers, writers, and activists in his lifetime.

Notes

Author's note: The author would like to sincerely thank Fitzhugh Brundage for the invitation to participate in this conference and for his generous and astute readings of this essay. I am grateful to David Leverenz and Louise Newman for invigorating comments during the weekend. Thanks also to my Portland State University colleagues Corey Olds and Kimberly Springer for helpful feedback and encouragement with this essay.

1. Booker T. Washington, *Up From Slavery: An Autobiography* (New York: Bantam Books, 1977). All future references to this book will be to this edition and cited parenthetically within the text.

2. "Reconsidering *Up From Slavery*" conference poster, 2001.

3. See Ida B. Wells-Barnett, *Crusade for Justice: The Autobiography of Ida B. Wells*, ed. Alfreda M. Duster (Chicago: University of Chicago Press, 1970), especially the chapter "Satin and Orange Blossoms." On *Crusade for Justice*, see Joanne M. Braxton, *Black Women Writing Autobiography: A Tradition within a Tradition* (Philadelphia: Temple University Press, 1989), 102–38; and Patricia A. Schechter, *Ida B. Wells-Barnett and American Reform, 1880–1930* (Chapel Hill: University of North Carolina Press, 2001), chapter 1.

4. Darlene Clark Hine, "Rape and the Inner Lives of Black Women: Preliminary Thoughts on the Culture of Dissemblance," *Signs* 14 (summer 1989): 912–20. See also Evelyn Brooks Higginbotham, "Beyond the Sound of Silence: Afro-American Women in History," *Gender and History* 1 (1989): 50–67.

5. My thinking here is guided primarily by Patricia L. Duncan, "A History of Un/Saying: Silences, Memory, and Historiography in Asian American Women's Narratives" (Ph.D. diss., Emory University, 2000), especially chapter 1.

6. See David Lionel Smith, "Booker T. Washington's Rhetoric: Commanding Performance," *Prospects* 17 (1992): 191–208; Charlotte D. Fitzgerald, "*The Story of My Life and Work:* Booker T. Washington's Other Autobiography," *Black Scholar* 21 (1991): 35–40; William E. Cain, "Forms of Self-Representation in Booker T. Washington's *Up From Slavery*," *Prospects* 12 (1987): 201–22; Frederick McElroy, "Booker T. Washington as Literary Trickster," *Southern Folklore* 2 (1992): 89–107; Donald B. Gibson, "Strategies and Revisions of Self-Representation in Booker T. Washington's Autobiography," *American Quarterly* 45 (September 1993) 370–93; William L. Andrews, "Booker T. Washington, Belle Kearney, and the Southern Patriarchy," in *Home Ground: Southern Autobiography*, ed. J. Bill Berry (Columbia:

University of Missouri Press, 1991), 85–97; James Olney, "The Founding Fathers: Frederick Douglass and Booker T. Washington," in *Slavery and the Literary Imagination*, ed. Deborah E. McDowell and Arnold Rampersad (Baltimore: Johns Hopkins University Press, 1989), 1–23; Raymond Hedin, "Paternal at Last: Booker T. Washington and the Slave Narrative Tradition," *Callaloo: A Journal of African-American and African Arts and Letters* 2 (October 1979): 95–102; Roger J. Bresnahan, "The Implied Readers of Booker T. Washington's Autobiographies," *Black American Literature Forum* 14 (1980): 15–20; Jane Gottschalk, "The Rhetorical Strategy of Booker T. Washington," *Phylon* 27 (1966), 388–95; and Donald B. Gibson, "Chapter One of Booker T. Washington's *Up From Slavery* and the Feminization of the African American Male," in *Representing Black Men*, ed. Marcellus Blount and George P. Cunningham (New York: Routledge, 1996), 95–110.

7. The only scholar to mention Washington's refutation of racist slander/libel of black women is Houston A. Baker Jr., *Turning South Again: Re-thinking Modernism/Re-reading Booker T.* (Durham: Duke University Press, 2001), 41. The following authors expertly analyze the politics of gender in *Up From Slavery* and in Washington's educational and political work: Kevin K. Gaines, *Uplifting the Race: Black Leadership, Politics, and Culture in the Twentieth Century* (Chapel Hill: University of North Carolina Press, 1996), 30–44; and Claudia Tate, *Domestic Allegories of Political Desire: The Black Heroine's Text at the Turn of the Century* (New York: Oxford University Press, 1992), 128–34. See also Louis R. Harlan, *Booker T. Washington: The Making of a Black Leader, 1856–1901* (New York: Oxford University Press, 1972) (hereinafter cited as Harlan, *BTW*, vol. 1), chapters 1–3 and chapter 9.

8. See Gibson, "Chapter One," 103: "The slave [presumed male] is represented in Washington's text as one whose sexual desire is nonexistent, suppressed by racial mythology. He has no sexuality, not even in relation to black women, for that would allow the potential of sexual threat to white women. He is at one stroke both feminized and neutered." Gibson does not square this statement with Washington's marriages and paternity.

9. Olney, "Founding Fathers," 21–23.

10. See especially Harvey G. Hudspeth, "Up from Disrepute: The Historiographical Accommodation of Booker T. Washington, 1901–1991," in *Booker T. Washington: Interpretive Essays*, ed. Tunde Adeleke (Lewiston, N.Y.: E. Mellen Press, 1998), 153–73. Hudspeth argues that "notwithstanding occasional lay attempts to portray Booker Washington as a proto-typical 'Uncle Tom,' objective historians have always seemingly followed their own brand of accommodation to credit Washington for doing what little he could do within the context of his unfortunate time" (154). Another good example of scholarly criticism—of calling Booker T. Washington a liar—can be found in Smith, "Commanding Performance": "In other words, [Washington] was willing to perform in any way necessary to get what he wanted.... Again and again he reveals himself as a man who can and will perform any verbal or physical gesture to achieve his goals" (193). "Washington ... spoke 'without bitterness'—that is dishonestly" (195).

11. David Levering Lewis, *W. E. B. Du Bois: Biography of a Race, 1868–1919* (New York: H. Holt, 1993), 397. See also William S. McFeely, *Frederick Douglass: A Biography* (New York: Norton, 1991), 185.

12. A good example of this last dynamic is found in Hedin, "Paternal at Last": "The Washington who appears in *Up From Slavery* is the public father of an extended family rather than the man of private thought; and his wives are primarily mothers to that family rather than Washington's private companions" (97–98). Hedin is flustered by Washington's characterization and labels it simply deceptive, rather than seeing it as quite consistent with those produced by African American leaders, male and female, at the time in the service of the agenda of racial uplift.

13. Harlan, *BTW*, 1:100, 152. On Douglass's ancestry, see Frederick Douglass, *Narrative of the Life of Frederick Douglass*, in *The Classic Slave Narratives*, ed. Henry Louis Gates Jr. (New York: New American Library, 1987), 255–56; and McFeely, *Frederick Douglass*, 6–7; 330–32. On Wells-Barnett's ancestry, see her autobiography, *Crusade for Justice: The Life of Ida B. Wells* (Chicago: University of Chicago Press, 1970), 4–9; and Schechter, *Ida B. Wells-Barnett*, 24–25.

14. The Civil Rights Act of 1964, specifically Title VII, included the word *sex* in its antidiscrimination provision. Though its inclusion was a cynical move by Democrats to derail the legislation in Congress, its existence was understood by advocates like Pauli Murray to be critical for the inclusion of black women under its protections.

15. Patricia Hill Collins, *Black Feminist Thought: Knowledge, Consciousness, and the Politics of Empowerment* (2d ed., New York: Routledge, 2000), 69–96. See also Beverly Guy-Sheftall, *Daughters of Sorrow: Attitudes toward Black Women, 1880–1920* (Brooklyn: Carlson, 1990); and Patricia Morton, *Disfigured Images: The Historical Assault on Afro-American Women* (New York: Greenwood Press, 1991).

16. Andrews, "Booker T. Washington," 89–91, 87. See also *Six Women's Slave Narratives*, ed. William L. Andrews (New York: Oxford University Press, 1988) (further citations to the women's narratives are to this edition).

17. For a founding text in combating this kind of move, see *All the Women Are White, All the Blacks Are Men, But Some of Us Are Brave: Black Women's Studies*, ed. Gloria Hull, Patricia Bell Scott, and Barbara Smith (Old Westbury, N.Y.: Feminist Press, 1982). Andrews commits precisely the errors that I spend most of my time teaching students about: free white married women under coverture were neither "slaves" nor "chattel" in the way that enslaved black women were; there is no such thing as "the patriarchy" with a unified point of view or politics; and references to "blacks and women" is a totally inadequate framework for dealing with the complexities of U.S. history.

18. Jacqueline Anne Rouse, "Out of the Shadow of Tuskegee: Margaret Murray Washington, Social Activism, and Race Vindication," *Journal of Negro History* 81 (1996): 31–46. Adele Logan Alexander, "School Days, School Days: Discovering My Grandmother, Adella Hunt Logan," *Journal of the Afro-American Historical and Genealogical Society* 9 (1985): 65–73; Carolyn A. Dorsey, "Despite Poor Health:

Olivia Davidson Washington's Story," *Sage* 2 (fall 1985): 69–72. See also Dorsey's entry, "Olivia America Davidson," in *Black Women in America: An Historical Encyclopedia*, ed. Darlene Clark Hine (Brooklyn: Carlson, 1993), 2:302–4.

19. Harlan, *BTW*, 1:155.

20. Ibid., 146.

21. On conservative gender ideology among northern free black communities, see James Oliver Horton, "Freedom's Yoke: Gender Conventions among Antebellum Free Blacks" *Feminist Studies* 12 (September 1986): 51–76. See also Barbara Welter, "The Cult of Domesticity," *American Quarterly* 18 (summer 1966): 151–74.

22. Delores S. Williams, *Sisters in the Wilderness: The Challenge of Womanist God-Talk* (Maryknoll, N.Y.: Orbis Books, 1993), 159–69. See also Schechter, *Ida B. Wells-Barnett*, 248.

23. Harlan, *BTW*, 1:152.

24. Andrews, introduction to *Six Women's Slave Narratives*, xxix–xxxi; Braxton, *Black Women Writing Autobiography*, 15–79. See also Frances Smith Foster, *Written by Herself: Literary Production by African American Women, 1746–1892* (Bloomington: Indiana University Press, 1993).

25. Roi Ottley, *The Lonely Warrior: The Life and Times of Robert S. Abbott* (Chicago: H. Regnery, 1955), 25–27, 297; Reverdy C. Ransom, *The Pilgrimage of Harriet Ransom's Son* (Nashville: Sunday School Union, 1949), 40–42.

26. Washington's discussion of his mother's passing in *The Story of My Life and Work* (1900), a text understood to have been written and marketed for an African American audience, is little—though perhaps significantly—embellished from that in *Up From Slavery*. Washington notes the "indescribable pain" incurred by his being absent in her dying hour. He also states, with rather more flair than he does in *Up From Slavery*, that "the lessons of truth, honor and thrift which she implanted in me while she lived have remained with me, and I consider them among my most precious possessions." Booker T. Washington, *The Story of My Life and Work* (1900; reprint, New York: Negro Universities Press, 1969), 62.

27. I agree with the otherwise sensitive reading of Frederick McElroy, that in *Up From Slavery*, Washington "for the most part . . . conceals the cultural traditions [namely, mother wit] developed by the slaves and their descendants to help them survive desolation and to affirm their worth as human beings" (*Washington as Literary Trickster*, 93). Yet I cannot help but think that this interpretation minimizes the importance of Jane Ferguson and her teachings in Washington's life. Similarly, Houston Baker may go a bit far in claiming that in *Up From Slavery* "the 'real' black mother is displaced by the bodies and morality of Mrs. Ruffner and Miss Mary Mackie" (*Turning South Again*, 51). In the main, I am sympathetic with McElroy's interpretation of Washington as "the obsequiously aggressive slave and consummate trickster" (104) and his conclusion that when "we probe beneath the surface of *UFS*, we find a residue of bitterness, a determined desire to outdo antagonists, which contradicts the professions of benevolence" (100). This desire, however, had an oppressive manifestation, as Baker points out: "In contrast to education that produces

excess, luxury, urbanity, book learning, and the accessorized body, Washington urges a clean, thrifty, rural, industrial, plain style—a *domesticated immobility*—as the regimen for the black body of the 'country districts.' . . . What this amounts to, of course, is a zealous aestheticization of slavery as 'modernity'" (emphasis in original, 60). Kevin Gaines similarly holds Washington accountable for the way he "exploited and legitimized the racial fears of his time" (*Uplifting the Race*, 40). See also James D. Anderson, *The Education of Blacks in the South, 1865–1925* (Chapel Hill: University of North Carolina Press, 1988).

28. Fitz Brundage and Orlando Patterson pressed this question upon me.

29. bell hooks, *Talking Back: Thinking Black, Thinking Feminist* (Boston: South End Press, 1989); Duncan, "A History of Un/Saying."

30. See Deborah Gray White, *Too Heavy a Load: Black Women in Defense of Themselves, 1894–1994* (New York: Norton, 1999), especially chapters 1–3.

31. I am reminded here of Claudia Tate's reading of *Up From Slavery*, in which she identifies "feminized" political rhetoric—laboring hands rather than voting citizens, for example—as a safer vehicle for Washington's message to whites. See Tate, *Domestic Allegories*, 128–30. It is also important to acknowledge critiques of the concept of "positive stereotypes" that can be confining and even oppressive. On racial identity formation in the twentieth century, see Beverly Daniel Tatum, *"Why Are All the Black Kids Sitting Together in the Cafeteria?" And Other Conversations about Race* (New York: Basic Books, 1999).

32. Virginia Lantz Denton, *Booker T. Washington and the Adult Education Movement* (Gainesville: University Press of Florida, 1993).

33. Harlan, *BTW*, 1:140.

34. Anna Julia Cooper, *A Voice from the South: By a Black Woman from the South*, ed. Mary Helen Washington (New York: Oxford University Press, 1988), 29–33; 55–56.

35. Harlan, *Booker T. Washington: The Wizard of Tuskegee, 1901–1915* (New York: Oxford University Press, 1983), 404.

8

Booker T. Washington's Strategies of Manliness, for Black and White Audiences

DAVID LEVERENZ

Patricia Schechter has argued that modern critics have invented Booker T. Washington's alleged silences about women. On the contrary, she declares, Washington counters stereotypes of black women as Jezebels by presenting his mother and his wives with dignity, decorum, and reticence, as befits his conservative southern manhood.[1] But a comparison of *Up From Slavery* (1901) with the first version of *The Story of My Life and Work* (1900), his earlier autobiography, written for black readers, suggests that Professor Schechter is wrong in one respect: there are indeed silences about women in both texts. More intriguingly, these silences differ. The differences confirm her larger argument that Washington presents his women tactically, in part to counter reigning white stereotypes, and in part to exemplify how a respectable man should talk about the women he has respected, honored, and loved.

Louis Harlan has disparaged *The Story of My Life and Work* as a "thoroughly bad book" produced by a "lazy and incompetent" young black journalist, Eugene Webber, whom Washington quickly fired. True enough; the narrative eventually disintegrates into a laundry list of speeches given and gifts received. Nonetheless, many of the passages in *Story* are very similar to their counterparts in *Up From Slavery*, written with the assistance of a white Vermonter, Max Thrasher.[2] Given the frequent paragraph-after-paragraph parallels, the differences in Washington's presentation both of his wives and mother at home and of his own body on the lecture platform become culturally significant.

Always a canny tactician, Washington pitches his portraits of women and other kinfolk to reflect his audiences' values. In presenting his body, he takes greater risks, especially with white audiences. *Story* stresses the dignity that black bodies can gain through manual labor. *Up From Slavery* gives more specific prominence to the phrase "keep under the body" and highlights his physical mastery of his audience, most notably in the Atlanta Exposition address.[3] Curiously, Washington does not emphasize such pleasures of control when writing to black readers.

Throughout these passages, Washington uses manliness for strategic theatricality, at the cost of considerable self-suppression.[4] He displays subtly different kinds of manliness not to affirm or alter his identity, as current theories of gendered performativity might suggest, but to be an example of self-uplift for his black and white audiences. For black readers, he presents himself as a father figure and race leader, civilizing the young, furthering racial uplift, and bragging about getting white handouts as well as white approval. For northern white readers, he presents himself as a C.E.O. of a subsidiary enterprise and a leading member of the professional-managerial class. For elite southern white readers, he appropriates characteristics of patrician honor in describing his public speaking to northern audiences. Finally, and most strangely to me, he features a white war correspondent's celebration of his body's multicolored mastery at his climactic moment of risk and success, the Atlanta Exposition address.

Washington's Manliness

For most people who know about Booker T. Washington, the *T.* subliminally stands for "Tom." In chapter 3 of *The Souls of Black Folk* (1903), W.E.B. Du Bois called him no kind of man in seven different ways, and the charge has stuck. Booker T. Washington is the wizard of accommodation, not the champion of resistance. It would be hard even to imagine a modern African American saying of him what Ossie Davis famously said of Malcolm X at his funeral: "Malcolm was our manhood, our living, black manhood!"[5]

Such charges of unmanliness presume two questionable dichotomies: between authenticity and performance, and between rebelliousness and accommodation. As several other essays in this volume emphasize, charges of unmanliness also minimize Washington's talent for race leadership in conditions of terror.⁶ In recent years, critics have begun to move toward the position Du Bois took near the end of his life, that Washington did the best that could be done for southern African Americans under extremely oppressive conditions.

Why is it, then, that while many other contemporary African American men exemplified dignity and moderation as race leaders, Booker T. Washington has been singled out for charges of unmanliness? The conflict between Washington's enormous personal power and his advocacy of temporary racial subordination invites charges that he hypocritically perpetuated a regional quasi-slave culture for his own national advancement. Yet the ad hominem attacks also respond to his crafty and crafted personas. From Houston Baker Jr. to Carla Willard, the best scholars of Washington have highlighted his uses of rhetoric to further his interests as well as to advance African Americans toward the then-impossible ideal of full middle-class citizenship.⁷

Many American readers, then and now, feel uncomfortable with manliness displayed as a deliberate performance, a means rather than an end. It seems "feminized," a gendered charge that still packs a manly wallop. In *Turning South Again*, for instance, Houston A. Baker Jr. calls Washington's life a servile, abject, feminized "masquerade" that represented his *"personal triumph in white drag."*⁸ To Baker and many other readers, Washington seems hidden and inauthentic, a Tom, an Oreo, all power on the outside, all imitative on the inside. By implication, manliness requires a strong oppositional self, not just success in managing the art of the possible with dignified self-control.

In chapter 3 of *The Souls of Black Folk*, for instance, W.E.B. Du Bois relentlessly accuses Booker T. Washington of being unmanly. Washington's "emasculating" effect helped to build a submissive "servile caste." Du Bois sees very clearly Washington's allegiance with the capitalist dynamics of "the rich and dominating North." The president of Tuskegee Institute "grasped the spirit of the age . . . the speech and thought of triumphant commercialism."⁹ In soliciting the money of northern whites, Washington sold out southern blacks—so runs the now familiar charge.

Du Bois's charge signals a clash in cultural constructions of manliness.¹⁰ Speaking from the privileged background that would eventually lead him to call for a "Talented Tenth," as if the other nine-tenths had no talents, Du Bois invoked his New England tradition of rights, freedom, and cultural entitlement to constitute an oppositional black elite. Washington, who rose from enslaved peasant beginnings, saw that national power was shifting to industrialists while southern power was shifting back to racist whites. He gained power and cultural authority by accepting black segregation and service roles as the most that whites would tolerate. With rigorous self-control, he presented the products of Tuskegee Institute as candidates for rural and working-class employment, and himself as a candidate for incorporative white uplift, or the crossover status that comes from white philanthropists' perception that he was "doing *our* work" (*Up From Slavery*, 185). For privileged black leaders, the manliness associated with resistance, confrontation, and assertions of independent social standing might have seemed viable. Yet Du Bois's charge avoids any awareness of the reciprocal mutuality crucial to survival for upwardly mobile black men like Washington. Implicitly, the charge signals the much greater price that ambitious lower-class black men had to pay for their racial as well as class crossovers.[11]

Psychological critiques of Washington tend to foreground his repressive self-control, his drive for upward mobility, and his need to assimilate to white norms. Certainly he took emulative pleasure in his patriarchal domination of his "plantation" at Tuskegee, as Louis Harlan emphasizes.[12] Yet Washington's tightropes were more social than psychological. His success required the enthusiastic assent of at least five conflicting audiences: white southern leaders, northern philanthropists, a black national elite, uneducated white southerners, and uneducated black southerners who were scrabbling for a toehold in a hostile environment. Only the black elite eventually dissented from Washington's public minimization of African American claims for full civic rights, and even Du Bois changed his mind about Washington several times.[13]

The nearly ubiquitous assumption that black manhood has to mean protest also blocks an appreciation of how Washington performed at least four kinds of southern and national manhood, in black and white. First, walking a tightrope over terror, he exemplified middle-class black male dignity and self-control, mixing assertiveness with civility, without craven submission, and without lower-class styles of flashiness, disrespect, and rebelliousness. In keeping with that conservative model of manhood, he presents the women in his life as illustrations of his quasi-patriarchal ability to revere and protect them.[14]

Second, maneuvering between subservience and independence at a time of intensified racist stigmatization, he affirms the dignity of freely laboring black bodies as an indispensable aspect of southern community. *The Story of My Life and Work* narrates his effort to reorient mostly rural ex-slaves from thinking about rights and civic status to dignifying their bodies through physical work. More audaciously, *Up From Slavery* presents white readers with the spectacle of his own body as a site of mastery, in private and public modes.

Third, incorporating two quite different ideals of manhood, Washington manages to perform the managerial agency that northern capitalists respected, while also exemplifying the southern ideal of honor, which requires competitive public display and gift giving to gain mutual obligation and peer respect among the white elite. His gift is racial uplift through social segregation and industrial training. For him, the gift of temporary accommodation is not an end but a necessary means, the first step on the long road toward achieving his ultimate goal of mutual racial obligations.[15] For himself at least, Washington was also able to minimize the obverse of honor, the collective shaming imposed by white people on black skin.

As Chief Justice Roger B. Taney wrote in the 1857 Dred Scott decision, African Americans did not deserve full citizenship because their blackness had "stigmatized" them with "deep and enduring marks of inferiority and degradation."[16] In the postbellum South, as ex-slaves threatened to unsettle white expectations of domination, many white people intensified shaming pressures, reducing black womanhood to the category of "loose women" and more stringently enforcing the humiliation of black men through terrorizing tactics such as lynchings. For Washington to be received and perceived as a gentleman, on nearly equal terms with whites, was a dangerous kind of heroism for a black man in the late nineteenth century.

Honor and manhood were not loner virtues in the white South. Across classes and races, manhood meant men's ability not only to be independent, but also to protect the reputation of the women in their lives. At the upper end of the social scale, male performances of honor maintained elite community and elite white male leadership, while presuming deference from those lower on the social scale.[17] Washington's educational goal of training rural black people in "civilized" manners and work habits reflects his realistic understanding that in white eyes, ex-slaves were starting in a condition of imposed collective shame, without any white respect, and therefore without the grounds for manhood or womanhood, and with honor as only a utopian possibility. As Washington knew very well, most white people wanted to keep it that way.

Current theories of performativity often presuppose a social condition of relative privilege, in which community respect and gendered ideological bonding can be presumed and played with. Judith Butler's field-shifting *Gender Trouble* has stimulated a great many studies emphasizing that men and women perform normative gender roles with varying mixtures of imitation and transgression.[18] These studies sometimes reduce the positive side of what Butler calls "performativity" to self-discovery through self-reflexiveness. From the turn of the last century to 2002, such self-reflexiveness has been a white middle-class luxury, a privileged and private version of the tensions between accommodation and resistance that have shaped all African American lives.

While postbellum black southerners were expert at covertly parodic subversions, they lacked any cultural entitlement, at least in white eyes. To gain full rights as citizens, they needed to establish minimal social standing along traditionally gendered lines. Such standing depended on securing a grudging respect from their white neighbors. For Washington, prejudice "is something to be lived down, not talked down" (*Story of My Life and Work*, 275). As he frequently repeated, before "political agitation" could have any effect, Negro men "must have industry, thrift, intelligence and property; . . . no race without these elements of strength could . . . gain the respect of its fellow citizens" (*Story*, 154, also 233–34, 317–21). That dream of manly independence is also a dream of interdependence. It will come through "the dignity, beauty, and civilizing power of intelligent labor" (*Story*, 82).

To place Washington in an individualistic Yankee tradition of upward mobility and self-reliance restricts his work ethic to his own ambition. It misses his southern strategy for making uneducated African Americans useful to people predisposed to be racist. How to teach independence and interdependence without impudence? His answer was to teach hard work, cleanliness, and property ownership as the lower-middle-class tickets to manhood and womanhood, which need social respect to convey a full measure of self-respect. As their conductor on that train, Washington reached still higher for the honor conferred on him by white leaders in the next car.

Washington's Women

Patricia Schechter has argued that modern critics, not Washington, have silenced the women in his life story. Displaying a "conservative, not compromised" valuing of women, *Up From Slavery* places Olivia Davidson "at the emotional center of Washington's adult married life," much as his mother was during his childhood. The "terse details" about women simply indicate that Washington treats them with respect. Like a proper conservative gentleman, he does not bring the ladies into the public sphere. It is only the white critics who either erase these women, or, worse, make those imagined silences into sites of resexualized fascination.

To qualify and amplify this argument, a comparison between Washington's two autobiographies shows that there are indeed some silences about women, and that these silences are strategic. We can begin with his mother's name. The first volume of Louis Harlan's biography notes that her full name was Jane Ferguson, probably because she was married to "Washington, a slave of Josiah Ferguson," and therefore took the name of her husband's owner. A Ferguson may well have been Booker's father, among several other white suspects. But Booker did not know that Ferguson had become his last name, and even Harlan minimizes it.[19]

More certainly, neither *Story* nor *Up From Slavery* mentions his mother's last name, and *Up From Slavery* does not mention her name at all. Whereas *Story* starts with an individualized picture of the woman he calls "Jane," *Up From Slavery* introduces her anonymously as a generic victim of slavery, who supported her son as any mother would, in the midst of oppressive circumstances. If that silences her individuality, it may be for two contrary reasons. First, Washington knows that to white people, all black women look alike. And second, he introduces her that way to make white readers feel a little heat about what slavery did to black women.

Story begins with female kinfolk. As the first paragraph announces, Washington is writing this book because his daughter, Portia, asked him to. In the second paragraph, he immediately turns to his mother. "The name of my mother was Jane. She, to me, will always remain the noblest embodiment of womanhood with whom I have come in contact." Right at the start, he mentions that she mysteriously provided food "many times"—usually "eggs and chickens" (30). Some "code of ethics" might call it "stealing," he says, "but deep down in my heart I can never decide that my mother, under such circumstances, was guilty of theft. Had she acted thus as a free woman she would have been a thief, but not so, in my opinion, as a slave" (32).

In sharp contrast, *Up From Slavery* begins without Portia or his mother.[20] Instead, Washington starts in the Frederick Douglass tradition, by recounting his birth and lack of ancestry, in a rather impersonal voice. Then he introduces his mother through white perceptions of her as a commodity, an animal, equivalent to "the purchase of a new horse or cow" (3). He never gives her a name. Instead, he always calls her "my mother," usually in connection with her domestic tasks. He reduces what *Story* calls the "many" instances of her mysterious providing to one example, cooking a chicken. Now, he says, "I should condemn it as theft myself." Then, however, "She was simply a victim of the system of slavery" (5). While he sneakily reduces her transgressions from many to one, he shifts the rhetorical frame from a complex, rather ambivalent rumination on individual ethics to a firm, succinct indictment of slavery as a system. While *Story* honors his mother, *Up From Slavery* uses his mother as a type, to gain white readers' sympathy for her as a struggling, resourceful "victim." Perhaps, as he does in his 1895 Atlanta Exposition address, he also indulges in a little stereotypical humor about chicken stealing, to gain white readers' indulgence.

These are little, yet not so little differences. Other examples make the differences more complicated and strange. For a black audience, Washington recounts that "just after the close of the war," his family went to the "'big house'" to hear some speeches. Afterwards "my mother leaned over and whispered, 'Now, my children, we are free'" (*Story*, 37–38). For a white audience, Washington says his mother took them to the "'big house'" to hear "the Emancipation Proclamation, I think." "My mother, who was standing by my side, leaned over and kissed her children, while tears of joy ran down her cheeks" (*Up From Slavery*, 20–21).[21] The *Story* version presents her as more emphatic and matter-of-fact, while *Up From Slavery* presents her as more emotional, fulfilling white conventions of sentimental mothering. The differences might also signal an homage to Lincoln for white people, contrasted with black people's more realistic awareness that southern slaves were not emancipated until the end of the war.

In a similarly sentimental mode, several passages in *Up From Slavery* emphasize his mother's unstinting support for his "ambition" as well as her moral and practical nurture. Chapter 2 emphasizes that support at considerable length (28–34). Only once, when he chooses to leave for Hampton Institute, does she balk a little, and Washington frames her sympathy with several ambiguous negatives. "I do not think that anyone thoroughly sympathized with me in my ambition to go to Hampton unless it was my mother, and she was troubled with a grave fear that I was starting out on a 'wild-goose chase.' At any rate, I got only a half-hearted consent from her" (45).

Curiously, the much shorter discussion of his ambition in chapter 2 of *Story* gives his mother only one sentence: "in some way, my mother secured a book for me, and although she could not read herself, she tried in every way possible to help me to do so" (43). Washington also restricts his account of his ambition to the desire to get an education, and he says nothing about his mother's reaction to young Booker's departure. Chapter 3 begins simply, "After my mother and brother John had secured me a few extra garments, ... I started for Hampton" (55). Does that silence her emotion, or emphasize her practicality? Or does Washington think succinct images of practical mothering would appeal to black readers, while amplified images of sentimental mothering would appeal to whites?

Even in describing his reaction to her death, *Up From Slavery* raises the emotional pitch. In *Story*, he announces straightaway that "Soon after my return to Malden my mother, who was never strong, died." His emotion has to do with his absence: "It has always been a source of indescribable pain to me that I was not present when she passed away" (61–62). In *Up From Slavery*, though he mentions long before that his mother "was rather weak and broken in health" (46), he dramatizes her death as a great shock. It "seemed to me the saddest and blankest moment in my life" (70). It is more arresting, but also stranger. Whereas the rest of the paragraph in *Story* focuses on her nurturing support for her son's educational goals, the rest of the paragraph in *Up From Slavery* focuses on himself. A great wash of powerlessness comes over him, as he thinks about not having been able to fulfill two contradictory desires: his "intense desire to be with her when she did pass away," and his desire to succeed enough to "make my mother comfortable and happy" (70).

What about Olivia? Both texts emphasize her indispensable contributions. Again, *Up From Slavery* is more emotional, and *Story* is more practical. In *Up From Slavery*, Olivia first appears as "a new and rare face . . . a co-teacher. This was Olivia A. Davidson, who later became my wife." He notes that "since she was so very light in colour," she could have passed, but chose not to. He really likes the word *rare:* she had "a rare moral character and a life of unselfishness that I think has seldom been equalled." As he sums it up, "No single individual did more toward laying the foundations of the Tuskegee Institute . . . than Olivia A. Davidson" (124–26). Most significantly, the next few paragraphs abound with "we." Only after seven paragraphs, in which "we" or "our" or "us" appear twenty-nine times, does Washington return to his usual first-person mode. Just remembering Olivia has given him a natural high.

In contrast, *Story* introduces Olivia without saying they later married (85). He mentions their marriage only after she dies, and praises her then mostly by reprinting a lengthy obituary written by a local minister (128–32), deleted from *Up From Slavery*. The earlier text says nothing about her ability to pass. It has a similarly strong though more qualified assessment of her importance: "The success of the school, especially during the first half dozen years of its existence, was due more to Miss Davidson than any one else" (85). He immediately turns to how Tuskegee grew in its enrollment and finances. There is no hint of "rare"; it is one professional praising another. Earlier, after he introduces her, "we" and "our" appear only four times, in half a paragraph, before "I" takes over again (86).

What do those differences mean? The silencing of Olivia's potential for passing stimulates several speculations. Perhaps Washington presents her to white people as almost one of their kind. Or perhaps he flaunts his possession of a woman who could have been mistaken for white. For a black audience, mentioning her light color might have tainted his image or manhood, or raised questions about his racial loyalty. Silencing it might have been his way of protecting her as well as himself from readers' grumblings.

But why the near-silencing of their intimacy? *Up From Slavery* displays his obvious, abiding love for her. *Story* does not allow that kind of response. Why not? I can only guess that in Washington's mind at least, a black audience wants a real man to be patriarchally controlling, firm, and resolute.[22] His emotional dependence on his wife should stay really private. At least in his imagination, more relaxed white middle-class expectations about manly yet companionable marriage invite a more expansive celebration of marital affection as well as respect. Different codes of manly honor frame his differing presentations of Olivia to white and black readers.[23]

Washington's briefer descriptions of his two other wives have far fewer points of contrast. In *Up From Slavery* he omits the four-paragraph obituary for Fannie Smith that appears in *Story* (89–90), and he introduces his third wife as "Margaret" (267) instead of the more informal "Maggie" in *Story* (139–40). In the earlier autobiography, Fannie was "completely one with me" (89), a phrase given to both Fannie and Margaret in *Up From Slavery* (147, 267). More tellingly, when Washington describes his stay with Viola Ruffner in *Up From Slavery*, he silences what he reveals in *Story*, that "I grew weary of her exact manner of having things done, and, without giving her any notice, I ran away and hired myself to a steamboat captain" (49), as if he too could be Mark Twain. Reluctantly, he came back. For black readers, he lets his youthful edginess about accommodation show a little.

As Frederick Douglass does in his revisions of his *Narrative* for *My Bondage and My Freedom*, Washington in *Story* gives much more attention to his kinship network—his brothers and sister as well as his wives and mother. Both *Story* and *Up From Slavery* present Washington's admiration for the women in his life as one aspect of how he performs personal dignity in a culture that made black skin a site for impersonal shaming. The textual differences reflect cultural differences, or at least Washington's assessment of each audience's code for how a respectable man should honor the women in his family. If Washington chooses to be more sentimental or emotional when he presents himself to white readers, and more matter-of-fact or practical when he writes for black readers, these choices bring different silences about women. For us, the differences make the silences speak. As strategic erasures, they have more to do with satisfying his conflicting audiences' expectations about honor, manhood, and womanhood than with fulfilling private obsessions.

160   David Leverenz

Washington's Body

To most postbellum southern white men, the free and masterless black male body was a daily reminder of the South's humiliation in the Civil War. General Sherman's march through Georgia and the Carolinas showed that white men had not even been able to protect their property and the women of their households. Every lynching of a black man for allegedly raping a white woman was a way of restoring precariously idealized chivalry, as if to say, "We might not have protected our ladies against the Yankees, but we sure can protect them against these black boys." As Orlando Patterson has suggested, the ubiquitous white charges of rape may also have been a way of denying manhood to young or prosperous black males. By charging that male ex-slaves desired white women's bodies, white men deflected and denied their challenge to white male dominance. "[T]he single most important reason for lynching was murder and assault by Afro-Americans against Euro-American men" to defend their manhood.[24]

Washington was not interested in what Patterson has recently called "macho suicide."[25] Instead of directly confronting the terrorizing practices that preserved white power and privilege, Washington performed a manliness based on self-control and mastery. Adopting the long African American tradition of chiasmus, or crossing and reversal, he turned the general shame and powerlessness imposed on black male bodies into personal honor and power. His example also enacted the equally long strain of African American manliness that emphasizes quiet dignity rather than hotheaded rebelliousness.[26]

At the most obvious level, Washington displays his access to white ideals of paternalistic power and honor through chiasmus in paying homage to his mentor and father figure.[27] He introduces General Samuel C. Armstrong, the head of Hampton Institute, as "a perfect man." That phrase alludes to the contemporary white middle-class fascination with bodybuilding, personified in Eugen Sandow, widely called "the perfect man." John Kasson's recent book on Houdini, Tarzan, and Sandow illuminates the sometimes bizarre theatricality and the male desires for metamorphosis underlying this cultural obsession.[28] Within sentences, however, Washington presents Armstrong as a cripple under his care. "General Armstrong spent two of the last six months of his life in my home at Tuskegee. At that time he was paralyzed to the extent that he had lost control of his body and voice . . . so badly paralyzed that he had to be wheeled about in an invalid's chair" (55–56). Washington turns his worship of his patron into his own benevolent care, while highlighting Armstrong's loss of bodily control.

A more subtle use of chiasmus occurs midway through *Up From Slavery*, when Washington reveals his two "rules" for "the science of what is called begging" (180). The first rule is "always to do my whole duty" to make his work "known"; the second rule is "not to worry about the results." Then, elaborating on the danger of worrying, he declares that he has succeeded by imitating "wealthy and noted men." "I have observed that those who have accomplished the greatest results are those who 'keep under the body'; are those who never grow excited or lose self-control, but are always calm, self-possessed, patient, and polite." President McKinley, he says, "is the best example of a man of this class that I have ever seen" (181).

At one level this passage flagrantly curries favor with the current president, the biggest man in the nation, who has just done him the honor of visiting Tuskegee (303–10). At another level, Washington lays claim to being "a man of this class" himself. More interestingly and problematically, the phrase "keep under the body" evokes a multitude of conflicting meanings.[29]

The phrase comes from St. Paul's first address to the Corinthians: "But I keep under my body, and bring it into subjection: lest that by any means, when I have preached to others, I myself should be a castaway" (9:27). St. Paul's context implies the restraint of sexual desires. As he says earlier, "It is good for a man not to touch a woman" (7:1), and, more infamously, "it is better to marry than to burn" (7:9). Strangely, as Washington uses it, the phrase seems on the verge of losing its own self-control, since it suggests exactly the opposite of what he says it means. "Keep under the body" might well command us to put the body above, as master. The phrase also hints at a homoerotic or conventionally feminine sexual position. By implying that it means the reverse, "keep the body under," which he translates as "never grow excited or lose self-control," Washington both affirms and denies a tension between body, subjectivity, and self-control. One has to know the biblical context to subdue these conflicting interpretations.

Since the context is Washington's northern fund-raising, "worry" and "excited" are probably euphemisms for shame and anger. To illustrate his self-control, he tells the story of two Boston gentlemen on whom he called. One became "abrupt," "ungentlemanly," and grew "so excited" that Washington had to leave his house. The other man wrote Washington a check, saying, "We in Boston are constantly indebted to you for doing *our* work." The second white man's paternalistic praise transforms Washington from supplicant to a field manager for a national corporate enterprise. As Washington rephrases it, "rich people" are coming to regard fund-raisers like himself "not as beggars, but as agents for doing their work" (*Up From Slavery,* 185). Wary of seeming too proud, he lets the white man speak the reversal of his status: These benevolent capitalists are "indebted" to him. They defer to his deference, while incorporating his leadership skills into their national agenda. Conversely, in a more subtle chiasmus, the "ungentlemanly" white man who throws him out of the house is shameful as well as shaming. It is only his loss of self-control that makes Washington feel like a beggar—or something that sounds like beggar.

The Story of My Life and Work does not tell that story. Instead of dramatizing his potential shaming as a seeker of northern funding, Washington details his successes as a speaker and fund-raiser, complete with speeches, facts, and figures. At one point he does mention "a rich gentleman in New York, who did not even ask me to take a seat, but in a gruff and cold manner handed me two dollars, as if to say, I give you this to get rid of you." Subsequently this man has given gifts of "as much as ten thousand dollars in cash" (398). For black readers, Washington presents himself as an exemplary success among rich white northerners, able to convert their initial disdain into large cash gifts and attentive audiences. When he does mention begging, it refers not to himself but to northern ministers who had cut him dead. Now they send letters "begging that I would deliver lectures in their churches, and naming large sums of money as compensation" (398). A little earlier, he quotes a New York Rector who said, "We allowed General Armstrong to go around begging, begging from door to door, ... until it killed him. It is our duty to save Mr. Washington from an untimely death" (375). Here the implications of unmanly supplication and dependence apply to a white man, not himself, and the white minister declares the "duty" of contemporary whites to raise Washington above his mentor's fate.

For white readers, Washington celebrates how he transforms his begging into mastery of rich white men, who give him man-to-man respect as well as money to serve their philanthropic desires. With a keen sense that white men ascribe shamefulness to male dependence and servitude, Washington gains power by transforming his black begging body into an outsourced version of white managerial agency. He has learned the knack of making northern capitalists feel dutiful and indebted to him for furthering "uplift," that enduring redundancy. For black readers, he restricts his accounts of fund-raising to the dollars received, while emphasizing his years of unstinting, often fruitless labor. Walking that tightrope shows his ability to embody emerging northern ideals of corporate management, while also embodying residual southern ideals of rural hard work.

In either region, to keep his cool among white people means to keep under a body branded as alien and inferior, by playing roles that mirror his conflicting audiences' perceptions of their ideal selves. This unstable fusion of submissiveness and mastery shapes the whole of the autobiography he wrote for white people. In *The Story of My Life and Work*, however, Washington presents his achievements with more generalized pride. In a way, he is showing off to the folks back home, sure of their approval and eager to rouse their own pride in a representative black man's accomplishments. His stories about fund-raising and public speaking do not try to teach white readers the difference between bad racism and good paternalism. Instead they teach a simpler lesson: you can do it, too.

Earlier in *Up From Slavery*, Washington recalls some "fatherly" advice from a white friend of General Armstrong: "Washington, always remember that credit is capital" (146). As Washington became the dominant African American of his time by assiduously securing his credit with wealthy whites, he learned that his credit depended on their trust that he could recirculate their surplus wealth for social profit. To gain that credit, he learned to imitate corporate managerial skills by keeping black bodies "under," from his emphasis on "the influence of the toothbrush" as one of the most important "agencies of civilization" (75) to his development of a useful and tractable labor pool. In both texts, Washington speaks about the necessary subordination of black bodily labor with a ruthless clarity, though the ambiguity in his accommodation becomes apparent to white readers only when he discusses Indian bodies, not black ones. As a young teacher, he made his Native American charges cut their long hair, give up their blankets, and stop smoking, all for a simple reason:

"no white American ever thinks that any other race is wholly civilized until he wears the white man's clothes, eats the white man's food, speaks the white man's language, and professes the white man's religion" (98).

Surprisingly, *Story* takes a muted and belated tack on the toothbrush and cleanliness. Where *Up From Slavery* emphasizes the toothbrush as a primary agent of "civilization" (75, 174), *Story* mentions it only briefly near the end, as an aspect of "parental" discipline, including "systematic regulations for bathing, eating, sleeping, the use of the tooth brush and care of health" (377). For white readers, Washington emphasizes his ability to clean up black bodies as one of his most important achievements. Critics have given a great deal of attention to Washington's seeming fascination with cleanliness. Yet that alleged obsession strategically mirrors white middle-class virtues, while allaying white anxieties about dirty or out-of-control black bodies. What modern readers take to be a nearly pathological fetishizing may reflect Washington's canny awareness of what his early twentieth-century white readers would like to hear.[30] For black readers, he frames his pedagogy of cleanliness as a minor aspect of parenting, while recounting the students' labors for Tuskegee in much more detail. Black readers would approve of his no-nonsense parenting skills, especially his ability to turn considerable student resistance to physical labor—unmentioned in *Up From Slavery*—into enthusiasm for building an institution (95–98).[31]

"Keeping under the body" achieves climactic impact in the Atlanta Exposition address, where a single sentence established Washington's national eminence: "In all things that are purely social we can be as separate as the fingers, yet one as the hand in all things essential to mutual progress" (*Up From Slavery*, 221–22).[32] Coming just a year before *Plessy v. Ferguson's* doctrine of separate but equal, this simile attracted northern capital to the New South by picturing a national body free of either black uppityness or—as Washington repeatedly assures his readers—any black bitterness. Tellingly, *Story* never mentions black people's lack of bitterness.[33]

So desperate was the racial atmosphere of the early 1890s that Washington merely codified what other black writers were also urging. In *The American Commonwealth* (1895), James Bryce notes various black spokesmen who have given up on hopes for entry into educated white society. They ask only for "a separate society" with equal opportunity, "equal recognition of the worth of their manhood, and a discontinuation of the social humiliations they are now compelled to endure." The one essay that Bryce cites, an 1891 article by the Rev. J. C. Price, emphasizes that respectable blacks want access to first-class railroad cars or restaurants for the company of their black peers, not for racial mixing. Detesting the smell of tobacco, "foul men and vile women," they seek "simply comfort, and not the companionship, or even the presence, of whites.... If he is left alone, the Negro will be contented with his own people." Washington had been saying the same thing, even with the same simile of the hand, for a decade.[34]

Washington's simile had a national impact, as Price's essay did not, in part because Price's essay highlights a growing black middle class wanting rights and comforts, while Washington's image of the national body fosters a less threatening image of black people content with separateness and subservience. Yet his image of the hand subliminally subverts what it stabilizes. To literalize, it makes the hand fall apart. Is it striped, like a zebra? Blended, like a mulatto? Which fingers are black, and which are white? How many of each are there? What happens at the base of the black fingers or fingers, when the black moves into the palm? Washington secures his national status by pointing to a blackness whose physicality momentarily protrudes, then all but vanishes into an abstracted racialized signifier of E Pluribus Unum. Metonymically representing a national work force, or "hands," the image promises mutual exclusiveness at the fingers and incorporation or even miscegenation in the palm as the basis for "mutual progress."

Yet as Washington spoke that compromising simile, his body flaunted its mastery over his Atlanta audience, his hand held high, his fingers extended. The threatening instabilities suddenly surface, not in Washington's own words, but in his reprinting of a white journalist's ecstatic report. Both *Story* and *Up From Slavery* reprint James Creelman's account, but *Up From Slavery* gives it much more prominence. *Story* tucks it away in the middle of chapter 10 (174–77), amid other newspaper accounts mixed into a narrative of his subsequent activities. Easy to skip over, it seems no more significant than the many other newspaper reports appended to his many other speeches. For black readers, the positioning says this report is just one minor illustration of Washington's success.

In *Up From Slavery,* Washington gives Creelman's account top billing by placing it right at the beginning of chapter 15, to show "how my address at Atlanta was received" (238). As *Story* has it, Creelman simply "wrote the following for the World" (174), nicely poised between a New York newspaper and the globe. In *Up From Slavery*, Creelman "telegraphed" his account, intimating more eagerness and urgency. Both narratives reprint his text identically. But for white readers, situating it so prominently says "Read this!" Ostensibly, the positioning invites white readers to appreciate or even identify with Washington's delight in getting a great review.

Startlingly, Creelman presents the speech almost entirely as a spectacle of Washington's masterful body. As "the noted war correspondent" tells the story, "all eyes were turned on a tall tawny Negro sitting in the front row of the platform." Creelman comes back to the relentless gaze of the audience: "the eyes of the thousands present looked straight at the Negro orator. A strange thing was to happen. A black man was to speak for his people." Already Washington is "tawny," "Negro," and "black." At last he "strode to the edge of the stage," faced down the "blinding" sunlight "without a blink of the eyelids, and began to talk." Thereafter Creelman recounts not one word of the talk except the famous simile. He is aroused and captivated by Washington's magnificent physique: "a remarkable figure; tall, bony, straight as a Sioux chief, high forehead, straight nose, heavy jaws, and strong, determined mouth, with big white teeth, piercing eyes, and a commanding manner. The sinews stood out on his bronzed neck, and his muscular right arm swung high in the air, with a lead-pencil grasped in the clinched brown fist. His big feet were planted squarely, with the heels together and the toes turned out.... And when he held his dusky hand high above his head, with the fingers stretched wide apart, ... the whole audience was on its feet in a delirium of applause." At the end the governor of Georgia "rushed across the stage ... and for a few minutes the two men stood facing each other, hand in hand" (*Up From Slavery*, 239–41).

This is an eroticism of combat. As Creelman frames Washington's appearance: "a Negro Moses stood before a great audience of white people ... the men who once fought to keep his race in bondage" (238, 241). A commanding black man's body brings a potentially hostile white audience to an orgiastic frenzy of excitement. But whose desire is being represented? A white male audience, personified by the governor, who wants to hold hands with a black man? The "fairest women of Georgia," who seemed "bewitched"? Or the war correspondent, who seems aroused less by the audience's frenzy than by Washington's strenuous muscularity—the sinews, jaw, mouth, fist, the "bronzed neck," the more stereotypical "big feet,"—and that "dusky hand" stretched skyward? Is it Washington himself, who puts Creelman's description in his book so that he can gaze at white people gazing at his mastery? Or is it Washington's canny knack of letting the northern reader, especially the potentially philanthropic capitalists who were this book's real constituency, gaze at all of the above with self-approval?

Creelman lingers on the various manifestations of Washington's virile erectness, twice calling him "tall," though Harlan calls him "small of stature and unprepossessing of appearance" (*BTW*, 1:206). But the reporter dallies more uncertainly with Washington's skin of changing colors, as if it were a floating signifier of mastery and desire. First the speaker seems "tawny," then "Negro," then "black," then "a Sioux chief" with "big white teeth," then "bronzed," then "dusky." Finally the correspondent settles on "this angular Negro," whose face never changed its "earnest" expression. Here is a body that cannot even keep under its own color. Nor could white observers; William Dean Howells called Washington "this marvellous yellow man" (see *Up From Slavery*, xxix). For Creelman, Washington's body has an oceanic flux of changing colors. What dominates those sea changes is the speaker's unchanging face. With rigid self-control, Washington stares down the sun itself amid the "wave" and "roar" of the audience's delirium.

Just as the eroticized "supreme burst of applause came," Creelman spots a "ragged, ebony giant" who had been watching the speaker "with burning eyes and tremulous face." Now, as he "squatted on the floor in one of the aisles," the man began to cry. From despair? From relief, that a black man was doing so well? From general tension? "Most of the Negroes in the audience were crying, perhaps without knowing just why" (241). Mirroring and reversing Washington's claim to "keep under the body," the uncontrollable tears of a nameless black man squatting at the bottom confirm Washington's exemplary rise from black unmanliness to biracial mastery.

Washington's story displays the tactical fictions of crossover necessary for a black man to gain power, manhood, and honor in deeply conflicting regional worlds, the white rural South and the white corporate North. We should not reduce this spectacle to Uncle Tomism, or to a suppression of black self-hatred. In the "burning" eyes of both Creelman and the ebony giant, this is Custer winning against all odds, when the Indians are white. "We are a mixed race in this country," Washington wrote in a private letter. Our business interests are "intermingled" (153), he emphasizes elsewhere in *Up From Slavery;* our lives are "interlacing," he declares in this speech (221).[35] Here, in a white man's eyes, he embodies that intermingling. Washington himself has become the perfect man.

Creelman's report introduces Washington's meditation—completely absent from *Story*—on his success as a public speaker. He revels in his ability to transform white audiences from being skeptical or hostile to being "completely one with me"—as he says of his wives. That public possession of his white listeners, their grudging or enthusiastic deference, and perhaps their implied feminization signal his access to white honor, previously the exclusive preserve of the white plantation elite. His greatest pleasure comes, he says, when he feels "I have really mastered my audience, and that we have gotten into full and complete sympathy with each other. It seems to me that there is rarely such a combination of mental and physical delight in any effort as that which comes to a public speaker when he feels that he has a great audience completely within his control" (*Up From Slavery*, 243). Saying "within" seems even more intimately masterful than the more conventional "under." While achieving equality by bringing white audiences into "sympathy" with him, he can also dominate when required.

"If in an audience of a thousand people there is one person who is not in sympathy with my views, . . . I can pick him out. When I have found him I usually go straight at him, and it is a great satisfaction to watch the process of his thawing out" (*Up From Slavery*, 243). To "go straight at him" declares his virile, penetrative power, and unmans or feminizes the resisting, independent listener. Symbolically, Washington can "thaw," warm, and melt the rigidity of the audience's most protruding hostile member. To "go straight at him" also goes beyond eroticized hostility to the language of the duel, the most combative ritual to establish and display honor among the antebellum white elite.[36] Typically, duels resulted from public insults or shaming, and Washington takes great pleasure in warding off that potential threat with a preemptive strike. Those who chastise Washington for his ingratiating jokes about stolen chickens should remember what he was up against.

Washington's delight in control is especially gratifying, he says, when a "dramatic effect" can make a white audience "entirely lose control of itself" (*Up From Slavery*, 253). In a Boston speech, Washington had just turned to honor a troop of black soldiers in the Civil War, when one of the wounded veterans spontaneously raised the flag that he had never lowered in battle. The ironies of mastery and deference in white and black gazing proliferate. A white audience erupts in sympathetic tumult at the sight of a symbolically erect black man, watched by another erect black speaker, who is praising the work of wounded black soldiers in the white fight to make black people free—all to dedicate a monument to a white man, Robert Gould Shaw, who had led a black regiment in the Civil War.

The greatest surprise here is that Washington struts his mastery over white audiences for white readers, but not for black readers. One can easily see how narrating Washington's appropriation of white honor would please himself. But here he walks an exceptionally dangerous tightrope, since he has to present his oratorical mastery in ways that gain white readers' credit. Yet he flagrantly celebrates his dominance of potentially hostile white listeners. Why does talking about all that please rather than offend? Preening is not Washington's style. For black readers he restricts himself to exemplifying dignity, character, and manly self-control. For white readers he goes considerably further.

Several contradictory interpretations come to mind. First, to adopt a Du Boisian reading, he presents himself to northern capitalists as a C.E.O. in the making, already on the way up their national corporate ladder, commanding and at ease with public speaking. Like so many executives then and now, inwardness is simply not his department, so he's not very subtle or self-reflective about his pride.[37] Executives and philanthropists might be pleased that he has remade himself in their image. As David Levering Lewis notes, "Andrew Carnegie recognized in him a black version of his better self." By imitating those "wealthy and noted men" who keep under the body, he shows that he deserves their credit and cash. They can feel proud of him as almost one of their own, so long as he keeps his distance. In a more radical version, Washington's body will keep under its work by supplying convertible "hands" to farms and factories. He offers a black version of regional primitivism, to satisfy a new transregional white elite who looked for power through cultural incorporation as well as profits.[38]

Second, Washington might actually feel more at ease bragging to white readers, especially northern readers a little removed from the South's intense racism. Later in his life, when his presence at private dinners with Theodore Roosevelt, John Wanamaker, and other northerners aroused great anger in the South, he defended himself by saying he adapted his manners to the region. While he continued to be circumspect and self-segregating with the southern elite, many in the northern white elite treated him as a near equal, and he could let his pride shine a bit.

Third, more mythically, he brings northern and southern white readers together by dramatizing an American Dream that transcends the otherness of race. The readers and audiences who take pleasure in his mastery might be congratulating themselves on their own imagined transcendence of the racial divide.

Fourth, his erotics of power may also be an erotics of honor. Here Washington walks a public tightrope between reciprocity and mastery, perhaps akin to a private tension between male dominance and sympathy in the bedrooms of the white elite. Perhaps Washington's flagrant otherness, in white eyes, gives him conditional license to exercise civic leadership, even dominate them temporarily for their own benefit, without making white listeners feel too slavish or submissive.[39]

The framework of honor and shame also helps to explain the equally surprising absence of reflection on body and oratory when he writes for black readers. Perhaps, in Washington's mind, black skin had become a general site of shame for black people, and the postbellum black male body had become a particular target for white shaming, humiliation, and murder. Therefore it might heighten black readers' anxiety rather than pleasure to see him strutting his embodied triumphs.[40] Conversely, for the northern middle-class readers Washington aimed at pleasing with *Up From Slavery*, the black male body was a site of potential incorporation and exotic appeal as well as a target for shaming.

In any case, the pleasure Washington takes in speaking and fund-raising is the pleasure of feeling just what Du Bois claims he lacks: independence and mastery. The drive for mastery extends to every aspect of his life. "I make it a rule never to let my work drive me, but to so master it, and keep it in such complete control, . . . that I will be the master instead of the servant" (*Up From Slavery*, 261). In these and many other ways, Washington uses his culture's incorporative whiteness for black agency, while resisting and deflecting white uses of race for collective shaming. Ultimately, by presenting himself with dignity on the nation's stage, his message of national community mixed with his calm, commanding otherness doesn't quite fit his message of temporary accommodation. He becomes a Rorschach test; listeners and readers, myself included, see what we want to see in him.

In a provincial white culture that scapegoated and shamed black men to atone for the honor lost in the Civil War, Washington performed several kinds of nonconfrontational manhood for conflicting audiences.[41] He exemplified managerial manhood to northern capitalists, honor and civic leadership to elite white southerners, and quasi-patriarchal civic leadership to African Americans of every class and region. He performed each version with great self-control and dignity. Using the tools of gender and honor, he tried to build communities of mutual respect where almost everyone else saw little but conflict and danger. To that end, "The more I read old Booker T., / The more it's all a strategy."

Notes

1. Patricia A. Schechter, "'Curious Silence'? African American Women in *Up From Slavery*," in the present volume.

2. Louis R. Harlan, *Booker T. Washington: The Making of a Black Leader, 1856–1901* (New York: Oxford University Press, 1972) (hereinafter cited as Harlan, *BTW*, vol. 1), 1:244. In "Strategies and Revisions of Self-Representation in Booker T. Washington's Autobiographies," *American Quarterly* 45 (September 1993), 370–93, Donald B. Gibson argues that Washington wrote three autobiographies: two editions of *Story* (1900, 1901), and *Up From Slavery*, which Gibson calls "a revised version of *Story*" (383–84). Gibson notes the "extraordinarily large number of actual word-for-word parallels" in the three versions (382). *Story* was sold door-to-door, and by 1904 sales of its two editions had reached 75,000, more than for *Up From Slavery*. See also Harlan, *BTW*, 1:245. I use *Story*'s first edition, which I like better than Gibson does.

3. Booker T. Washington, *The Story of My Life and Work* (Toronto: J. L. Nichols & Co., 1900); Booker T. Washington, *Up From Slavery* (1901; reprint, New York: Penguin, 1986). Both books are cited parenthetically in the text.

4. On the psychic cost of Washington's self-suppressions, see Maurice Wallace, "Constructing the Black Masculine: Frederick Douglass, Booker T. Washington, and the Sublimits of African American Autobiography," in *Subjects and Citizens: Nation, Race, and Gender from Oroonoko to Anita Hill*, ed. Cathy Davidson and Michael Moon (Durham: Duke University Press, 1995), 245–70. Wallace argues that black men's masks have been constructed to resist the ubiquity of white-imposed stereotypes, especially the symbiotic twins of the black rapist and the abject or feminized Uncle Tom. For both Washington and Frederick Douglass, manhood becomes a phobic posture renouncing the libidinal and the feminine. For a similar attack that finds more performative femininity in Washington, to his discredit, see Houston A.

Baker Jr., *Turning South Again: Re-thinking Modernism/Re-reading Booker T.* (Durham: Duke University Press, 2001).

5. Ossie Davis, "Our Shining Black Prince: Eulogy Delivered by Ossie Davis at the Funeral of Malcolm X," Faith Temple Church of God, Harlem, February 27, 1965. Text available at various Internet sites.

6. See Peter A. Coclanis, "What Made Booker Wash(ington)? The Wizard of Tuskegee in Economic Context"; and Robert J. Norrell, "Understanding the Wizard: Another Look at the Age of Booker T. Washington"; I refer also to Orlando Patterson's keynote address at the October 2001 University of Florida conference that gave rise to the present collection.

7. See Houston Baker Jr., *Modernism and the Harlem Renaissance* (Chicago: University of Chicago Press, 1987); and, most recently, Carla Willard, "Timing Impossible Subjects: The Marketing Style of Booker T. Washington," *American Quarterly* 53 (December 2001): 624–69, which illuminates Washington's uses of mass-media story techniques and photographs to present an African American professional-managerial class that did not yet exist.

8. Baker, *Turning South Again*, 69 (his italics), also 73, 75.

9. W.E.B. Du Bois, *The Souls of Black Folk*, in *Three Negro Classics*, ed. John Hope Franklin (New York: Avon Books, 1965), 252, 247, 246, 241.

10. In *Race Men* (Cambridge: Harvard University Press, 1998), Hazel V. Carby critiques Du Bois's patriarchal presumptions in making Washington "the metaphorical equivalent of the black mother (or the black female prostitute) who succumbs to the lust of white men" (39). Baker's *Turning South Again* updates that version of Du Bois's argument. Conversely, argues Ross Posnock, Washington enduringly stigmatized black intellectuals as unmanly; see his *Color and Culture: Black Writers and the Making of the Modern Intellectual* (Cambridge: Harvard University Press, 1998), 15; see also 58–61 on Washington's complicity with "white terror of black literacy" (59), and 16, 222, which link Washington to the Black Power movement.

11. In secrecy, Washington tried to undermine racial discrimination as well as his critics, as Harlan's two-volume biography shows in detail. Nonetheless, Harlan follows Du Bois's lead by arguing that Washington's consuming ambition for power and dominance subsumed his individuality in role-playing to please whites. For Houston Baker, in *The Journey Back: Issues in Black Literature and Criticism* (Chicago: University of Chicago Press, 1980), "a self distinguishable from . . . white capitalists never emerges" (47). In *Blues, Ideology, and Afro-American Literature: A Vernacular Theory* (Chicago: University of Chicago Press, 1984), Houston Baker argues that Washington's voice is "slavishly imitative" in its assimilationism and assumed gentility, though perhaps with some signifying against white masks at the anecdotal margins (115). Baker's *Turning South Again* takes those charges even further.

12. See Harlan, *BTW*, vol. 1, especially chapter 14.

13. Du Bois supported Washington's compromise at first, and he came close to taking a position at Tuskegee. At the end of his life, he rebuked a Ghanian student

who compared Moise Tshombe to Washington: "Don't you forget that that man, unlike you, bears the mark of the lash on his back.... [Your fight] is nothing like as tough as what he had to face in his time and in his place." Quoted by David Levering Lewis, *W. E. B. Du Bois: Biography of a Race* (New York: Henry Holt, 1993), 569; on the Tuskegee offer, see 229–32.

14. As Orlando Patterson has argued at the University of Florida conference, given the context of terror during the aftermath of Reconstruction, and given the limited African American choices of flight (spiritual or physical), accommodation, or resistance, subsequent African Americans unfairly limit manhood to resistance. In *Slim's Table: Race, Respectability, and Masculinity* (Chicago: University of Chicago Press, 1992), Mitchell Duneier analyzes the self-presentations of black men who frequented a cafeteria near the University of Chicago. Their dignified civility, moral responsibility, and self-control opposed not only male ghetto styles of flashiness and disrespect (66) but also white expectations of black male rebelliousness. In *Uplifting the Race: Black Leadership, Politics, and Culture in the Twentieth Century* (Chapel Hill: University of North Carolina Press, 1996), Kevin K. Gaines notes Washington's "talent for speaking simultaneously to differently situated audiences" (39).

15. Lewis, *W. E. B. Du Bois: Biography of a Race*, 175; Harlan, *BTW*, 1:218.

16. Chief Justice Roger Taney's assertion of black stigmatization is quoted in Brook Thomas's "Citizen Hester: *The Scarlet Letter* as Civic Myth," *American Literary History* 13 (summer 2001), 202. Thomas notes that the Thirteenth Amendment forbade all "badges and incidents" of slavery as well as slavery, and he develops distinctions between badge and stigma (202).

17. On honor among elite southern white men, three classic texts are Bertram Wyatt-Brown's *Southern Honor: Ethics and Behavior in the Old South* (New York: Oxford University Press, 1982); Steven M. Stowe's *Intimacy and Power in the Old South: Ritual in the Lives of the Planters* (Baltimore: Johns Hopkins University Press, 1987); and Kenneth S. Greenberg's *Honor and Slavery* (Princeton: Princeton University Press, 1996). Edmund S. Morgan's "The Price of Honor," *New York Review of Books*, May 31, 2001, 36–38, succinctly reviews the scholarly tradition. Joanne B. Freeman's *Affairs of Honor: National Politics in the New Republic* (New Haven: Yale University Press, 2001) emphasizes that the culture of honor was a source of national as well as southern stability, defining genteel status, enforcing gentlemanly behavior, and proving who was fit for civic and political leadership (xv, 170–71).

18. Judith Butler, *Gender Trouble* (New York: Routledge, 1990).

19. Harlan, *BTW*, 1:9. Harlan does not cite Jane Ferguson's last name until p. 52, and Washington, the man she lived with, did not use his cruel master's last name much (29, also 17–18). Booker "resented Wash Ferguson for his greed and shortsightedness," and "he never became a father" in any positive sense (32). After the boy "blurted out Washington" as his last name (36), he never quite disowned the connection to George Washington, though he was probably thinking of his semi-stepfather. See Gibson, "Strategies," 375–76.

20. Gibson decries the "mawkishness" of using Portia to introduce *Story* ("Strategies," 385–86); however, I like the more intimate initial focus on kinship.

21. The references to "the big house" are a fiction, since the Burroughs house "was actually an unpretentious farmhouse with five rooms" (Harlan, *BTW*, 1:7).

22. Recent historians of postbellum black families disagree about the prominence of patriarchal expectations. In *A Short History of Reconstruction, 1863–1877* (New York: Harper and Row, 1990), Eric Foner argues for "the increasingly patriarchal quality of black family life" (40). Patricia Hill Collins emphasizes the "woman-centered kin unit" and "the centrality of mothers" in *Black Feminist Thought: Knowledge, Consciousness, and the Politics of Empowerment*, 2d ed. (New York: Routledge, 2000), 178, while Jacqueline Jones's *Labor of Love, Labor of Sorrow: Black Women, Work, and the Family, from Slavery to the Present* (New York: Basic Books, 1995) asserts that black working women in the South had "more equal" domestic relationships than did "unproductive" middle-class white women who "derived their status from that of their husbands" (99). Laura F. Edwards's *Gendered Strife and Confusion: The Political Culture of Reconstruction* (Urbana: University of Illinois Press, 1997), which focuses on Granville County, North Carolina, discusses gender roles in postbellum black families at length (145–83). Property ownership was crucial, both as "a symbol of manly independence" and as a means of establishing a man's social identity as provider (174, 161–62). Edwards gives several examples of highly independent black wives.

23. As Willard emphasizes in "Timing Impossible Subjects," Washington took a great deal of care to present stories and photographs showing refined black families at leisure. Washington also highlighted photographs that showed white guests visiting them, in the garden or at tea. Much as Olivia Davidson was for Washington, the black woman becomes "a midwife of mutual admiration between the races" (643–44).

24. Orlando Patterson, *Rituals of Blood: Consequences of Slavery in Two American Centuries* (New York: Basic Civitas, 1998), 224.

25. Patterson, keynote address at University of Florida conference, October 2001.

26. See Duneier, *Slim's Table*.

27. On African American uses of chiasmus, see Henry Louis Gates Jr., *The Signifying Monkey: A Theory of Afro-American Literary Criticism* (New York: Oxford University Press, 1988), 153–54 (on Olaudah Equiano) and 172 (on Frederick Douglass).

28. In *Houdini, Tarzan, and the Perfect Man: The White Male Body and the Challenge of Modernity in America* (New York: Hill and Wang, 2001), John F. Kasson analyzes the middle-class fascination with unclad, muscular white male bodies in the 1890s (8, 22), and the equal avidity for theatrical performances of manhood as a metamorphosis from weakness to physical virility, personified in Teddy Roosevelt as well as Tarzan and Sandow (23, 32, 194).

29. In *Turning South Again*, Baker says the praise of President McKinley makes

a "courtier-like appeal" that smacks of "racial cross-dressing, homoerotic display and liaisons dangerous" (62). Earlier, he says "there existed a deeply homoerotic bond between Booker T. Washington and *all* white men" (73), and later, Baker links "keep under the body" to speculations that Washington died of syphilis. Baker also memorably sexualizes Washington's broom (47–49).

30. In "What Made Booker Wash(ington)?" Peter Coclanis argues that Washington's emphasis on cleanliness was a realistic and healthy response to rural conditions rife with various diseases.

31. Harlan, *BTW*, 1:272, emphasizes Washington's "paternalistic and even dictatorial" rule over Tuskegee staff and students. He disciplined teachers who failed to attend morning devotional exercises, and peremptorily dismissed students or even long-term faculty for any misbehavior that might compromise the institution's image (277–79). In *Uplifting the Race,* Gaines notes "a none-too-subtle language of empire" in *Up From Slavery* (38; see also 32–42 on Washington's "missionary" and elitist aspects, emulating Samuel C. Armstrong)

32. Edward L. Ayers, *The Promise of the New South: Life after Reconstruction* (New York: Oxford University Press, 1992), 322–26, highlights the drama of the Atlanta address. When the governor started to introduce Washington, for instance, the crowd applauded at the words "great Southern educator," then stopped abruptly when they realized the speaker was black (324). Ayers portrays Washington as a realistic tactician in a racial situation that was "impossible, and deteriorating" (326). On cultural resonances of the hand simile, see Eric J. Sundquist, *To Wake the Nations: Race in the Making of American Literature* (Cambridge: Harvard University Press, 1993), 251–52.

33. Gibson, "Strategies," 389. The disavowal of bitterness appears five times in the opening chapter of *Up From Slavery,* Gibson notes. It should be added that the theme appears in *Story*'s reprinting of the Atlanta Exposition address. Gibson points out that the second edition does include the story of the ex-slave who returns "to compensate his owner for his loss" (382).

34. James Bryce, *The American Commonwealth,* 2 vols., 3d ed. (1889: London: Macmillan Co., 1895), 2: 508–9; Rev. J. C. Price, "Does the Negro Seek Social Equality?" *The Forum,* 10 (January 1891), 558–64. On Washington's recycling of his decade-old metaphors, see Harlan, *BTW,* 1:204. In *Promise of the New South,* Ayers argues that the first segregation laws in the 1880s arose from the visible presence of respectable, nonlaboring blacks in railroad cars (136–46).

35. Washington, letter to R. Underwood Johnson, editor of the *Century,* October 1, 1908, quoted by Willard, "Timing Impossible Subjects," 655. In context, Washington is resisting white claims that mulattoes differ racially from darker blacks, but I am applying his "we" to whites as well. Curiously, Washington's emphasis on "interlacing our industrial, commercial, civil, and religious life" (*Up From Slavery,* 221) seems not to have threatened southern whites, perhaps because the phrase introduces the "hand" simile, which overrides it. Later, when he ventured a seemingly

less radical version in a Chicago speech that urged "the blotting out of race prejudice in 'commercial and civil relations'" (256), he received vitriolic criticism for suggesting social mixing.

36. On honor and duelling, see Wyatt-Brown, *Southern Honor,* 166–67, 350–61 (the relation of virile honor to feminized shame is discussed on pp. 154–57); see also Greenberg, *Honor and Slavery,* xi–xii, 53–65, 74–75, 81–82. Greenberg argues that duels were forms of exchange that reestablished reciprocity, elite community, and honor threatened by personal insults or shaming. The insults created an imbalance in status evoking mastery and slavery, or perhaps domination and feminized dependence or inferiority (62).

37. In *Turning South Again,* Baker argues that Washington "suffered panic attacks" about public speaking (37–39). In my opinion, Washington's nervousness before speaking was a way of preparing himself for a battle or duel that he thoroughly enjoys. In *Booker T. Washington: The Wizard of Tuskegee, 1901–1915* (New York: Oxford University Press, 1983), Louis R. Harlan marvels at Washington's lack of inwardness amid his political machinations: "not a single love letter, nor a cry of joy . . . he seemed incapable of passion or even affection" (403).

38. Lewis, *W. E. B. Du Bois: Biography of a Race,* 256. On the shift from local gentry orders to "translocal" national elites, which relished regional primitivism as a leisure outlet for fantasies of cultural homogeneity, see Richard H. Brodhead, *Cultures of Letters: Scenes of Reading and Writing in Nineteenth-Century America* (Chicago: University of Chicago Press, 1993), chapter 4, especially 135–36. In *Whiteness of a Different Color: European Immigrants and the Alchemy of Race* (Cambridge: Harvard University Press, 1998), Matthew Frye Jacobson is exceptionally good on the contradictory cultural responses to a "crisis of over-inclusive whiteness" (8). Immigration debates made Celts, Italians, Hebrews, and Slavs "less white," while these same groups "were becoming whiter and whiter in debates over who should be granted the full rights of citizenship" (75).

39. Another possibility is that whites enjoyed a more unconscious mixture of fear and awe in responding to him as a commanding, yet socially distant father figure. As Wyatt-Brown suggests, while the code of honor demanded a "formal role of virility," a "submissiveness to those in higher authority was part of the training in honor and the avoidance of shame." That submissiveness is modeled on "instant, outward deference" to fathers (*Southern Honor,* 307, 157).

40. In *Rituals of Blood,* Orlando Patterson emphasizes the complex dynamics of shame and eroticized envy that whites have projected onto the black male body (xviii, 211, 234–54). See also Eric Lott, *Love and Theft: Blackface Minstrelsy and the American Working Class* (New York: Oxford University Press, 1993), on white obsessions with black bodies in blackface minstrelsy.

41. Patterson, *Rituals of Blood,* 192–93 on scapegoating, and 171–232 on lynchings as ritual sacrifices.

9

Moving Beyond the Accommodation/Resistance Divide

Race and Gender in the Discourse of Booker T. Washington

LOUISE NEWMAN

> Perhaps psychoanalysis or role psychology would help us to solve
> Booker T. Washington's behavior riddle, if we could only put him on the couch....
>
> Louis R. Harlan, 1972

> What implicit ideals, standards, images must loom in the conscious and unconscious
> of a southern black boy who seeks to outperform the Great White Father?
>
> Houston A. Baker Jr., 2001

One of the themes to emerge from these essays on Booker T. Washington is a dissatisfaction with the ways in which scholarship so often has promulgated a construction of Booker T. as an "Uncle Tom" whose acquiescence to Jim Crow and segregation was disastrous for black people. Since the 1960s, scholars following August Meier's lead have characterized Booker T. Washington as disingenuous or two-faced in his response to racial discrimination: seemingly acquiescent in public but more resistant in private.[1] Such an approach, while it has the advantage of bringing nuance and complexity to Washington's politics, often results in a questioning of Washington's character: Washington as not just an Uncle Tom but also the Wizard of Tuskegee, a man skilled in deception who would "play a different role, wear a different mask" depending on the situation.[2] More recently, scholars have admired Washington's strategic political genius, while trying to come to terms with him as a "master of masquerade."[3] But for Waldo Martin, masquerade is problematic from the outset: Washington kept his private radicalism so well hidden that it failed utterly as a political strategy. By contrast, his public accommodationism was so very influential that it continues to shape the image we have of Booker T. Washington and his legacy, even today.[4]

The contributors to this volume collectively attempt to move beyond the usual dichotomies of accommodation/resistance and conservative/radical that so often emerge when Washington's life and work are discussed. For some scholars, Washington's so-called accommodationism does not appear so compromised if we remember that these strategies enabled Washington, an ex-slave whose goals and anxieties were fundamentally shaped by the institution of slavery, to establish a prominent educational institution and exert significant political influence while continuing to live and work in the Deep South. Washington's political strategies were the only viable and effective means of resistance in an age when more direct forms of resistance resulted in death or exile. Orlando Patterson, therefore, emphasizes that Washington's accommodationism was "conservative" in a more fundamental sense than the one usually ascribed—that is, conserving of Washington's life and of the possibility for future political and social change.[5]

Robert J. Norrell also emphasizes the need to reassess Washington's seeming capitulation to white power and white racism by reevaluating the public relations campaign that Washington tirelessly waged against whites' presumption that blacks were a savage race, incapable of assimilating into American society. To quote Norrell: "The overarching message that Washington intended was not acceptance of disfranchisement and segregation but rather a message of progress, of movement forward and upward." Reassessing Washington's public activities means fully apprehending the harsh realities that Washington faced: not just the violence of white mobs or the discriminatory policies of white politicians, but also the hegemonic power of white discourses that characterized the black race as both uncivilized and uncivilizable. As Norrell argues, Washington consciously worked "to improve the image of African Americans," to counter the "Negro-as-beast" stereotype that so often dominated the popular and political discourses of whites, whether in the form of minstrel show, coon song, comic strip, trade card advertisement, newspaper editorial, or political speech. Although Norrell concedes that Washington ultimately "failed in his larger purpose of persuading whites that African Americans were progressing rather than degenerating," nonetheless Norrell insists on a revaluation of Washington's actions in this regard: "His efforts to shape his own symbolism, and that of African Americans as a group, should be marked as a shrewd and valiant effort to lift his people."[6]

Indeed, Booker T. Washington was a brilliant publicist, one who clearly understood the need to engage in a discursive struggle with the dominant, racist representations of the Negro. In relation to the other masterful African American orators and publicists of the nineteenth century (Frederick Douglass and Ida B. Wells for example), Washington holds his own as a great speech maker who understood the potential transformative power of the spoken and written word.[7] Washington's discursive skill was already evident in 1895, in the speech he delivered at the Cotton States and International Exposition in Atlanta. As Glenda Gilmore argues, when Washington proclaimed, "Cast down your buckets where you are," whites and blacks heard two different things. Whites focused on what they understood as Washington's "acceptance of a separate black place in the agrarian south," while blacks heard "an argument for the inclusion, not the exclusion of African Americans in the urban industrial order." Washington formulated his message to white captains of industry (that they needed to hire black workers) in the form of a prediction, rather than entreaty: blacks will "run your factories." "It is in the South that the Negro is given a man's chance in the commercial world."[8]

Historians sometimes overlook or underplay the significance of these kinds of discursive struggles, considering them merely rhetorical or ideological, secondary in impact and significance to apparently more overt political and economic struggles. Yet reformers in the late nineteenth century who committed their lives to overcoming racial and/or gender discrimination understood the critical importance of altering the dominant discourses that helped maintain white women's subordination to white men and black peoples' subjection to the white race. Increasingly, as historians have come to adopt a Foucaultian understanding of discourses—as not just ideas but as material practices that constitute the power relations of a given society—greater attention and appreciation has been given to the discursive battles waged in the nineteenth century.[9]

Washington's discursive challenges were immense: how to appear dignified, intelligent, self-assured, manly, and virile without becoming a figure of scorn to whites who viewed educated black men as dandies and uneducated ones as beasts? Washington faced this dilemma not just in his writings about his life, but in his public speaking as well, which caused him acute anxiety throughout his life. He also faced this psychosocial challenge while fund-raising for his institution. The difficulty of maintaining a manly dignity while asking white people for money was especially fraught, given that the position of a supplicant was implicitly a feminized and submissive one. His sensitivity to the potentially degrading aspects of his situation is evident in the lengths he goes to distinguish his method of asking for money from "begging": "I often tell people that I have never 'begged' any money, and that I am not a 'beggar.'" He insisted that he merely educated his white patrons as to the "facts": "I have usually proceeded on the principle that the mere making known of the facts regarding Tuskegee, and especially the facts regarding the work of the graduates, has been more effective than outright begging."[10] Thus did Washington attempt to establish the right modicum of manly independence so that he would appear worthy of the financial contributions he sought. His great personal and political accomplishment was his ability to establish himself as a credible and authoritative *black* patriarch.

In other words, Washington's public relations campaign to refute whites' ideas of blacks as lazy, stupid, immoral, and criminal depended upon getting whites to see blacks as normatively gendered human beings who conformed to evolutionary constructions of separate spheres and hence manifested the appropriate "civilized" sexual characteristics. Social evolutionary discourses set the terms for understanding race (racial difference and racial inferiority) in Washington's era and were fundamentally rooted in specific understandings of gender—a belief in a type of sexual specialization that historians have termed the Victorian ideology of "separate spheres."[11] Separate spheres prescribed that men and women should perform different activities (man's sphere was supposedly the public one of politics and work; woman's sphere the private one of home and family) and in the performance of their gender-specific activities, men and women would supposedly develop different sexual traits. The most civilized or advanced races were purportedly those who manifested the most pronounced sexual differences: the most manly men and womanly women. Womanly women were supposed to be pure, pious, submissive, and domestic. Manly men were supposed to be economically independent, physically strong, and emotionally restrained.[12] Civilization thus denoted a precise stage in human evolution, a stage following savagery and barbarism that was characterized by this specific configuration of gender roles and sexual traits.

If Washington was to refute the racism of social evolutionary discourses, he had to convince whites that black people believed in and embodied "civilized" norms of manliness and womanliness. Teaching black women to maintain clean and well-ordered homes, and training black men so that they could become economically self-reliant, was critical to asserting the black race's equality with the white race, however traditional or patriarchal it may have been in its assertion of proper gender relations. Washington understood that blacks as a race would not be able to make effective claims to equal citizenship so long as they were unable to demonstrate their adherence to dominant discourses of gender and race. Thus, however reactionary Washington's program of industrial education at the Tuskegee Normal and Industrial Institute may appear from the perspective of the twenty-first century, from the perspective of its engagement with social evolutionary discourses of the late nineteenth century, it was a crucial and critical tool in the struggle for racial equality (with both progressive and reactionary elements and effects).

Moreover, although social evolutionary theories opened up a way to conceive of how so-called lower races could become more like higher races (that is, adopt the gendered practices inherent in the Victorian ideology of separate spheres), many whites doubted whether savage and primitive races had developed sufficient evolutionary capacity for learning and adaptation. Herein lay the critical import of Booker T. Washington's educational vision. Whites were not convinced that education could produce the more advanced racial and sexual traits needed for assimilation into whites' advanced civilization. Washington fashioned Tuskegee to prove that this was in fact the case, and he was careful to structure the curriculum for young men and women in ways that would develop in each of them respectively the appropriate masculine and feminine traits and roles.

In these endeavors, using education to bring about racial uplift, Booker T. Washington was certainly not alone. Nor was he alone in understanding the critical importance of countering white racist discourses with a demonstration of blacks' capacity for civilization, in which adherence to Victorian patriarchal norms was key.[13] Scholars have explored how some African American women asserted themselves as "true women" (pious, virtuous, and refined) in order to demonstrate that their race already was or would soon become civilized.[14] Middle-class black women reformers (and those aspiring to middle-class status) assumed it as their moral duty and responsibility to "elevate" and "uplift" the masses of black women ("lifting as we climb" was the official motto of the National Association of Colored Women).[15] These women articulated and disseminated the values of chastity, temperance, and piety because they believed that these things were in fact necessary for and evidence of a civilized race. In the words of Olivia Davidson (Booker T. Washington's second wife): "We cannot too seriously consider the question of the moral uplifting of our women, for it is of national importance to us. It is with our women that the purity and safety of our families rest, and what the families are, the race will be."[16] When Davidson asserted "what [our] families are, the race will be," she believed, as the precepts of social evolution held, that race characteristics were formed and acquired in the home and passed on via the mother to her children—in a Lamarckian process involving the partial transmission of acquired traits.[17] For racial advancement to occur, mothers had to establish good, clean homes, in order to raise children who could become the moral and intellectual equals of whites.

In short, social evolutionary discourses of civilization were fundamental to black reformers' advocacy of racial advancement in the postbellum period. Notwithstanding the challenge to black male leadership that was articulated by women such as Anna Julia Cooper, Ida B. Wells, and Mary Church Terrell, inherent in black women's notion of racial uplift was an acceptance of certain patriarchal precepts. This is one of the most profound ironies in the history of both black (and white) women's struggles for racial and sexual equality during this period. For example, Cooper drew from hegemonic discourses the argument that civilizations were measured by the status of women, and this argument permitted her to formulate a powerful corollary: black women's status and treatment were key to the Negro's racial progress. But for Cooper that status was still dependent on a notion of black women's purity, chastity, and essential moral goodness, as normatively defined. And to ensure that black women would be able to manifest these qualities, Cooper insisted that black men needed to protect and defend the women in their families from the sexual abuses of white men. What was progressive in this claim was the insistence that black women were not sexually promiscuous but sexually unprotected. Still, Cooper's call for protection was a call to black men to act as manly men and to black women to embody the characteristics of true womanhood.[18]

Scholars have also analyzed how black women resisted various aspects of these hegemonic discourses of race and gender to represent themselves as legitimate political actors. Glenda Gilmore, for example, argues that black women reformers in North Carolina often encountered the ideology of separate spheres in prescriptive literature and from white northern teachers, but did not themselves advocate the cult of southern ladyhood. Rather they articulated "an evangelically driven ethos of 'usefulness,'" that gave them a "middle space between the spheres into which they might venture on the business of the race."[19]

In a similar vein, Patricia Schechter describes what she calls the "authenticating strategies" of Ida B. Wells's autobiography *Crusade for Justice*, which enabled Wells to downplay the threat and transgression of a black woman assuming personal power. According to Schechter, Wells framed her political actions in terms of a religious commitment, describing herself as an "instrument of justice," and was able to move beyond the private sphere of domesticity—wife, mother, daughter—by drawing on the southern black women's long-standing protest traditions. Nonetheless, Wells was careful to "mask passion and feeling in order to avoid the appearance of unrestraint or immortality that so easily attached to African American women."[20] Moreover, Wells's refusal to accept financial compensation for her speeches owes something to the way in which wages were deemed to be a corrupting influence on white women in the Victorian period.

Although Wells transgressed the sexual politics of the postbellum South in her antilynching writings, nonetheless both she and Cooper argued for the inclusion of black women in civilization's construct of femininity (as virtuous and pure) even as they struggled against the constraints of that discourse, which mandated middle-class women's confinement to the domestic sphere.

Similarly, to assert his authority as a patriarchal race leader, Booker T. Washington had to maneuver carefully within the discourses of civilization and manliness that were used to deny black men the economic, political, and social status of the (white) patriarch.[21] It will change our perspective dramatically if we see how Washington conceptualized his problem of securing racial equality, not in liberal or Lockean terms of attaining individual citizenship rights for blacks, but in terms of attaining social recognition for black men as patriarchs. In the rural South in this period, the family was still considered a political unit: white men attained social and political status not just as individuals, but as patriarchs or heads of families, protectors, and providers for dependents (women, children, servants, apprentices, employees). Only recently had "democratic" or Lockean notions of a citizenry composed of individuals begun to replace a "republican" or Filmerian notion of a citizenry composed of household heads.[22]

Blacks, even free backs in the North, had long been denied the status of patriarchal heads of family. What were the supposedly inherently racial traits of patriarchs—of Great White Fathers? First and foremost, they had to be good providers: materially prosperous and economically independent of others. Waged labor, although sometimes deemed to be honorable, especially in the North, could also be taken as indicative of dependency—and the ultimate goal for a white patriarch was economic independence, for upon this basis their political independence could rest. By the end of the nineteenth century, this myth of republican democracy would clearly be rejected as hopelessly outdated, but it still functioned as a political ideal in the 1870s and even in the 1880s; advocates of women's suffrage, for example, proposed the enfranchisement of women as a way of returning to this older republican ideal.[23]

Moreover, in addition to their ability to support families and dependents economically, patriarchs were identified by their physical strength and virility, their role as protectors of their dependents, their wise governance of their families. Washington's feelings of attraction toward General Samuel Armstrong, as so many other scholars have emphasized, stemmed from Washington's consideration of Armstrong as "'the most perfect specimen of man, physically, mentally and spiritually'" that Washington had ever seen; "a great man—the noblest, rarest human being that it has ever been my privilege to meet."[24] How, then, was Washington to rise to this standard, especially given whites' expectations of subserviency and deference from blacks? How could he manifest sufficient virility as to be considered manly but not so oversexed as to risk affirming white's belief in the Negro-as-beast or black-male-as-rapist? How was he to represent or assert black political power without seeming uppity or out of place? The burden upon individual race leaders to embody the traits of manliness (or true womanhood) was especially acute in this period, particularly because the current understanding of evolution held that racial advancement depended upon individual development. As Gail Bederman explains, "manliness was the achievement of the perfect man, just as civilization was the achievement of a perfect race."[25] Given that his own early childhood and home life were far from the model that whites insisted was necessary for the transmission of civilized race traits, how was Washington to assert his own manliness in the face of whites' (even Armstrong's!) presumption of black racial inferiority? What claims to manliness and racial progress could this exslave of mixed racial ancestry make?

The beginnings of an answer to these questions may be found in rereading *Up From Slavery*—this time not as a flawed autobiography that hides as much as it reveals about the "true" Washington, but as a text that sheds insight into how Washington attempted to manipulate discourses of civilization and masculinity for particular political purposes.[26] This approach is quite different from the ways in which *Up From Slavery* has traditionally been read: either straightforwardly as autobiography (but one that the reader has to navigate carefully, given Washington's predilection for dissembling), or as a type of postbellum slave narrative whose central argument is economic—that is, advocacy of the Protestant work ethic and gospel of wealth as the basis for Negro uplift.[27] The proof that evolution could bring about racial progress is manifest in the way that Washington's own education at Hampton Institute was represented as having brought about the remarkable transformation of a poor, illiterate slave to the influential patriarch of Tuskegee—a process that, as we shall see, was initiated by white women. Moreover, the import of *Up From Slavery* derives not so much from anything Washington says about his own masculinity, but from the success of the text itself—its extraordinary and enduring popularity, not just in its own time, but into our own day as well, as a racialized myth of individual and social progress.

Reading *Up From Slavery* against the dominant discourses of gender and civilization will deepen our understanding of Washington's seeming obsession with cleanliness and order, which played a critical role in Washington's efforts to counter the racist stereotype of blacks as uncivilized and dirty beasts and lay a basis for his claiming of racial equality for blacks in the late nineteenth century. It is easy enough to miss the full significance of this critical aspect of Washington's character by viewing it solely as an idiosyncratic personality trait, a source of humor or pathos.[28]

Peter Coclanis helps us take seriously this dimension of Washington's discourse by calling attention to its economic and materialist aspects. In other words, Washington considered cleanliness a precondition for the ultimate goal of economic independence, which in the rural agricultural South in this time period necessitated individual landownership, because there was not enough of a capital base within rural black communities to support an extensive middle class from professional occupations.

Coclanis thus spells out Washington's logic of how personal hygiene was required to achieve the end result of economic independence, not just for an individual, but for an entire race. This "transubstantiation process . . . of virtue into property," to quote Coclanis's wonderful phrase, involved beginning with a healthy body—healthy physically and healthy spiritually. For Victorians, cleanliness was next to godliness. It was impossible to imagine how a clean soul could long inhabit a dirty body. So the first step was care of the body—washing. The second step was care of the soul. Education—a term that in the nineteenth century often connoted moral education, to which of course Washington was adding the concept of industrial education—inculcated industry, sobriety, and thrift—moral values of the northern middle class that Washington considered essential for the accumulation of property.

But the transubstantiation of virtue into property did not stop here. The third step was care of the family and home, conceived as the province of women. This was the lesson that Washington was taught by northern middle-class white women—first Viola Ruffner and later Mary Mackie, and it explains the essential need that Washington felt to have prominent and powerful lady principals in his institution. Home management, a place where women were in charge, was critical to racial progress in ways I have mentioned above (providing the necessary physical environment for the transmission of civilized race traits), but it was also critical for the ultimate goal of landownership, for without proper home management—the woman's sphere—the family would never be able to save enough from their labor to effect the transformation of virtue and character into property.

Landownership was also of particular importance to a southern black population just recently permitted to own land, not simply as a matter of material necessity, but also because of what it signified in terms of personal freedom. As Jacqueline Rouse, in an article on Margaret Murray Washington, Washington's third wife notes, "it is difficult to understand southern African American culture without grasping this concept of personhood [manliness] through land ownership."²⁹ For Washington, the role of patriarch extended well beyond his nuclear family to Tuskegee itself, or rather he saw Tuskegee and black people more generally as part of his extended family. He was certain that cleanliness was essential to Tuskegee's (and the race's) development, and he constantly impressed on his teachers the idea "that the school will always be supported in proportion as the inside of the institution is kept clean and pure and wholesome" (*Up From Slavery*, 139).

In *Up From Slavery*, Washington's depictions of Samuel C. Armstrong present him as a "perfect man," even when in the last declining months of his life he is confined to a wheelchair and his strength and vigor are clearly gone. Washington is unafraid to express his admiration and affection toward Armstrong, giving literary critics and historians plenty of evidence to later speculate as to the homoerotic nature of Washington's attraction toward this man who was "more than a Father."³⁰

But if it was culturally permissible for Washington to emphasize the love he felt for a white man, he would have to be more circumspect in expressing his feelings for the two white women, Viola Ruffner and Mary Mackie, who had such a tremendous influence on him during his formative years. Ruffner, his employer when he was an adolescent, was the northern wife (from Vermont) of General Lewis Ruffner, the owner of the Malden mines. Washington worked for her as her houseboy. In *Up From Slavery*, written for white elites whose support Washington was seeking, Washington represents Ruffner as one of his most significant *teachers*, from whom he has learned the most important and valuable "life lessons": "the gospel of thrift, propriety, cleanliness and hard work." Washington's decision to represent her as an educator, not employer, enabled him to liken her to the legions of Yankee schoolteachers who came south to educate the freedmen during Reconstruction, some of whom stayed and found permanent employment in southern schools in the 1870s and 1880s, serving as models for the black women Washington himself would later hire to staff Tuskegee.

Washington's relationship with the real Viola Ruffner (not just the textual one) was, to use Baker's phrase, one of "'obsessive' purification." Their shared activities centered around cleaning and domestic work—activities that were thought to both embody and foster the virtues of "true womanhood"—purity, piety, domesticity, and submissiveness.³¹

For white men—who had other, better options—domestic work would have been emasculating, but Washington saw how he could adapt these "life lessons" to foster his own manliness: the hard work Ruffner put into her domestic activities, he put into his role as institution builder; piety he adapted straightforwardly, and submissiveness he reconfigured into propriety.

Cleanliness and fastidiousness were signs of a white woman's sexual purity—and it was the white woman, for a host of cultural reasons, who was considered the person most suited to civilizing blacks.[32] Thus, there was no shame in acknowledging the key role that Mrs. Ruffner had on his life—indeed it gave Washington the particular credential he needed in the eyes of northern whites: he had passed the civilization test, as administered by the strictest of Yankee women, not just once but twice (Mary Mackie will ask Washington to sweep out Hampton's recitation room before she decides to admit him as a student).

The issue of how intimate Washington was with Ruffner, or how he handled the intimacy in actuality (a question that has interested some modern readers), is unresolvable, given the current state of historical knowledge. Whatever sexual undertones there might have been in Washington's actual relationship with Ruffner (who was a young, shy woman prone to hysteria, a disease that was understood by many in this period to be caused by sexual frustration), were sublimated in their shared activities; if not fully repressed, then any such feelings were probably kept secret from each other and others. What is evident from the textual evidence, though, was that it was socially acceptable for young Negro men to have these types of intimate relationships with schoolteachers, particularly if they were from the North, because these were socially sanctioned relationships, duly fitting to transform a black slave boy into an independent patriarchal man.

The second most important white woman in Washington's young life was Miss Mary F. Mackie, another northern émigré—the head teacher at Hampton Institute. Mackie is also depicted in terms of the Yankee schoolmarm trope, even though as Houston Baker points out, using evidence from Louis Harlan's biography, the real Mary Mackie did not conform to the caricature that Washington invoked. Miss Mackie, in flesh and blood, was young and attractive, one of the "maiden ladies of exquisite sensibility and devotion to genteel culture and self-improvement" that General Samuel Chapman Armstrong recruited to staff Hampton Institute.³³ Washington's account in *Up From Slavery*, however, gives us an image of Mackie as stern taskmaster, summarily administering what Washington immediately understands to be a test of his character upon which his future depends. She tells him that the recitation room needs sweeping: "Take the broom and sweep it." Confident that this is a test he can pass with flying colors ("I knew I could sweep, for Mrs. Ruffner had thoroughly taught me how to do that when I lived with her"), Washington goes about the endeavor with "delight": "I swept the recitation room three times. Then I got a dusting-cloth and I dusted it four times. The woodwork around the walls, every bench, table, and desk, I went over four times with my dusting-cloth" (40).

This test—Washington's entrance exam as it turns out—allows each of them to size up the other. Washington recognizes that Miss Mackie is no ordinary lady with the usual standards of housekeeping. "She is a Yankee woman who knew just where to look for dirt." Miss Mackie, for her part, is compelled to grant Washington his due—for, although she "inspected the floor and closets; then ... took her handkerchief and rubbed it on the wood work about the walls and over the table and benches, ... she was unable to find one bit of dirt on the floor, or a particle of dust on any of the furniture." Washington conveys Mackie's respect in terse language, befitting of the strictest Yankee schoolmarm: "I guess you will do to enter this institution" (40). Houston Baker characterizes these "sweeping" moments in the narrative (as well as the actual relationships Washington had with Ruffner and Mackie) as "framed rituals" in which the usual taboos of intimacy across the color line are suspended, with the result that Booker is transfigured from dirty "*blackness* into 'Booker Taliaferro Washington'—a 'New Negro,' ahead of his time with respect to 'civilization,' and white womanist intimacy."³⁴ I would modify this claim by suggesting that Washington was not ahead of his time—this was exactly how New Negroes were to be fashioned, and Washington's experience served as evidence that the cultural process worked. This is why Washington can proudly recount these moments in *Up From Slavery*, emphasizing the mutual respect that develops between him and these women, whom he can culturally claim as female mentors, and who, in turn, are represented as proud to be known publicly as his benefactors. Mackie, Washington writes, "proved one of my strongest and most helpful friends," and her value to him was as much spiritual as practical: "her advice and encouragement were always helpful and strengthening to me in the darkest hour" (41).

If we take this type of approach to *Up From Slavery*, reading it for the ways in which Washington represents his own manliness to northern whites, then Louis Harlan's assessment, that "The image of modesty, rectitude, and compromise that he had presented in *Up From Slavery* needed to be revised," assumes ironic resonance.[35] If, as Harlan argues, Washington was careful not to reveal himself fully as an individual, such a strategy nonetheless tells us a great deal about how Washington appropriated discourses of masculinity to fashion himself into the Father of his race, and in so doing he demonstrated his own and his race's advancement in human evolution—progress that Washington himself, as well as the whites for whom he wrote, found remarkable for a black man recently emancipated from slavery.

Notes

1. August Meier, *Negro Thought in America, 1880–1915* (Ann Arbor: University of Michigan Press, 1963).

2. Louis T. Harlan, *Booker T. Washington: The Making of a Black Leader, 1856–1901* (New York: Oxford University Press, 1972) (hereinafter cited as Harlan, *BTW*, vol. 1), viii.

3. See Houston A. Baker Jr., *Turning South Again: Re-thinking Modernism/Rereading Booker T.* (Durham: Duke University Press, 2001), 40–78.

4. Waldo Martin, "In Search of Booker T. Washington: *Up From Slavery*, History, and Legend," in the present volume, represents one such attempt to understand Washington as a master of masquerade or masterful dissembler.

5. Orlando Patterson, in keynote address at the October 2001 University of Florida conference that gave rise to the essays in the present collection.

6. Robert J. Norrell, "Understanding the Wizard: Another Look at the Age of Booker T. Washington," in the present volume, 61.

7. For a provocative psychoanalytic analysis of Washington's anxiety about speech making, see Baker, *Turning South Again*, 37–40.

8. Glenda Gilmore, *Gender and Jim Crow: Women and the Politics of White Supremacy in North Carolina, 1896–1920* (Chapel Hill: University of North Carolina Press, 1996), 25.

9. Gail Bederman, *Manliness and Civilization: A Cultural History of Gender and Race in the United States, 1880–1917* (Chicago: University of Chicago Press, 1995), 25. See also Patricia Schechter, *Ida B. Wells-Barnett and American Reform, 1880–1930* (Chapel Hill: University of North Carolina Press, 2001), and Louise Newman,

White Women's Rights: The Racial Origins of Feminism in the United States, 1870–1915 (New York: Oxford University Press, 1999).

10. Booker T. Washington, *Up From Slavery* (1901; reprint, New York: New York Public Library Collector's edition, Doubleday 1998), 136. All future references to *Up From Slavery* are taken from this edition and will be cited parenthetically in the text.

11. For an overview of how women's historians have used this phrase, see Linda K. Kerber, "Separate Spheres, Female Worlds, Woman's Place: The Rhetoric of Women's History," *Journal of American History* 75 (June 1988): 9–39.

12. Bederman, *Manliness and Civilization*, 25.

13. See Kevin K. Gaines, *Uplifting the Race: Black Leadership, Politics, and Culture in the Twentieth Century* (Chapel Hill: University of North Carolina Press, 1996), especially 12–13, 41–43, 128–51.

14. See Shirley Carlson, "Black Ideals of Womanhood in the Victorian Era," *Journal of Negro History* 77 (spring 1992): 61–73; Gaines, *Uplifting the Race*, 13, 42–43; and Gilmore, *Gender and Jim Crow*. See also Evelyn Brooks Higginbotham, *Righteous Discontent: The Women's Movement in the Black Baptist Church, 1880–1920* (Cambridge: Harvard University Press, 1993), and Elsa Barkley Brown, "Negotiating and Transforming the Public Sphere: African American Political Life in the Transition from Slavery to Freedom," *Public Culture* 7 (1994): 107–46.

15. Elizabeth L. Davis, *Lifting as They Climb: The National Association of Colored Women* (Washington, D.C.: National Association of Colored Women, 1933); Beverly W. Jones, "Mary Church Terrell and the National Association of Colored Women, 1896–1902," *Journal of Negro History* 67 (spring 1982): 20–33.

16. Cited in Newman, *White Women's Rights*, 9.

17. Ibid., 30–31.

18. Gaines, *Uplifting the Race*, 134, 135.

19. Gilmore, *Gender and Jim Crow*, 36.

20. Schechter, *Ida B. Wells-Barnett*, 25.

21. See, in the present volume, David Leverenz, "Booker T. Washington's Strategies of Manliness, for Black and White Audiences," and Martin, "In Search of Booker T. Washington."

22. See Mary Beth Norton's *Founding Mothers and Fathers: Gendered Power and the Forming of American Society* (New York: Vintage, 1997).

23. See Newman, *White Women's Rights*, 59–60.

24. Harlan, *BTW*, 1:56, 57.

25. Bederman, *Manliness and Civilization*, 27.

26. For excellent examples of this type of approach, see Leverenz, "Booker T. Washington's Strategies of Manliness," and Patricia Schechter, "'Curious Silence'? African American Women in *Up From Slavery*," both in the present volume.

27. For an example of the former tendency, see Louis Harlan, "*Up From Slavery* as History and Biography"; for an example of the latter, see Wilson J. Moses, "More Than an Artichoke: The Pragmatic Religion of Booker T. Washington"; both are essays in the present volume.

28. Once, toward the end of Washington's life, when he was ill, he purportedly came down the stairs "picking up every little speck of paper, every little bit of lint, and anything on the floor that seemed to be something that should not be there." A faculty member who witnessed the incident reported that "he was calling for his wife.... As he picked things up he'd say, 'Maggie.' Then he'd pick something else up and again say 'Maggie.' ... [H]e went on picking up every little bit of something that ought not to have been on the floor and calling his wife's name." As reported by Ophelia Cooper and cited in Linda Rochell Lane, *A Documentary of Mrs. Booker T. Washington* (Lewiston, Maine: Edwin Mellen Press, 2001), 8–9.

29. Jacqueline Anne Rouse, "Out of the Shadow of Tuskegee: Margaret Murray Washington, Social Activism, and Race Vindication," *Journal of Negro History* 81 (winter–autumn 1996): 34.

30. Harlan, *BTW*, 1:56.

31. Barbara Welter coined this term almost forty years ago, and it has endured as a descriptive label of nineteenth-century gender ideology. See Welter, "The Cult of True Womanhood, 1820–1860," *American Quarterly* 18 (summer 1966): 151–74.

32. For a discussion of white women as the supreme civilizers and purifiers of the black race, see Newman, *White Women's Rights*, 22–55.

33. Harlan quoted in Baker, *Turning South Again*, 45.

34. Ibid., 48–49; emphasis in original.

35. Harlan, "*Up From Slavery* as History and Biography," 34 in the present volume.

10

Up From Slavery for South Africans

Booker T. Washington's Classic Autobiography Abridged

HUNT DAVIS

Booker T. Washington's *Up From Slavery* appeared in abridged form in South Africa in 1929. The abridgment was the work of a white South African educator, Charles Templeman Loram. Loram suggested in his preface that the book "seems to have a special significance for the people of Africa today, many of whom are at the same stage of national development as the Negro people to whom Booker Washington preached his great message."[1] As a member of a white triumvirate who dominated education in anglophone Africa during the post–World War I era (the other two being Thomas Jesse Jones, education director of the Phelps-Stokes Fund, and J. H. Oldham, secretary of the International Missionary Council), it is not surprising that Loram would undertake an abridgment of Washington's classic autobiography. Loram, along with Jones and Oldham, "preached the doctrine of the education of the head, the heart, and the hand,"[2] and he asserted that Washington also advocated the same doctrine. The trio believed further that the determination of what was best for black people, both in the United States and Africa, should rest with whites.[3] Again, Loram implied that Washington shared the same outlook: "Like every other wise leader of the Negro race, he saw how necessary it was for his people to have ... the sympathy, advice and practical help of the best ... of the white race."[4] Loram thus sought to capture Washington (who, having died in 1915, could not speak for himself) as an ally in his efforts to shape the education of Africans (and also African Americans) along the lines that he and like-minded white educators believed appropriate. *Up From Slavery* provided an excellent vehicle for these efforts, but it would be even better if shaped more to Loram's dictates—hence the abridgment.

It wasn't only white educators, however, who found Washington's message appealing and who sought to appropriate it for their own ends. Many African educators of the era also found great merit in what Washington had to say and would agree with Loram that *Up From Slavery* held "a special significance for the people of Africa today." Foremost among them was Davidson Don Tengo (D.D.T.) Jabavu, the sole African member of the academic staff at the South African Native College at Fort Hare.[5] He tirelessly promoted Washington's views, particularly those on education and agriculture, as a model for South Africa to adopt. Jabavu collaborated with Loram in this effort, but he did so on the basis of his own motives and objectives.

Loram for the most part abridged the autobiography by excising lengthy passages of text and in some instances entire chapters rather than altering the wording of sentences and paragraphs.[6] This approach produced a certain awkwardness that mars the flow of the prose in the original. At times it also eliminated crucial information. One example stems from removing the entire chapter 16, "Europe." Other than the reference to friends forcing "Mrs. Washington and myself to spend three months in Europe" that Loram retained, readers of the abridgment would perhaps be puzzled by the first sentence of the final chapter, which begins: "Before going to Europe."[7] The fuller significance of the elimination of Washington's chapter 16 is discussed below. Another and perhaps more significant example has to do with the passage in chapter 8 of the autobiography where Washington discusses the important contribution of Olivia Davidson to Tuskegee's development. Included in this passage is his tribute to her: "No single individual did more toward laying the foundations of the Tuskegee Institute . . . than Olivia A. Davidson."[8] Since Loram eliminated this material, the reader is abruptly introduced to "Miss Davidson" with only a footnote stating that she was "Booker Washington's assistant and subsequently his wife."[9] He thus presents Davidson to his readers in the subordinate role of wife and helpmate rather than as an important individual in her own right. Loram's depiction of her was very much in keeping with the prevailing views on the role of women in white English-speaking South African circles.

Loram eliminated Washington's brief preface, replacing it with one of his own, and reduced the seventeen chapters of the original to ten chapters. He retained three chapters in their entirety, fully excised three others, and significantly abridged another three chapters.[10] Loram considerably shortened the remaining eight chapters and combined them as pairs to form four chapters.[11] A closer comparison of the contents of the original and the abridged edition reveals those aspects of the autobiography that Loram wished to emphasize as well as those he sought to deemphasize or ignore altogether.

As an educator Loram clearly wished to highlight the "experience of a whole race beginning to go to school for the first time" from the earlier portions of the book.[12] This experience was particularly relevant to Loram in light of his comments in the preface that Africans were at the same stage of development in 1929 as African Americans were when Washington began his work among them. Loram wanted to stress as well Washington's comments on the individual effort and initiative it took to gain an education. This emphasis was in keeping with his own philosophy of self-help. Furthermore, accounts of "the best . . . of the white race" aiding Washington and other young blacks in their quest were important. Hence, the passages on Viola Ruffner, wife of the Malden, West Virginia, salt-furnace and coal-mine owner, Mary F. Mackie, head teacher at Hampton, and, most importantly, General Samuel E. Armstrong, Hampton's founding principal, were critical to Loram's version of Washington's life.[13] After all, such individuals formed a "Christlike body of men and women who went into the Negro schools at the close of the war by the hundreds to assist in lifting up" the race.[14] Loram no doubt wished to be included in the later South African manifestation of this "body." And not the least important was what Washington had to say about the content of his Hampton education: "I sometimes felt that almost the most valuable lesson I got . . . was in the use and value of the bath." Bathing not only cleaned the body but also inspired self-respect and virtue.[15] "The education . . . out of the text-books was but a small part of what I learned there." "I also learned a valuable lesson . . . by coming into contact with the best breeds of livestock and fowls." "Perhaps the most valuable thing that I got out of my second year was an understanding of the use and value of the Bible." These were themes to which Washington returned in his final chapter.[16]

Embedded in the first four chapters of the autobiography were the two basic premises of Loram's own thinking on African education.[17] First, whites were the rulers and Africans the ruled. Outstanding individual blacks, such as Washington or, as we shall see, D.D.T. Jabavu, could provide leadership, but the masses were to be ruled. The second premise was that Africans were inherently rural and their future resided in the countryside. Loram had already written in 1917 about the need for "inducing the Native to take up farming, the occupation most in keeping with his nature and view of life, and one that he can pursue without entering into competition with the European."[18]

Three principal themes regarding African education emerged from his basic premises, themes that also found expression in the early chapters of the autobiography. One theme was that the education of African Americans was relevant to that of Africans, a point already noted with regard to his preface.[19] A second was that existing African education was too "bookish" and needed to be adapted "to the everyday needs of the African people." As he wrote in 1929, "Which is really more important in the African villages today—practical hygiene or the ability to read? Elementary agriculture or geography? Wise recreation or arithmetic?"[20] The notion of adapted education in turn flowed readily into the third concept, that of "education for life," a life that was supposedly that of the rural villager. In reality, however, as even Loram acknowledged, Africans were increasingly as unlikely to remain on the land as were African Americans, particularly following the Great Depression of 1929.[21]

The story of the founding and early years of Tuskegee remains in the abridged edition, though in abbreviated form. Loram also ensured that the key portions concerning the content and nature of Tuskegee's curriculum were retained. Although "most of the students wanted to get an education because they thought it would enable them to earn more money as school teachers," Washington had learned that they mostly came from rural areas and that "about eighty-five per cent of the coloured people in the Gulf states depended upon agriculture for their living." Accordingly, "we wanted to be careful not to educate our students out of sympathy with agricultural life." The title "Working with the Hands," which Loram gave to the combined chapters 10 and 11 of the original, further emphasized the industrial nature of the Tuskegee curriculum. Also retained was the sense that Washington conveyed concerning accommodation with whites. Particularly important in this regard was the Atlanta Exposition address, the full text of which appeared in the abridgment.[22] Other significant speeches that Washington included in his autobiography, however, such as the address to the National Education Association in Madison, Wisconsin, or the speech at the dedication of the Robert Gould Shaw Monument in Boston, do not appear in the abridgment, nor does his participation in the delegation to Washington to secure funding for the Exposition from Congress. Perhaps, though, one should not make too much of these omissions, because Loram retained Washington's concluding chapter in its entirety. It included the lengthy discussion of the honorary degree that Harvard conferred on Washington, his comments at the dinner following the ceremony, and the newspaper coverage of the event. It also contained the description of President McKinley's visit to Tuskegee.[23]

The contents of the abridgment are instructive as to the "message" that Loram wished to convey, but the omissions are equally instructive if somewhat more speculative with regards to Loram's motives. One can assume that condensing the first two chapters was largely for purposes of brevity. Also, issues such as the debate over slavery, the celebration of the "day of freedom," and the extended discussion of Reconstruction would have held limited interest and relevance to Loram's largely South African readership.[24] Other omissions, however, are far more serious. When one takes into account the three chapters that were excised in full the suspicion emerges (though lacking in documented evidence) that Loram was consciously minimizing Washington's agency and that of his associates (especially Olivia Davidson). Washington makes it clear, for instance, that it was due to the concerted effort on his and Davidson's part, leading to many "anxious days and sleepless nights," that Tuskegee managed to survive its early "trying seasons." "I knew," he wrote, "that . . . we were trying an experiment—that of testing whether or not it was possible for Negroes to build up and control the affairs of a large educational institution."[25] This experiment was of little interest and perhaps even threatening to Loram, given his firm and unquestioned conviction that whites were to rule and thus set the agenda and that Africans were at best "junior partners in the firm."[26] Likewise, Washington's account of his fundraising activities on behalf of the school in chapter 12 did not fit well with Loram's interpretation of the appropriate nature of black-white relationships in the field of education. The exclusion of the entire chapter "In Europe" perhaps can best be explained for its social implications. After all, as Washington writes, "On various occasions Mrs. Washington and I were the guests of Englishmen in their country homes."[27] Such events seem to belie and contradict the argument of the Atlanta Exposition speech that "In all things that are purely social we can be as separate as the fingers, yet one as the hand in all things essential to mutual progress."[28] Social separation was integral to the South African order as Loram perceived it.

Although the South African abridged edition of *Up From Slavery* is of interest in its own right (if for no other reason than it provides additional evidence for the far reach and extensive influence of the autobiography), the main concern of this paper is with the South African context itself. Specifically, why did this abridged edition appear when it did and for what purpose? This in turn takes us to Charles Templeman Loram. Who was he? What was the political milieu in which he operated? Who was the intended audience for his *Up From Slavery*?

Charles Templeman Loram (1879–1940) was born and raised in Natal, which was the South African province with the largest percentage of Africans in its population.[29] In 1906, following receipt of his bachelor's degree from Cambridge University, he began working for the Natal education department as an inspector of schools. This work involved him directly with issues of African education, issues he was to address in his 1917 doctoral dissertation from Teachers' College, Columbia University. Loram entered Teachers' College in 1914 with the intention of writing about the "complex and difficult subject ... [of] the Native Question" based in part by "studying a similar problem in the United States."[30] Soon after his arrival in New York, he wrote to Washington about his interest in Tuskegee in connection with his focus on African education. In December he again wrote to Washington, stating that "I am taking advantage of my stay in this country to attempt to convince my fellow whites in South Africa that the example of the United States proves that with proper training and education the Negro can be made a valuable asset to any country."[31]

Returning to his employment with the Natal education department, Loram was soon appointed to the new position of chief inspector of native education. In 1920 he became one of the initial members of the South African Native Affairs Commission and served in this position until 1930 when Prime Minister J. B. M. Hertzog dismissed him. He returned to Natal and became superintendent of education, but only for a short time. In fact, this was not the job that he preferred. As he wrote to Thomas Jesse Jones in 1929: "Let me repeat my preferences. First, a useful job in

Native Affairs such as Superintendent General of Native Education for the Union. Second, the Principalship of Hampton [Institute]. Third a job at Teachers College [Columbia University] in charge of the training of educators in retarded countries. Fourth the [Superintendent of Education] job in Pitermaritzburg [Natal]."[32] Loram was becoming increasingly frustrated with the policies of the National Party toward Africans and especially African education. He indicated as much in a 1929 letter to Anson Phelps Stokes: "The work here grows increasingly more difficult. . . . [Prime Minister] Hertzog has said publicly that he will do nothing to advance the Native cause as long as by his vote he remains a danger, to the Europeans."[33] In 1931 he accepted the offer to become Sterling Professor of Education at Yale, where he remained until his death. There he continued to pursue his interest in education in Africa and the American South.

Loram's publications and administrative work in African education in Natal and on the Native Affairs Commission helped earn him the reputation among his contemporaries as "the leading authority on Native education."[34] As Saul Dubow has noted, Loram's *The Education of the South African Native* constituted a "landmark work on the 'native question.'" The book's significance lay "in its attempt to articulate a detailed and differential educational policy" for Africans.[35] Loram's high standing as an educator gained him a position on the first (to South Africa and Rhodesia in 1921) and second (to East, Central, and Southern Africa in 1924) Phelps-Stokes Commissions on African Education. Serving on the two commissions in turn led to an active engagement with the Phelps-Stokes Fund and, subsequently, the Carnegie Corporation.[36] Loram's thinking on education was very much in keeping with that of Thomas Jesse Jones, the fund's education director. His ties with major U.S. philanthropic organizations provided him with resources to promote his own views, including advising on and administering Carnegie grants in South Africa. These connections, moreover, enable him to obtain the Yale professorship. Yet these same ties also created problems for him, because the South African government viewed his American ties with suspicion.[37]

Within South Africa Loram belonged to a circle of like-minded English-speaking white liberals who were concerned with race relations and solving "the Native Question."[38] Other prominent members included the academic Edgar Brookes, who also served as a senator representing African interests in Parliament, Lovedale principal James Henderson, the Quaker philanthropist Howard Pim, and John David Rheinallt Jones, who was another senator representing African interests.[39] When it came to race relations, their political ideology was one of segregation, which was "primarily a defensive political strategy intended to contain the vast social forces unleashed by the industrial process."[40] According to John Cell, the formulation of this ideology "was desperately needed" to resolve "the conflicting approaches to the Native Question among the various sections of the white community." Fundamental disagreements existed among whites over the best government policy for administering Africans. It thus "was remarkably convenient that all of these competing interests could be contained, however uneasily, under the umbrella of segregationist rhetoric." The effect was to screen off "the most potentially divisive issue of them all, the Native Question . . . from the rest of the white man's politics." This in turn enabled "the white community to carry on a common political discourse."[41] Whites thus were able to diffuse intramural tensions in what they interpreted as a competitive racial situation. Or, as Loram put it, to "go round with the oil can and reduce friction wherever I can."[42] Adherence to the ideology of segregation, however, did not mean an unyielding commitment to it. For instance, Loram noted in 1924 that: "It seems certain that uniformity in the details of Native policy and methods of administration is quite impossible. . . . In the fundamentals of Native policy and administration, however, there is needed a standard and united opinion. We shall in the long run be compelled to admit it, that 'segregation' is not a panacea for our racial ills, and that 'differential treatment' is only possible to a limited extent."[43]

The principal white liberal institutional forum for addressing racial issues was the Joint Council movement, launched in Johannesburg in 1921 and based on the older Native Welfare Associations. Its antecedents were also partially American, for its founders patterned it after the Commission on Interracial Co-operation, which had been founded in Atlanta in 1919 with the backing of the Phelps-Stokes Fund. Moreover, the immediate impetus was the arrival in 1921 of the Phelps-Stokes Education Commission, which was a project of a philanthropic foundation keen to support an organization in South Africa patterned after the Atlanta group. Crucial to this process were two commission members: Thomas Jesse Jones, its chair, and the American-educated colonial Ghanaian educator James E. K. Aggrey. They consciously presented an image of interracial cooperation.[44]

Especially important to the white liberals associated with launching the Joint Councils was the representation of Aggrey, both by himself and by Jones, as the "good African." Kenneth King utilizes this term as "convenient shorthand" to describe an African "with certain characteristics: a co-operative attitude in race relations . . . ; readiness to take advice on his education abroad, and abjure politics; pride in remaining African, with a high determination to return to serve his people as soon as possible; a capacity to serve on his return within the existing colonial framework."[45] Aggrey's 1921 address to the Transkei Territories General Council, a quasi-legislative body with a joint membership of white officials and leading African notables, encapsulates the "good African" approach to race relations: "He was glad to see that they [Africans] got along with the white man in the Transkei. When the white man went to America there were about one million Indians there. The Indians said 'we won't let you come here, we will fight,' and they fought every year, and today there were only 30,000 Indians. The black man went to America and said we are not going to fight, we are going to work. The black people numbered 50,000 when they went to America, and today there were 10 million. Work and love increased, fighting and fighting decreased. The strongest weapon the black man had was the weapon of work and love."[46]

Aggrey's image of the black man's "weapon of work and love" was no doubt intentionally evocative of the "pliant and hardworking Negro" who was, as Waldo Martin notes elsewhere in this volume, "a staple in Washington's rhetoric and ideology." And, in the same way that Washington's imagery "earned him, among his antagonists, the popular epithet of 'Uncle Tom,'"[47] so too Aggrey engendered strong opposition from Africans. Black South Africans often heckled him (though not, one supposes, the Transkei Councilors), because they considered accommodation of whites an invitation for them to be even more repressive.[48]

The Joint Councils provided forums "where small groups of Whites, Africans, Coloureds, and Asians met to discuss racial problems."[49] The 1923 Conference on Native Affairs, convened by the Federal Council of the Dutch Reformed Churches, exemplified such a forum. As Loram noted in his preface to the published papers and addresses from what he termed "the largest and most important unofficial Conference on Native Affairs ever held in South Africa": "Many Europeans and many more

Natives must have been surprised to see forty Europeans ... sitting down in open round table conference with an equal number of Natives ... and conducting a conference on a race question with rare skill, hard facts and the greatest good feeling.... [T]hroughout there was a feeling of friendliness and trust and a willingness to see the point of view of the other side. It was a good omen for the future."[50] Of the eight published papers and addresses, five were by whites and three by Africans. Although meetings such as that in 1923 might well generate "the greatest good feeling," Loram was sadly mistaken about their serving as "a good omen for the future." For despite Loram's characterization of participants as representing a fairly broad spectrum, in fact, of the thirty-two white participants (all male, as were the African participants), twenty-six were ministers or missionaries. The Africans were a more diverse group, but they had very little clout outside their own circles.[51] As Leonard Thompson as so appropriately commented, "few white South Africans, however, were susceptible to the influence of ... [such gatherings]. Most whites were determined to maintain their own privileges and power." Before the end of the decade, Loram had reached a similar conclusion as well. Writing in 1928 to Carnegie Corporation president Frederick Keppel, Loram observed that "white South Africans don't want Native education to improve too much. Consciously or unconsciously there is the fear that the Natives will equal the whites."[52]

Somewhat ironically, then, Loram's *Up From Slavery* appeared in print at a time when he was growing increasingly pessimistic about the future of his work on behalf of Africans within South Africa. Yet, this pessimism does not need to cloud too much the question of the audience he had in mind for the abridged edition. His broadest objective was, as he had written to Washington in 1914, "to convince my fellow whites in South Africa that the example of the United States proves that with proper training and education the Negro can be made a valuable asset to any country." Proper training, he concluded, was one that had "definite and demonstrable utility," because it would "definitely function in the life of the pupil." To this end, he proposed courses of study from the elementary through the higher education level that imparted practical knowledge and a strong dose of industrial education. Furthermore, the example of African American education in the United States and particularly in the South provided the model that South Africa should adopt, since, as he argued, Americans faced a problem similar to the "Native

Question." *Up From Slavery* conveyed that model to its readers better than any other single work; Loram particularly emphasized "the spirit which animates the work at Hampton and Tuskegee," a spirit which was "much more valuable . . . than all the courses offered."[53]

Loram eventually had to acknowledge that he could not convince a majority of whites and in particular the National Party government about how best to make Africans "a valuable asset" to the country.[54] He continued, however, to refine his understanding of what constituted education with "definite and demonstrable utility." His audience began to shift and focus more on his immediate circle of white liberals and those working more generally in African education not only in South Africa but also elsewhere on the continent. In this connection his ties with the Phelps-Stokes Fund and the Carnegie Corporation became increasingly important. In 1926, as he informed "my colleagues in African education" in a pamphlet published by the Phelps-Stokes Fund, "About the middle of October, 1926, I had the pleasure of spending a few days at Penn Normal, Industrial and Agricultural School on St. Helena Island . . . South Carolina. . . . I saw that this was the school which, more than any other I had seen, exemplified my ideal for African education, with the school as the center and chief factor of village development. I was delighted when I learned that Miss Rosa B. Cooley, the Principal . . . had written a charming account of the work . . . published under the attractive title *The Homes of the Freed.*"[55]

On the same trip to the United States, Loram also encountered the system of Jeanes visiting teachers. This program provided supervising teachers for rural black schools who assisted the teachers in these schools to augment the traditional three r's with practical work. Additionally, the Jeanes system had the objective of making schools centers for community betterment.[56] In order to promote this community-based American model for African education, Loram, with Carnegie Corporation funding, organized tours of southern black educational institutions for mostly white educators from Africa. They received a "very select number of works on the Negro and his education," including *Up From Slavery*, Monroe Work's *The Negro Yearbook*, T. J. Woofter's *The Basis of Racial Adjustment*, Thomas Jesse Jones's *The Four Essentials of Education*, and, later, Rosa Cooley's *Homes of the Freed*.[57]

White liberals in general and whites involved in African education more specifically were a significant component of the audience that

Loram sought for his *Up From Slavery*. But they did not constitute the entire audience. Africans, and more particularly those working in education, also constitute part of Loram's intended audience, because he needed their active participation in the assimilation process.[58] Paul Rich underscores this argument: "Some of the liberals in the Cape ... appealed to [the model provided by] ... Tuskegee Institute ... [because] its ethos of 'industrial training' for rural black farmers and sharecroppers was combined with a missionary zeal supportive of European colonization in Africa. To many race experts its importance lay in the fact that, despite extensive financial backing from white philanthropic interests, it represented an apparent endorsement of rural industrial training by blacks on their own initiative."[59]

Kenneth King, whom Rich cites, argues even more succinctly that Washington's "value [to Loram and company] ... was ... [the] example of twenty years' success in technical expansion, but, much more important, Tuskegee ... was the first outstanding example of the black man's turning to industrial education of his own accord."[60]

Loram, in the preface to his abridgment, also argues for the active participation of Africans. Not only was he seeking to capture the symbol of Washington to convince Africans of his own educational and development agenda, but he was also invoking an African contemporary. "He [Washington] was the chief pleader for and exponent of the doctrine of racial co-operation—a doctrine which as been endorsed and preached in another continent by his devoted admirer and disciple—Aggrey of Africa."[61] Much earlier, Loram had already suggested that "The progress of a nation is largely the result of the efforts of the great men of its own and other races. The South African Native Question must, to a large extent, be solved by the Natives themselves through the efforts of their leaders; and if the European section of the community is wise, it will hasten the day of this solution by affording the very best education in its power to the talented few, who will not only be able to transfer to their own people the results of European civilization, but will, by their example, influence, and studies, effect a rapid uplift of the Native people."[62]

Aggrey, of course, was one of "the talented few," but Loram had another member of this small band much closer to home. He was D.D.T. Jabavu (1885–1959), professor and one of the two initial faculty members of the South African Native College at Fort Hare.[63] As already noted, he was an open admirer of Washington and a promoter of his educational philosophy. In fact, Jabavu was in many ways a potential African Booker T. Washington. When it came to manual and agricultural education, he argued, "We need a native Booker Washington to galvanise natives to action in this matter."[64] Jabavu shared his admiration of Washington with many of his contemporaries. Two of the most important were John L. Dube (1871–1946) and Sol Plaatje (1876–1932). Dube, sometimes called "the Booker T. Washington of South Africa," in 1901 founded Ohlange Institute in Natal, which he consciously modeled after Tuskegee. He was also the first president of the African National Congress (ANC).[65] Plaatje, a journalist, political activist, literary figure, and general promoter of African welfare, was the original secretary-general of the ANC. He had particularly close ties with R. R. Moton, Washington's successor at Tuskegee, and he actively promoted the school and its founder by means of a traveling bioscope (a type of film projector) in South Africa.[66]

It was Jabavu, rather than Dube or Plaatje, who Loram selected to promote and support as an advocate of applying Washington's educational philosophy to African schooling in South Africa. Possibly, part of the reason for this choice was because he was not an ANC activist. In 1920, for instance, Loram gave fulsome praise to Jabavu's *The Black Problem* in a review for the *Natal Mercury:* "These papers and addresses give evidence of a clear and disciplined mind, wide reading, and an extraordinary command of the English language." Furthermore, "Mr. Jabavu . . . is a constructive thinker on social and political problems of the Booker-Washington type." The book, Loram concluded, made a "very valuable . . . contribution towards the solution of the Native problem." Consequently, "No patriotic South African, European, or Native, can afford to leave this book unread."[67] Loram also helped to arrange for an annual Phelps-Stokes grant for Jabavu and his wife during the later 1920s to support outreach to rural Africans, including teaching domestic skills to women. The two men were also active in the Joint Council Movement, and Loram no doubt backed Jabavu's selection as one of the organization's vice presidents.[68] Jabavu in turn firmly endorsed Loram's work and educational philosophy. Acknowledging his deep debt to Loram "for encouragement in the genesis of this venture," in the preface to *The Black Problem*, Jabavu at several points in the book commented favorably on his educational leadership and ideas.[69] He explicitly embraced the organizational scheme that Loram had proposed for African education in *The Education of the South African Native* in a 1923 paper on the administration and scope of African education, stating that it was "to be commended for the general organization of the whole of native education."[70]

A near contemporary in age with Loram, Jabavu was born into a prominent eastern Cape Methodist family.[71] His father, John Tengo Jabavu, was a pioneer African newspaperman who became editor of the weekly *Imvo Zabantsundu* [African opinion]. His mother, Elda Sakuba Jabavu, was the daughter of one of the first ordained African Methodist ministers. When D.D.T. married, it was to Florence Makiwane, the daughter of a prominent Presbyterian minister. John Tengo was also very active and influential in Cape politics, since Africans in the former Cape Colony continued to exercise the franchise. Ambitious for his son, who was denied admission to the local government high school on racial grounds, John Tengo in 1903 sent D.D.T. to Britain for his education. D.D.T. first studied at Colwyn Bay in Wales and then went on to the Universities of London and Birmingham, where, respectively, he earned a B.A. degree and a Secondary Teacher's Diploma. Jabavu returned to South Africa in 1914 as one of the best educated Africans of his generation. His university education and his father's political connections secured him a faculty position at Fort Hare, where he would remain until his retirement in 1944. As a longtime advocate for a college for Africans within South Africa, John Tengo became one of the two Africans on Fort Hare's eleven-member governing council.[72] His family background clearly differed greatly from that of Washington.

Jabavu's faculty position provided him with a high degree of visibility both within South Africa and internationally. He utilized this visibility to become a spokesperson for African advancement and African rights, which in turn inevitably led him to enter the political fray. He was, however, a political moderate in the Cape liberal tradition. Another Loram African protégé, Z. K. Matthews, retrospectively characterized this political strategy: Following military conquest, "Africans reluctantly accepted the rule of the white man but endeavored to fight for the amelioration of their lot and the removal of the disabilities under which they labour by the usual democratic methods of persuasion and discussion. . . . They fondly believed that the disabilities under which they laboured were due to their backwardness in the arts of modern civilization and that as they adapted themselves more and more successfully to the new ways of life, they would be accorded more and more recognition as fellow citizens of the white man."[73]

Such a political philosophy stemmed from an African sense of minority political status. As George Fredrickson has noted, power and leverage, not demographics, were what mattered. In South Africa "territorial and political segregation served to make a numerical majority into a functional minority that had little or no power within the ... state or polity." He argues further that this sense of minority status was "perhaps the most fundamental source of the [black] ideological parallelism" between the United States and South Africa.[74]

Jabavu operated in a political milieu where he seemed destined to be forever in the minority. Washington's messages of self-help and of being "as separate as the fingers" in the social sphere but "one as the hand in all things essential to mutual progress" therefore seemed to point the way for Africans to accommodate themselves to their situation. By way of contrast, Loram operated with the assurance that comes from being a member of the dominant group. *Up From Slavery* helped buttress the hold of the majority rather than challenge it. Loram intended its depiction of whites providing blacks "sympathy, advice and practical help" to be instructive for Africans on how to conduct themselves and to relate to "the best of" whites. Jabavu's Washingtonian political tactics and strategy appeared increasingly irrelevant to a rising generation of African political leaders that included his former Fort Hare students Nelson Mandela and Oliver Tambo. The apartheid election of 1948 brought final closure to the liberal political tradition that Jabavu and Loram, respectively, represented.

Jabavu first encountered Washington's ideas within the context of his own family, for his father's newspaper columns regularly brought them to his readers' attention and argued for their applicability to the South African context.[75] His association with Washington's ideas took firm root during a South African government-sponsored trip to Tuskegee in 1913 to observe and report on its educational programs and their appropriateness for South Africa. "In my country," he wrote to Emmett J. Scott, "our Government supports Academic Education, and Industrial Training is only in its infancy. They want to know how they can correlate these two and to adjust our schools, or some of them, experimentally, on your model."[76] His first introduction to Tuskegee left a lasting impression. After a long and tiring train trip, he arrived at "the celebrated Institute" on July 12 in "fierce heat." When he walked around the campus, he found it "covered with scores of Negro young men and women students and teachers, whose sight thrilled my heart and reminded me of home." Eating supper in "the gigantic Dining Hall which seats 1,700 people," he noted that there was "not a white face anywhere, managers, janitors, waitresses, chefs, being all Negroes!" He was to reiterate this impression in his report to the South African government: "The absence of white men [in] the successful administration of a purely Negro faculty, in an intellectual village of this sort is not among the least significant phenomena of Tuskegee."[77] While Tuskegee impressed Jabavu, he also impressed the Tuskegee community. In part, at least, it was due to the two musical recitals he presented at Tuskegee, which included vocal, violin, and piano solo pieces.[78] As Waldo Martin notes, "Washington provided a stunning counterimage [to "old-time Negro," and "old darky"]: middle-class refinement, culture, and respectability."[79] Jabavu's recitals projected the same image. It is thus no surprise that Washington described Jabavu as "a fine fellow, one of the best men we have ever had from Africa."[80]

Jabavu duly prepared a 305-page report on Tuskegee that contained both his observations on the school's curriculum and his recommendations.[81] Not surprisingly, he recommended the adoption in South African schools of many of the practical aspects of the curriculum such as hygiene, bookkeeping, cooking and housekeeping, child nurture, and agriculture. He also called for "the dissemination of suitable literature (e.g., Booker T. Washington's 'Working with the Hands') on the value of Industrial Training."[82] Jabavu had anticipated that the government would publish his report, but the First World War intervened and postponed its publication. He wrote the Minister for Native Affairs in 1920 urging its publication. "The time is now ripe," he stated, "that this report should see the light of day and that it should constitute a guide to those Natives and Europeans who throughout the Cape Province are just now much exercised by the question of Native Secondary Education." He also asked, and received, permission to publish the report on his own if the government did not intend to do so. It appeared in condensed form in *The Black Problem*.[83]

Jabavu considered Washington's educational philosophy as directly relevant to South Africa, a belief conveyed in the title of the chapter containing the condensed report—"Booker T. Washington"—and its subtitle, "What he would do if he were in South Africa." Although "it is far harder to guess what Booker Washington would have done had he been in South Africa than to detail what he has actually accomplished in

America," nevertheless "the best approximation of a satisfactory answer" lay in "an accurate description of what Washington has done in Tuskegee, together with tentative suggestions as to what can be done here." Jabavu presented a number of suggestions about the relevance of Tuskegee Institute to South Africa in terms of teaching the dignity of labor, the need for cleanliness and neatness, and so forth, but it was the agricultural curriculum that most caught his attention. "It is as much a practical lesson to South Africa as anything else Tuskegee can offer. The question, therefore, is not whether it be adopted or no, but how best to introduce it on the model of Tuskegee."[84]

It was through attempting to apply the institute's "practical lesson" to agriculture in the eastern Cape that Jabavu worked the hardest to promote the Tuskegee model. His objective was to improve the lot of African farmers. These farmers were mostly smallholders engaged in a mixture of commercial and subsistence agriculture. Beginning in 1918, Jabavu started collaborating with the African American missionary James Edward East to organize African farmers into Native Farmers' Associations. The associations were to promote modern farming techniques and also advocate African interests in a situation where white commercial agriculture was dominant. Jabavu helped found the South African Native Farmers' Congress in 1925 and remained active in promoting the associations well into the 1930s. By 1934, the congress had over forty affiliated Native Farmers Associations.[85]

The basis of Jabavu's deep commitment to bettering the lot of African farmers lay in the fact that, in contrast to many in the African middle class, he grew up and remained in the rural setting of the eastern Cape. There were important economic and social components to Jabavu's agricultural extension work. Beyond these concerns, however, was the moral value of the land itself. Thomas Spear places this concept in the context of a moral economy, which he defines in terms of "world views that held that everyone had a right to land and subsistence, that labour working the land conveyed rights in and responsibilities for the land, [and] that individual wealth and power carried social responsibilities for the general welfare of all." Furthermore, "moral economy must be seen as a dynamic set of values . . . that continually inform people's perceptions of and accommodations to their often changing conditions." One can argue that a similar belief in the moral right of eastern Cape Africans to land and subsistence underlay Jabavu's agricultural extension efforts.[86] From this perspective, perhaps the greatest moral condemnation of white South Africa was that decades of land alienation, codified in the 1913 Land Act that limited African landholding to 7 percent of the country's land surface, had denied Africans their moral right to land and subsistence. Jabavu was thus utilizing Washington's ideas on agricultural extension to affirm traditional beliefs about landownership and to support his argument that farming was important to Africans' future. Loram and many other whites dealing with "Native Affairs" would concur, but they saw only the social and economic dimensions of land. For them, subsistence farming was in keeping with the imagined inherent rural nature and outlook of Africans. It also could keep Africans out of the urban areas where they would compete with whites. Jabavu, in contrast, operating as he did from a minority political position, sought space for advancing African economic and social interests. Through advocating a Washingtonian vision and agenda he thus sought allies among sympathetic whites. Africans nevertheless understood not only the economic and social rationale of his actions but also the moral imperatives.

Jabavu went beyond Washington, as he did in other ways as well, when it came to the centrality of land. He was not an uncritical Bookerite. He thought, for instance, that Washington downplayed too much "the intrinsic merit" of the academic side of Tuskegee. "Somewhere in the 'Story of my Life' he claims, modestly I think, that the aim is rather to teach little and thoroughly, than much and insufficiently." Jabavu stated that the Tuskegee curriculum refuted such a proposition. Furthermore, Tuskegee and other industrial schools drew their faculty from "the great Northern White University colleges.... Without them, Tuskegee would, in the words of a Northern critic, 'have been unthinkable,' (Prof. Du Bois) and, in my opinion, impossible in its present constitution and Southern locality."[87]

On the issue of higher education, Jabavu also differed with Loram. Loram thought that American black universities served "a very definite and useful purpose," but that there was not yet a need for such institutions in South Africa. Indeed, "we should take cognizance of the danger (so apparent in India and Egypt) of educating any considerable number of individuals beyond the requirements of their race." Fort Hare should thus provide "a practical education, one that can actually be made use of by the Native." Jabavu, in contrast, bemoaned the fact that "in South Africa we have only one college offering ambitious and talented native youths with the degree education such as is available at the Atlanta, Wilberforce and Howard Universities for negroes."[88] Yes, it was important for South Africa to develop its own Tuskegees, but there were also young Africans who could profit from a South African Howard.

C. T. Loram and D.D.T. Jabavu, holding as they did vastly different positions of power and authority in the segregated South Africa of the 1910s and 1920s, came together around the educational philosophy of Booker T. Washington. Indeed, it is possible to envisage a less busy Jabavu abridging *Up From Slavery* himself. If he had done so, however, his Booker T. Washington would surely have exercised more agency than did Loram's. Part of the explanation for their mutual admiration of Washington and avocation of transplanting the Tuskegee model to South Africa lies in their individual personalities, temperaments, and circumstances. The appeal of *Up From Slavery* to South Africans, however, involves more than just personalities. It rests in the social and political ambiguities of interwar South Africa. Historian Shula Marks has suggested that the term *ambiguity* covers "two distinct but related phenomena: ambiguity of meaning and structural ambiguity, for which the term contradiction would be equally, if not more, appropriate."[89] Ambiguity of meaning often flowed from structural ambiguity. The meaning of what Washington symbolized was inherently ambiguous, certainly when placed in the South African context. Loram sought to make Africans "a valuable asset" to the country—that is, to the white population that controlled the country. He saw in *Up From Slavery* a blueprint for accomplishing this, a blueprint that was all the more valuable because a black man wrote it. Jabavu, on the other hand, worked to uplift his people. As a young man, Washington had been advised "to do something for his people, not to get something out of them."[90] *Up From Slavery* also offered him a blueprint for reaching his objectives. An added bonus was that its author was the era's most famous black man.

The structural ambiguities of preapartheid South Africa certainly underlay the ambiguity of the meaning of Washington's classic autobiography for South Africans. While rapidly fading, Rhodes's dictum of "equal rights for every civilized man south of the Zambezi" retained some political value as long as Africans in the Cape Province retained the franchise. White liberals such as Loram unabashedly affirmed the right of whites to rule Africans as subjects, though in a paternalistic manner. They thought it strategically necessary, however, to accord political rights to the talented few among Africans, for they needed them as allies. From this perspective, Washington served as an appropriate model for the Jabavus to emulate. They were to draw inspiration and guidance from Washington and devote their energies to improving the African masses and thereby making them "valuable assets." Jabavu and other African proponents of Washington, however, saw a different individual, someone who had overcome great odds, in an analogous situation of white supremacy, to build Tuskegee into the impressive institution it had become. Tuskegee, where "there was not a white face anywhere," served as an example of how black people could have some modicum of control over their lives in white-dominated South Africa.

Notes

Author's note: I would like to thank Daryl Scott for his helpful comments on the original draft of this paper in his role as a discussant when it was initially presented. Nicholas Southey, University of South Africa, similarly provided assistance through his thoughtful comments as a discussant for a subsequent draft of the paper when it was it presented to a Department of History Seminar, University of Pretoria.

1. Booker T. Washington, *Up From Slavery*, abridged by C. T. Loram (1929; reprint, Cape Town: Maskew Miller, 1958), preface (hereinafter cited as Loram abridgment).

2. This characterization of Loram, Jones, and Oldham is by Kenneth J. King, *Pan-Africanism and Education: A Study of Race Philanthropy and Education in the Southern States of America and East Africa* (Oxford: Clarendon Press, 1971), 52.

3. See Richard D. Heyman, "C. T. Loram: A South African Liberal in Race Relations," *International Journal of African Historical Studies* 5 (1972): 49–50, and R. Hunt Davis Jr., "Charles T. Loram and an American Model for African Education in South Africa," *African Studies Review* 19 (1976): 90–93.

4. Loram abridgment, preface.

5. For Jabavu, see Catherine Higgs, *The Ghost of Equality: The Public Lives of D. D. T. Jabavu of South Africa, 1885–1959* (Athens: Ohio University Press, 1997).

6. The abridged edition under consideration is a 1969 reprint of the 1958 edition published by Maskew Miller, Cape Town. This in turn appears to be a reprint of the original 1929 edition published by Harrap. The format is 4¾ by 7, with a preface of 3 unnumbered pages and the main text consisting of 133 pages.

7. Booker T. Washington, Up From Slavery: *Authoritative Text, Contexts, and Composition History, Criticism*, ed. William L. Andrews (New York: Norton, 1996), 120 (hereinafter all page references to the original text come from this edition); Loram abridgment, 111; Washington, *Up From Slavery*, 133; and Loram abridgment, 115.

8. Washington, *Up From Slavery*, 59–60.

9. Loram abridgment, 68.

10. Chapter 3, "The Struggle for an Education," chapter 4, "Helping Others," and chapter 17, "Last Words," were retained; chapter 9, "Anxious Days and Sleepless Nights," chapter 12, "Raising Money," and chapter 16, "Europe," were excised; and chapter 1, "A Slave among Slaves," chapter 2, "Boyhood Days," and chapter 15, "The Secret of Success in Public Speaking," were abridged.

11. Chapters 5 and 6, "The Reconstruction Period" and "Black Race and Red Race," took the latter title; chapters 7 and 8, "Early Days at Tuskegee" and "Teaching School in a Stable and a Hen-House," became "Early Days at Tuskegee and Teaching School"; chapters 10 and 11, "A Harder Task Than Making Bricks without Straw" and "Making Their Beds before They Could Lie Down," became "Working with Hands"; and chapters 13 and 14, "Two Thousand Miles for a Five Minute Speech" and "The Atlanta Exposition Address," took the latter title.

12. Loram abridgment, 15.

13. Ibid., 23–24 and 43, 30, and 43–44, and 31–33, 79–81, and 115–16, respectively.

14. Ibid., 33.

15. Ibid.

16. Ibid., 39, 127–30.

17. The following is based on Davis, "Charles T. Loram," 90–93.

18. Charles T. Loram, *The Education of the South African Native* (1917; reprint, New York: Negro Universities Press, 1969), 238.

19. This belief infused his *Education of the South African Native*, which was based on his doctoral dissertation for Teachers' College, Columbia University.

20. Charles T. Loram, "A National System of Native Education in South Africa," *South African Journal of Science* 26 (December 1929): 927.

21. Charles T. Loram, "The Phelps-Stokes Education Commission in South Africa," *International Review of Missions* 10 (October 1921): 502–3. As William Beinart has noted, "By the 1920s African small-scale farmers in the reserves [the approximately 7 percent of South Africa where Africans owned the land] and on the white-owned farms still produced nearly a quarter of the maize and held nearly half the cattle in the country.... But fewer and fewer peasants were able to produce a surplus. Perhaps 30–40 per cent of the economically active men in rural reserve areas were away at labour centers at any one time.... [M]arried men were having to migrate over a long period in order to help meet the subsistence needs of their families. An increasing number were interested in moving to towns permanently." "As population grew [over the course of the 1920s] so did the herds.... [R]ising stock numbers ... took their toll on the land, as revealed especially in the depression and droughts of the early 1930s." William Beinart, *Twentieth-Century South Africa* (New York: Oxford University Press, 1994), 33, 129.

22. Loram abridgment, 67, 68, 94–99.

23. Washington, *Up From Slavery*, 91–93, 113–15, and 94–95; Loram abridgment, 116–27.

24. Loram abridgment, 9–10, 14–16, and 40–43.

25. Washington, *Up From Slavery*, 68.

26. Anson Phelps Stokes to Arthur Keppel, June 21, 1928, box 28, folder 465, Anson Phelps Stokes Family Papers, Sterling Memorial Library, Yale University, New Haven. Stokes was commenting with approval on Loram's use of the phrase in a speech.

27. Washington, *Up From Slavery*, 130.

28. Loram abridgment, 97.

29. For fuller biographical details on Loram, see Davis, "Charles T. Loram"; Heyman, "C. T. Loram"; and R. Hunt Davis Jr., "Loram, Charles Templeman," in *Dictionary of South African Biography* (Pretoria: Tafelberg-Uitgewers, 1977), 3: 537–38.

30. Loram, *Education of the South African Native*, vii.

31. Loram to Washington, September 28, 1914, box 508, and December 27, 1914, box 523, Booker T. Washington Papers, Manuscript Division, Library of Congress, Washington, D.C. (hereinafter cited as BTW Papers). Some references to the Washington Papers are based on research that took place prior to the Library of Congress's microfilming of the collection, hence the reference to boxes instead of reel numbers.

32. Loram to Thomas Jesse Jones, October 6, 1929, folder Loram '29, files, Carnegie Corporation, New York. Subsequent correspondence in the Loram Folders (including Loram to Keppel, December 14, 1929, and January 6, 1930, and Keppel to Loram, January 3, 1930) indicates Loram's interest in landing a position in the United States, due to his growing dissatisfaction with his circumstances in South Africa.

33. Loram to Stokes, January 10, 1929, box 31, folder 512, Stokes Family Papers. Loram continued to bemoan the Hertzog government's handling of African affairs. For example, the Minutes of the Trustees Meeting of November 16, 1932, of the Phelps-Stokes Fund, noted: "Dr. Loram stated that the racial situation in South Africa at present is very bad, with little prospect of improvement under the Hertzog administration." Further, the "offer of [the] Rockefeller Foundation to contribute £70,000 toward native medical education" was withdrawn because of the South African government's inaction. See box 14, folder 2, Moton Family Papers, Manuscript Division, Library of Congress, Washington, D.C. According to Saul Dubow, however, Loram was slower than his liberal contemporaries to break with Hertzog. He noted that as late as 1930 Loram "remained a supporter of Hertzog." See Dubow, *Racial Segregation and the Origins of Apartheid in South Africa, 1919–36* (New York: St. Martin's Press, 1989), 48–49. It would seem, then, that Loram was undecided about Hertzog's policies at this time.

34. Thomas Jesse Jones, *Education in East Africa: A Study of East, Central, and South Africa by the 2nd African Education Commission under the Auspices of the Phelps-Stokes Fund, in Co-operation with the International Education Board* (1925; reprint, New York: Negro Universities Press, 1970), xxi.

35. Dubow, *Racial Segregation*, 27.

36. The correspondence referenced in notes 32 and 33 is indicative of the close nature of this relationship.

37. See especially Heyman, "C. T. Loram," 46.

38. For a thorough discussion of South African white liberals and race, see Paul B. Rich, *White Power and the Liberal Conscience: Racial Segregation and South African Liberalism, 1921–1960* (Manchester: Manchester University Press, 1984). For their role in formulating a segregationist ideology, see Dubow, *Racial Segregation*, 21–50.

39. Among Edgar H. Brookes's many books are *The History of Native Policy in South Africa from 1830 to the Present Day* (Cape Town: Nasionale Press, 1924), and *The Colour Problems of South Africa: Being the Phelps-Stokes Lectures, 1933, Delivered at the University of Cape Town* (Lovedale, S.A.: Lovedale Press, 1934). He was elected as one of four white senators representing African interests following passage of the Natives Representation Act of 1936. He later helped found the multiracial Liberal Party, which the government banned in 1960 as part of its apartheid-era suppression of political opposition. For Henderson, see Paul Rich, "The Appeals of Tuskegee: James Henderson, Lovedale, and the Fortunes of South African Liberalism, 1906–1930," *International Journal of African Historical Studies* 20 (1987): 271–92. Lovedale had long been the country's leading secondary school for Africans. For Pim, see Dubow, *Racial Segregation*, 23–26. Pim's wide-ranging interests included education, the welfare of Africans, race relations, politics, economics, and Johannesburg municipal affairs. Rheinallt Jones represented Africans in the Senate in 1937–42 and served as director of the South African Institute of Race Relations in 1930–47. His early views on policy toward Africans appear in Pim, "The Need for a Scientific Basis for South African Native Policy," *South African Journal of Science* 23 (1926).

40. Dubow, *Racial Segregation*, 9.

41. John W. Cell, *The Highest Stage of White Supremacy: The Origins of Segregation in South Africa and the American South* (Cambridge: Cambridge University Press, 1982), 213–14.

42. Loram to Stokes, January 10, 1929, box 31, folder 512, Stokes Family Papers.

43. C. T. Loram, preface to "European and Bantu: Being Papers and Addresses Read at the Conference on Native Affairs Held under the Auspices of the Federal Council of the D.R. Churches at Johannesburg on 27th to 29th September, 1923," pp. 5–6, MSS British Empire, S22 G195, Rhodes House, Oxford, England.

44. Higgs, *Ghost of Equality*, 96; George M. Fredrickson, *Black Liberation: A Comparative History of Black Ideologies in the United States and South Africa* (New York: Oxford University Press, 1995), 147. Aggrey had lived in the United States for more than twenty years prior to his appointment to the Phelps-Stokes Commission and was a faculty member at Livingstone College in North Carolina.

45. King, *Pan-Africanism and Education*, 232.

46. "Address by Professor J.E.K. Aggrey," Transkei Territories General Council,

Proceedings and Reports of Select Committees at the Session of 1921 (Umtata: Government Printer, 1922), 168–69. In the same address, he noted that he "went to the same school [Teachers' College] as Dr. Loram" (167). The precise wording is that of the council's recording secretary and not verbatim from Aggrey's speech.

47. Waldo Martin, "In Search of Booker T. Washington: *Up From Slavery*, History, and Legend," 52 in this volume.

48. Fredrickson, *Black Liberation*, 147.

49. Leonard Thompson, *A History of South Africa* (New Haven: Yale University Press, 1995), 175.

50. Loram, preface to "European and Bantu," 5.

51. Roster of Delegates, "European and Bantu," 56.

52. Thompson, *History of South Africa*, 176; Loram quoted in Heyman, "C. T. Loram," 45.

53. Loram, *Education of the South African Native*, 279, 312. See chapters 14 and 15, "Proposed Courses of Study" and "The South African Native College," ibid., 279–312.

54. The National Party took office in 1924, with J.M.B. Hertzog as prime minister.

55. Charles T. Loram, *Adaptation of the Penn School Methods to Education in South Africa* (New York: Phelps-Stokes Fund, 1927), 3. For a more detailed discussion of Loram's views regarding the Penn School, see R. Hunt Davis Jr., "Producing the 'Good Africa': South Carolina's Penn School as a Guide for African Education in South Africa," in *Independence without Freedom: The Political Economy of Colonial Education in Southern Africa*, ed. Agrippah T. Mugomba and Mougo Nyaggah (Santa Barbara: ABC-Clio, 1980), 83–112.

56. For a fuller discussion, see Davis, "Charles T. Loram," 93–96.

57. King, *Pan-Africanism and Education*, 180–81.

58. Here I take issue with Richard Heyman's assessment. Loram, he argues, had spent his entire working life in African education and on improving race relations. In keeping with white liberal thought of the time, he believed in "the premise that nonblacks were in the best position to decide what was best for blacks." If blacks were ever to "achieve their 'potential equality' . . . through a process of cultural assimilation," then they had to remain "passive rather than active in white-dominated societies." Heyman notes Remi Clignet's observation that assimilation "requires the active participation of the group assimilating" and then argues that Loram "did not allow for such activism on the part of the black" (Heyman, "C. T. Loram," 50). Heyman was citing Clignet's "Inadequacies of the Notion of Assimilation in African Education," *Journal of Modern African Studies* 8 (1970): 425–44.

59. Rich, "Appeals of Tuskegee," 271–72.

60. King, *Pan-Africanism and Education*, 47.

61. Loram abridgment, preface.

62. Loram, *Education of the South African Native*, 306.

63. The other founding member was the principal, Alexander Kerr, from Scotland. Fort Hare was located in Jabavu's home region of the eastern Cape Province, in

large part because so many of the college's African and missionary advocates hailed from the region.

64. D.D.T. Jabavu, *The Black Problem: Papers and Addresses on Various Native Problems* (1920; reprint, New York: Negro Universities Press, 1969), 97. King, *Pan-Africanism and Education*, 191–92, discusses how white missionaries and government officials saw in Aggrey an "African Booker T. Washington." Higgs suggests that King's description of the "good African" "fit D. D. T. Jabavu almost as well as it did Aggrey" (*Ghost of Equality*, 96).

65. See R. Hunt Davis Jr., "John L. Dube: A South African Exponent of Booker T. Washington," *Journal of African Studies* 2 (1975/1976): 497–528, and Shula Marks, "The Ambiguities of Dependence: John L. Dube of Natal," *Journal of Southern African Studies* 1 (1975): 162–80.

66. See Brian Willan, *Sol Plaatje: South African Nationalist 1876–1932* (Berkeley: University of California Press, 1984), especially 278–79. Thomas Jesse Jones facilitated his visit in 1922 to Tuskegee with a $100 grant from the Phelps-Stokes Foundation. For his relationship with Moton, see Plaatje to Moton, September 22, 1924, in *Sol Plaatje: Selected Writings*, ed. Brian Willan (Athens: Ohio University Press, 1997), 329–34.

67. C. T. Loram, review of *The Black Problem*, in *Natal Mercury*, n.d., contained in a scrapbook of clippings, D.D.T. Jabavu Collection, acc. #47, file 5, Documentation Centre for African Studies, University of South Africa, Pretoria. This scrapbook also contained another review, by J. D. Rheinallt Jones, which appeared in the December 1920 issue of the *South African Quarterly*. He concluded that "throughout the book there breathes a spirit of sweet reasonableness and patience. It will be to our eternal disgrace if we drive such a man as the writer of this book to lose all faith in the even-handedness of white justice. We must encourage Mr. Jabavu and others like him to voice the feelings and aspirations of the native peoples, and this volume is welcomed if only for that reason." There were four sections to "The Black Problem": political problems, educational problems, agricultural and economic problems, and social problems.

68. Higgs, *Ghost of Equality*, 70, 108. Higgs does not state that Loram facilitated the grant, but given his close ties to Jones and the fund, he no doubt had a say in the monetary award to the Jabavus. The 1927–28 and 1928–29 Phelps-Stokes budgets for the fund's work in South Africa each allocated $500 to the Jabavus (Phelps-Stokes Fund Budget for 1928–29, box 14, folder 5, Moton Family Papers).

69. Jabavu, *Black Problem*, preface, and 95, 132, and 155.

70. D.D.T. Jabavu, "The Administration and Scope of an Educational System," in "European and Bantu," 19. Loram set out his proposed organization of African schooling in chapters 14 and 15.

71. This biographical sketch is based on Higgs, *Ghost of Equality*.

72. Loram chaired the council in 1930–31, according to Alexander Kerr, *Fort Hare, 1915–48: The Evolution of an African College* (London: Humanities Press, 1968), 272.

73. Z. K. Matthews, "The Road from Nonviolence to Violence," a speech delivered at a conference sponsored by the World Council of Churches, Kitwe, Northern Rhodesia, May 1964, in *From Protest to Challenge: A Documentary History of African Politics in South Africa, 1882–1990*, vol. 5, *Nadir and Resurgence, 1964–1979*, ed. Thomas G. Karis and Gail M. Gerhart (Bloomington: Indiana University Press, 1997), 347–48. Matthews was the first Fort Hare B.A. recipient; he went on to Yale under Loram's sponsorship, where he earned his M.A. in anthropology. He then joined the Fort Hare faculty in 1936 as a lecturer in social anthropology and native law and administration. See Z. K. Matthews, *Freedom for My People* (Cape Town: D. Philip, 1981), especially 92–99 and 117.

74. Fredrickson, *Black Liberation*, 6.

75. See, for instance, *Imvo Zabantsundu*, May 3, 1899.

76. D.D.T. Jabavu to E. J. Scott, September 5, 1913, box 927, BTW Papers.

77. D.D.T. Jabavu, "My Tuskegee Pilgrimage" (typescript), pp. 27–28, file 3.1, Jabavu Collection, UNISA; Davidson Jabavu, "A Report on the Tuskegee Institute Alabama, U.S.A., for the Minister of Native Affairs, South African Union Government" (typescript), appendix 1, pp. 36–37, Helen Notando Jabavu Crosfield Collection, in the possession of Harrison M. Wright, professor emeritus of history, Swarthmore College. The same comment appears in the published edition of the report in Jabavu, *Black Problem*, 61.

78. See program for August 13, 1913, included in Jabavu to Emmett J. Scott, September 4, 1914, box 927, BTW Papers, and program for September 24, 1913, included in Jabavu, "My Tuskegee Pilgrimage." In his letter to Scott, he noted that there was "a widespread and insistent demand for me to repeat the concert I gave . . . last month."

79. Martin, "In Search of Booker T. Washington," 54 in this volume.

80. Washington to Rev. John H. Harris, London, September 9, 1913, reel 353, BTW Papers.

81. See note 77.

82. Jabavu, "Report on Tuskegee," 237.

83. D.D.T. Jabavu to Minister of Native Affairs, March 4, 1920, and Secretary of Native Affairs to Jabavu, March 23, 1920, file 2941/13/639, NAS, box 268, South African National Archives, Pretoria. The passage about people throughout the Cape Province being exercised on questions of African education is in reference to the 1919 report of the Cape Province Commission on Native Education. Jabavu, *Black Problem*, 27–70.

84. Jabavu, *Black Problem*, 28, 45–46.

85. Higgs, *Ghost of Equality*, 37–42. See also the section on "Agricultural and Economic Problems," in Jabavu, *Black Problem*, 99–142. For additional information on the Native Farmers' Associations and the roles of East and Jabavu, see Farieda Khan, "Rewriting South Africa's Conservation History: The Role of the Native Farmers Association," *Journal of Southern African Studies* 20 (1994): 499–516. The

uphill nature of this struggle can be seen from what William Beinart, cited in note 21, had to say about the declining prospects of African farming.

86. Thomas Spear, *Mountain Farmers: Moral Economies of Land and Agricultural Development in Arusha and Meru* (Berkeley: University of California Press, 1997), 12–13. The moral right of Africans to land and subsistence found expression in the redistributive homestead idiom whereby a political leader was the "father" and the people his "children." Children possessed the inherent right to expect sustenance from their fathers. See J. B. Peires, *The House of Phalo: A History of the Xhosa People in the Days of Their Independence* (Berkeley: University of California Press, 1981), 31–32. The Xhosa were the principal African inhabitants of the eastern Cape.

87. Jabavu, *Black Problem*, 37, 41.

88. Loram, *Education of the South African Native*, 310, 309; Jabavu, *Black Problem*, 41.

89. Shula Marks, *The Ambiguities of Dependence in South Africa: Class, Nationalism, and the State in Twentieth-Century Natal* (Baltimore: Johns Hopkins University Press, 1986), vii.

90. Higgs, *Ghost of Equality*, 159.

Contributors

W. Fitzhugh Brundage is the William B. Umstead Professor of History at the University of North Carolina, Chapel Hill. He is the author of *Lynching in the New South: Georgia and Virginia, 1880–1930* (1993) and *A Socialist Utopia in the New South: The Ruskin Colonies of Tennessee and Georgia, 1894–1901* (1996) and editor of *Under Sentence of Death: Lynching in the South* (1997) and *Where These Memories Grow: History, Memory, and Southern Identity* (2000).

Peter A. Coclanis is the George and Alice Welsh Professor and History Department chair at the University of North Carolina, Chapel Hill. He is the author of *The Shadow of a Dream: Economic Life and Death in the South Carolina Low Country, 1670–1920* (1989) and coeditor of *Ideas, Ideologies, and Social Movements: The United States Experience since 1800* (1999). He has also published numerous articles and essays.

Hunt Davis is professor of African history and former director of the Center of African Studies at the University of Florida. His publications include *Bantu Education and the Education of Africans in South Africa* (1972) and *Mandela, Tambo, and the African National Congress: The Struggle against Apartheid, 1948–1990* (1991).

Louis R. Harlan, professor emeritus, University of Maryland, is the author of *Separate and Unequal: Public School Campaigns and Racism in the Southern Seaboard States, 1901–1915* (1958), *Booker T. Washington: The Making of a Black Leader, 1856–1901* (1972), and *Booker T. Washington, the Wizard of Tuskegee, 1901–1915* (1983) and editor of *The Booker T. Washington Papers* (1972–83).

David Leverenz is professor of English at the University of Florida. His publications include *The Language of Puritan Feeling: An Exploration in Literature, Psychology, and Social History* (1980) and *Manhood and the American Renaissance* (1989).

Waldo Martin is professor of history at the University of California, Berkeley. He is the author of *The Mind of Frederick Douglass* (1984) and coeditor of *Civil Rights in the United States: An Encyclopedia* (2000).

Wilson J. Moses is professor of history at Penn State University. His publications include *The Golden Age of Black Nationalism* (1978), *Alexander Crummell* (1989), *The Wings of Ethiopia* (1990), and *Afrotopia: The Roots of African American Popular History* (1998).

Louise Newman is associate professor of history at the University of Florida. She is the author of *White Women's Rights: The Racial Origins of Feminism in the United States* (1999).

Robert J. Norrell is the Bernodette Schmitt Professor of History at the University of Tennessee, Knoxville. He is the author of *Reaping the Whirlwind: The Civil Rights Movement in Tuskegee* (1985), *A Promising Field: Engineering at Alabama, 1837–1987* (1990), and *James Bowron: The Autobiography of a New South Industrialist* (1991).

Patricia A. Schechter is associate professor of history at Portland State University. She is the author of *Ida Wells-Barnett and American Reform, 1880–1930* (2001).

Index

Abbott, Lyman, 22–23, 86
Abbott, Robert S., 139
Adair, Douglass, 111
Africa: Washington's influence in, 11, 14, 193–219
African National Congress, 205
Aggrey, James E. K., 201, 204
Alexander, Adele Logan, 135, 136
Alger, Horatio, 108, 109
Andrews, William, 43, 134
Arena, 59, 60, 64
Armstrong, Samuel Chapman: educational and racial philosophy of, 31–32, 87; influence of, on Washington, 31, 86, 89, 111, 160–61, 162, 163, 184, 187, 195
Atlanta Constitution, 66
Atlanta Exposition address, 2, 19–20, 34, 43–45, 58, 61, 118, 150, 156, 164–68, 179, 196; as performance, 165–68; white responses to, 10, 165–68
Atlanta University, 211
Atlantic Monthly, 59

Baker, Houston, 45, 46, 82, 89, 90, 151, 172n10, 172n11, 187, 188, 189
Bederman, Gail, 185
Bellah, Robert, 111
Birmingham Age-Herald, 62
Birth of a Nation, 75
Black Belt Gems, 116
Black critics of Washington, 2, 39–40, 59, 107–8
Broadhead, Richard H., 176n38
Brookes, Edgar, 199

Brownsville affair, 73
Bryce, James, 164–65
Butler, Judith, 154

Calhoun, William P., 64
Cambridge University, 198
Carby, Hazel, 172n10
Carlyle, Thomas, 84
Carnegie, Andrew, 2, 26, 27, 109, 111, 169
Carnegie, Dale, 86
Carroll, Charles, 64, 86
Character Building, 116
Chesnutt, Charles W., 85
Civil Rights Act (1964), 146n14
Civil Rights Movement, 39, 74
Coclanis, Peter, 7, 8, 9, 12, 186
Collins, Patricia Hill, 134, 174n22
Columbia University, 198
Commission on Interracial Co-operation, 200
Conference on Native Affairs (1923), 201
Cooley, Rosa B., 203
Cooper, Anna J., 10, 135, 182, 183
Councill, William Hooper, 64
Creelman, James: on Atlanta Exposition speech, 165–68
Crum, William D., 66–67
Crummell, Alexander, 113, 118–19, 120–21, 123–24, 125
Crumpacker, Edgar D., 68
Czolgosz, Leon, 69

Davis, Hunt, 11, 14
Davis, Ossie, 150

Delaney, Lucy, 139
Dewey, John, 112
Disfranchisement: campaign in the South, 6, 20; Washington's response to, 3
Dixon, Thomas, Jr., 65, 71, 72, 73
Dorsey, Carolyn A., 135, 136
Douglas, Mary, 89
Douglass, Frederick, 19, 38, 41, 42, 47, 48, 76, 95, 114, 120, 128n19, 132, 133, 156, 159, 179
Drumgoold, Kate, 139
Dube, John Langalabelele, 205
Du Bois, William Edward Burghardt: criticizes industrial education, 85, 104n47; *Souls of Black Folk*, 58, 150–52; on *Up From Slavery*, 25, 150–52; on Washington's career, 2, 39, 58, 76, 105n49, 113–15, 124, 170, 172–73n13
Dubow, Saul, 199

Eagleton, Terry, 90
East, James Edward, 209
Easterlin, Richard, 94
Eastman, George, 26–27
Edwards, Laura F., 174n22
Elias, Norbert, 89
Ellison, Ralph, 42, 43, 55, 109

Fairclough, Adam, 82
Federal Council of Dutch Reformed Churches, 201
Felton, Rebecca Latimer, 6, 66
Ferguson, Jane, 138, 139, 140, 155, 156–57
Foner, Eric, 174n22
Fort Hare South African Native College, 194, 204, 206, 210
Forum, 59, 64
Franklin, Benjamin, 41, 42, 109, 112, 113, 132
Frederickson, George, 207
Friedman, Milton, 83
Fukuyama, Francis, 93

Garvey, Marcus, 1, 26, 39
Gates, Henry Louis, Jr., 130n50
Genovese, Eugene, 100n20, 105n49
Gilmore, Glenda, 179, 183

Gourou, Pierre, 92
Grimké, Francis J., 117

Harlan, Louis R., 3, 5, 12, 41, 44, 59, 61, 74, 86, 98n10, 112, 136, 152, 188
Harper's Weekly, 59
Harris, Thomas, 63
Harrison, Lawrence E., 93
Heflin, J. Thomas, 69–70
Henderson, James, 200
Hertzog, J. B. M., 198, 199
Himmelfarb, Gertrude, 95
Hine, Darlene Clark, 131
Hoffman, Frederick Ludwig, 60
Holmes, Oliver Wendell, 62
Howard-Pitney, David, 13
Howard University, 211
Howells, William Dean, 25, 167
Hudspeth, Harvey G., 145n10
Huntington, Samuel P., 93

Independent, 64
Industrial education: at Hampton, 32, 84; at Tuskegee, 84, 99n14, 181; white hostility toward, 64, 65, 68–69; in South Africa, 196, 208–10

Jabavu, Davidson Don Tengo, 11, 194, 196; influence of Washington on, 204–11; education and career, 206; trip to Tuskegee, 207–8; criticisms of Washington, 210
Jacobson, Matthew Frye, 176n38
James, William, 109, 112, 113, 122
Jones, Jacqueline, 174n22
Jones, John David Rheinallt, 200
Jones, Thomas Goode, 66
Jones, Thomas Jesse, 193, 198, 199, 200, 203

Kasson, John, 160
Keppel, Frederick, 202
King, Kenneth, 201, 204
King, Martin Luther, Jr., 38, 76

Langston, John Mercer, 114
Leslie's Weekly, 68
Leverenz, David, 10, 11

Lewis, David Levering, 133, 173n13
Lincoln, Abraham, 113
Logan, Adella Hunt, 135
Loram, Charles Templeman, 11, 193; abridges *Up From Slavery*, 194–98; education and career of, 198–99; ideas of, about "native" education, 195–96
Lynching: extent of, 6; Washington's response to, 51, 61–62, 63

Mackie, Mary Fletcher, 40, 88, 89, 110, 125, 186, 188–89, 195
Malcolm X, 1, 150
Mandela, Nelson, 207
Marks, Shula, 211
Martin, Waldo, 3, 5, 7, 177, 201, 208
Mathews, Z. K., 206
McElroy, Frederick, 147n27
McKinley, William, 69, 161, 197
Meier, August, 3, 12, 100n20, 177
Memphis Scimitar, 66
Miller, Kelly, 73, 75
Montgomery Advertiser, 66, 71–72
Moton, Robert R., 205
My Larger Education, 35

National Association for the Advancement of Colored People, 75, 77
National Association of Colored Women, 140, 182
National Negro Business League, 2
National Party, 203
Native Americans: Washington's ideas about, 163–64
Newman, Louise, 9–10, 11
New Negro for a New Century, 54
Niagara Movement, 73
Norell, Robert, 4, 5, 7, 178
North American Review, 59, 64

Ohlange Institute, 205
Oldham, J. H., 193
Olney, James, 132
Outlook, 22, 24, 59, 96

Page, Thomas Nelson, 64
Page, Walter Hines, 21, 23, 24

Patterson, Orlando, 160, 173n14, 178
Payne, David Alexander, 117, 119
Penn Normal, Industrial, and Agricultural School, 203
Phelps-Stokes Commission on African Education, 199
Phelps-Stokes Fund, 193, 200, 203
Pim, Howard, 200
Plaatje, Sol, 205
Plessy v. Ferguson (1896), 6, 164
Pocock, J. G. A., 111
Pope, Alexander, 112
Popular Science Monthly, 59
Posnock, Ross, 126n1, 172n10
Price, Joseph C., 114, 165

Racial stereotypes: in popular culture, 52–53, 60–61; and social Darwinism, 177–92
Ransom, Reverdy C., 139
Reed, Adolph, 45, 46
Republican Party, 65–67
Respectability: Victorian emphasis on, 9, 10
Rich, Paul, 204
Richardson, Heather Cox, 12, 98n7, 100n20
Riis, Jacob, 102n38
Rockefeller, John D., 2, 26
Roosevelt, Theodore: relationship with Washington, 2, 65–66, 67, 72, 73, 170
Rosenwald, Julius, 2
Rouse, Jacqueline Anne, 135, 136, 186
Ruffner, Lewis, 31, 87, 188
Ruffner, Viola, 31, 87, 89, 110, 125, 159, 186, 187–88, 195
Russell, Bertrand, 113

Sachs, Jeffrey, 92
St. Paul: first address to the Corinthians, 161
Sandow, Eugen, 160
Schechter, Patricia, 10, 11, 149, 183
Scott, Daryl, 54
Scott, Dred, 153
Scott, Emmett J., 207
Smiles, Samuel, 84
Smith, Adam, 111
Smith, James P., 92
Social Darwinism, 10, 180–81

South African Native Affairs Commission, 198
Southern Workman, 32
Spencer, Samuel R., Jr., 100n20
Stein, Gertrude, 88
Storer College, 120
Story of My Life and Work, The, 4, 21, 33, 147n27, 149–76, 210
Story of the Negro, The, 53
Stowe, Harriet Beecher, 52
Sundquist, Eric, 44
Swee, Goh Keng, 95

Tambo, Oliver, 206
Taney, Roger B., 153
Tate, Claudia, 148n31
Tengo, John, 206
Terrell, Mary Church, 182
Tillman, Benjamin R., 66, 67, 68, 73
Thomas, William H., 64–65, 96
Thompson, Leonard, 202
Thrasher, Max Bennett, 21–22, 29, 86, 149
Togo, 14
Transkei Territories General Council, 201
Trotter, William Monroe, 3, 116
Tuskegee "machine," 2, 34, 80n30
Tuskegee Normal and Industrial Institute: coeducation at, 104n45, 142–43, 181; founding of, 2, 63, 81, 87–88; industrial education at, 88; Negro conferences at, 2; white attitudes toward, 67

University of Birmingham, 206
University of London, 206
Up From Slavery: and African American autobiographical tradition, 46–49; historical accuracy of, 28–35; paean to success, 42, 44, 63, 185; prose style of, 29; publication of, 23–24; published in South Africa, 193–98; response to, 1, 24–25; reviews of, 25; writing of, 4–5, 20–23

Vardaman, James, 65, 66, 67, 68, 73
Veblen, Thorstein, 115, 122

Walker, Benjamin, 69
Wallace, Maurice, 171n4
Wanamaker, John, 71–72, 170
Washington, Booker Taliaferro: acquires full name, 140; admitted to Hampton, 40; Armstrong's influence on, 31, 160–61; Atlanta Exposition Address, 2, 19–20, 34, 43–45, 150, 156, 164–68; birthplace described, 30; briefly interested in law and politics, 33; childhood of, in slavery, 30; childhood work of, in salt furnace, 86; early education of, 86; influence of Ruffners on, 30; education of, at Hampton, 40–41; and founding of Tuskegee, 2, 81, 87–88; furtive opposition of, to racial discrimination, 3; fund-raising efforts of, 26–27, 162–63, 180; later perceptions of, 39–40, 59, 107–8; physical appearance of, 166–67; on segregation, 61–62, 72; and Theodore Roosevelt, 2, 65–66, 67, 170; threats against, 72, 80n27; in Washington D.C., 142
—thought and influence: black jeremiad tradition, 13; cleanliness, 41, 81, 82, 89–90, 92–93, 163–64, 187–88; economic equality, 45, 93–94; economic thought, 7–8, 81–106; free labor ideology of, 12, 99n13; gender roles, 131–48, 149–76, 177–92; honor, 153–54, 170–71; iconic representations of, 14; Native Americans, 163–64; "new Negro," 49, 53, 54; oratorical devices of, 14, 164–68; Protestant work ethic, 48, 87, 99n13, 107–30, 186; self-mastery of, 161–62, 164; slavery and history, 49–53, 121–22; suffrage and electoral politics, 62, 67
—works: *Black Belt Gems*, 116; *Character Building*, 116; *My Larger Education*, 35; *Man Farthest Down*, 128n22; *New Negro for a New Century*, 54; *The Story of My Life and Work*, 4, 21, 33, 149–76, 210; *The Story of the Negro*, 53. See also *Up From Slavery*
Washington, Fanny Norton Smith (first wife), 136, 159
Washington, John H., 132
Washington, Margaret James Murray (third wife), 131, 132, 136, 143, 159, 186
Washington, Olivia A. Davidson (second

wife), 131, 136, 137–38, 141, 155, 158, 182, 194, 197
Washington, Portia M., 136, 155
Watson, Thomas, 70–71
Webber, Eugene, 21, 149
Weber, Max, 109, 110, 112, 114, 116, 117, 125
Wells-Barnett, Ida B., 3, 131, 133, 141, 179, 182, 183
White House dinner incident, 65–66, 69
Whittington, Richard, 108

Wilberforce University, 211
Willard, Carla, 151
Woodson, Carter, 53
Woodward, C. Vann, 59, 74
Woofter, Thomas J., 203
Work, Monroe N., 203
Wright, Richard, 47
Wyatt-Brown, Bertram, 176n39

Yale University, 199

www.ingramcontent.com/pod-product-compliance
Lightning Source LLC
Chambersburg PA
CBHW032250150426
43195CB00008BA/389